COMPUTER AUDIT GUIDELINES

COMPUTER AUDIT GUIDELINES

The Comprehensive Guide to
Auditing in Computerised
Environments

Fourth Fully Revised Edition

Published by

CIPFA, THE CHARTERED INSTITUTE OF PUBLIC FINANCE AND ACCOUNTANCY

3 Robert Street, London WC2N 6RH, United Kingdom. Tel: 071-895 8823. Fax: 071 895 8825

First published 1978
Second edition 1983
Third edition 1987
Fully revised fourth edition 1994

© 1994, CIPFA

ISBN 0 85299 595 4

Foreword

Over the last four years, significant changes have occurred in the information and information technology industry. Users have experienced an expansion in the number and complexity of their application systems together with major improvements in the hardware to support them. While the traditional mainframe environment is still popular, notable developments have occurred in distributed mainframe, mini and microcomputer networks.

This movement towards 'user driven computing' has been achieved through new communications infrastructures. Within organisations there has been a widespread adoption of local area networks to connect departmental microcomputers and wide area networks to provide a link to the wider environment. The result has required a consequential change in working practices for IT professionals, users, and auditors alike.

The primary objective of this and previous editions of the *Guidelines* has been to focus upon the responsibility of management to install good controls and adopt best practice in this changing environment. The auditor's task is still to assess the adequacy of the control mechanisms and compliance with best practice but to recognise the changing applications of the technology throughout organisations.

While the principles supporting computer audit have not changed over time, their application needs to keep pace with new developments both in the technology and its use. This fourth edition of the *Computer Audit Guidelines* retains the advice from earlier editions which has stood the test of time and includes much new material to reflect the developments in technology.

It provides a comprehensive approach to computer auditing and has been written for the auditor working in a computerised environment whether as part of the private or public sector. It will be relevant, too, to the user of technology who wants to understand the procedures which need to be in place to protect the substantial investment in and reliance upon IT.

Grateful thanks are due to those members of the Audit Panel's Information Technology Group (listed overleaf) who devoted generous time and effort in the compilation of this publication. Thanks are due too to others who have provided valuable commentary and advice during the compilation of the *Guidelines*.

Chris Hurford

Chairman, CIPFA's Audit Panel

Martin Adfield (*Chairman*) .... Audit Commission
Paul Garner .... Audit Commission
Peter Job .... Devon County Council
Rowena Johnson .... Hart District Council
David Lang .... Mercury Communications Ltd
Tim Nichols .... Woking Borough Council
Ken Odgers .... City of London Corporation
Vernon Poole .... Aid to Industry (part of Touche Ross)
Diane Skinner .... Audit Commission

Contents

NB: *Each chapter has an individual contents listing complete with page references.*

CHAPTER 1

INTRODUCTION

1

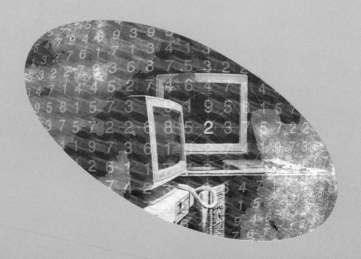

1.1 Purpose of the Guidelines

The provision of information technology (IT) within organisations varies considerably. Some will use sophisticated mainframes together with a range of networked minicomputers and microcomputers. Others will be satisfied with a single processor. In some organisations the auditor may have a number of separate installations to audit in various departments. Providing guidelines for such a range of computerised environments is a daunting task and so the approach adopted by the authors has been to focus on the best practice which management might adopt. The auditor will need to adapt these *Guidelines* to suit the environment in which audit operates.

Computer audit principles are no different from those which operate in all other spheres of audit but the technical qualities of computers and their associated software make the application of audit objectives more difficult. It is with this in mind that these *Guidelines* have been prepared to provide the auditor with a framework to use when considering how best audit objectives can be satisfied.

Auditors will always need to exercise their own initiative and the *Guidelines* have been written to provide for the clear definition of objectives, principles and guidance on work to be undertaken within discrete areas. Sufficient material is provided to allow auditors to define their own specific programmes of work.

1.2 Structure of the Guidelines

The *Guidelines* consist of seven sections and fifteen chapters. The topics range from the management of computer audit and information technology through to the detailed audit of operating systems, databases and networks. Within this revision the opportunity has been taken to address a number of new issues, including national and European legislation. The *Guidelines* have also been re-structured to provide both a logical approach to computer audit for those new to the subject and specific chapters concerning the more complex topics.

The structure of the *Guidelines* is therefore:

Computer Audit Management

Chapters 2 and 3 are concerned with the principles of computer audit and the philosophy behind these Guidelines. Chapter 2 addresses the issues facing those responsible for managing computer audit resources whilst Chapter 3 provides guidance concerning recruitment and training and assesses the changing use of technology and the resultant skills that a competent auditor should possess.

The Management of IT

Chapters 4 and 5 consider the processes by which an organisation ensures that it is achieving value for money from its computer resources and describes ways in which the auditor should be reviewing those processes. Subjects discussed include strategies and arrangements for IT, control over the development and implementation of applications, costing and charging procedures for computing facilities, monitoring the performance of IT resources, capacity planning and the acquisition of IT.

Installation Controls

Chapters 6 and 7 describe the range of controls governing the day-to-day operation of the computer installation. The section deals with the auditor's interest in the overall general security and control mechanisms governing the computing facilities within an organisation. This includes not only the need for physical security but also the safeguards incorporated into system software.

Application Controls

Chapters 8 and 9 are concerned with the need for management control of the development and operation of application systems. All systems should be produced and implemented in a logical and controlled manner whether they are written in house or obtained from an outside contractor. The section describes the procedures that should be established by management to ensure that systems meet their objectives, are delivered on time, are properly tested and are written to a defined quality. It discusses the areas of system maintenance and change control and normal practice in these two areas.

Auditing the Technology

Chapters 10 to 12 cover a number of discrete subjects concerning operating systems, databases, and networks. They expand upon the principles and controls detailed within the Installation Controls and Application Controls sections and provide guidance on the control and audit of each topic.

Computer Assisted Auditing

Chapter 13 addresses the need for auditors to keep pace with technological change and maintain efficiency and high quality in their work, whilst coping with an apparently growing workload. In the light of the pressures caused by these conflicting needs, the section addresses two areas in which audit can make use of computers both to help them work more efficiently and to produce a higher quality product. These areas are audit administration and computer assisted audit techniques.

Computer Audit and the Law

Chapter 14 is concerned with European legislation relating to IT and discusses the need for auditors to be aware of the European framework and its impact on the public sector. Chapter 15 is concerned with national legislation and identifies the different areas that are generally covered by UK statutes. Subjects covered include, data protection, computer misuse, fraud, health and safety, intellectual ownership and the acquisition of IT.

CIPFA

COMPUTER AUDIT GUIDELINES

COMPUTER AUDIT MANAGEMENT

2 MANAGEMENT OF COMPUTER AUDIT RESOURCES

3 RECRUITMENT AND TRAINING

CHAPTER 2

MANAGEMENT OF COMPUTER AUDIT RESOURCES

2

2.1 Introduction

The following extract from the UK Auditing Practices Board's Guideline *Guidance for Internal Auditors* (1990) reflects the general responsibilities of audit which can be applied to all computer audit activities:

'It is a management responsibility to maintain the internal control system and to ensure that the organisation's resources are properly applied in the manner and on the activities intended. This includes responsibility for the prevention and detection of fraud and other illegal acts'.

The main objectives of internal control systems are:

— to ensure adherence to management policies and directives in order to achieve the organisation's objectives;

— to safeguard assets;

— to secure the relevance, reliability and integrity of information, so ensuring as far as possible the completeness and accuracy of records; and

— to ensure compliance with statutory requirements.

Internal audit is an independent function established by the management of an organisation to appraise and report on the internal control system and audit amongst other things objectively examines, evaluates and reports on the adequacy of internal control as a contribution to the proper, economic, efficient and effective use of resources.

Over the past decade there has been a significant change in the range of products and speed of operation and complexity of the facilities provided by the IT industry. Costs of IT facilities continue to fall and this has facilitated the large scale development of decentralised systems and their associated local and wide area networks. IT has thus become central to the effective and efficient provision of services within the public and private sectors.

All auditors must be aware of the scope of IT within their organisation, and how it is structured and managed. IT is integral to an organisation's systems and such details are essential to the planning and conduct of any audit. Similarly, without access to the information that these systems contain, managers and auditors alike will be unable effectively to undertake their responsibilities. Information is now the life-blood of most organisations, and without it their services cannot be undertaken.

Because of the pervasiveness of IT, the effective use of software can assist auditors in achieving their objectives. In the past, however, this has been left to the specialist. The long term aim should be to enable the whole of an audit section to use IT facilities thus allowing the specialist auditor to operate as an adviser giving technical support, developing audit techniques and dealing with those areas of computing which require a high level of technical skill.

The use of retrieval software and interrogation techniques to test and verify the quality of data held on computer files and the adequacy and proper functioning of controls built into computer applications is of great value to the auditor. It is also an effective way of communicating with key computer personnel to discuss the contents of data files and computer applications and it will develop the auditor's understanding of systems design. Much of the knowledge acquired during the development of interrogation programs will have a direct bearing on the auditor's effectiveness in the other areas of computer audit.

2.2 Planning Audit Activities

Planning the audit of a computer environment is in essence no different from planning any audit activity. Indeed the principles of computer auditing are no different from those which operate in all other spheres of audit: what is different, though, is the application of those principles. It is important to emphasise, too, that the systems-based approach to audit should be the cornerstone of the audit process.

Developments in IT require the auditor to consider the use of technology throughout the organisation, whereas previously the view was of a self-contained computer installation. Organisations may be exploiting a combination of mainframe, mini and micros to provide for the overall needs of their departments. Some of these will be linked, others acting as stand-alone machines. However, in most organisations the trend will be for IT to be decentralised and, whatever the mode of operation chosen, that will call for distributed auditing. No longer can auditors concern themselves solely with the central IT department; in future they will need to consider the use of computing facilities as a whole throughout the organisation: this may include audit coverage of local and wide area networks or of facilities managed by an external contractor.

As more processing becomes distributed so auditors must be aware of its impact upon their own organisations. User-driven computing inevitably means that the user is in direct control of their systems rather than being reliant upon IT services. The demand placed upon the auditor's skills and resources to assess the procedures and controls at each of the end-user points will be considerable.

One of the many questions for audit management which can only be resolved individually by each organisation, concerns the balance between the various aspects of auditing in an IT environment, given that limited and fixed resources are available. In practical terms this often raises questions such as how much time should be spent on installation security, rather than on the examination of financial applications, what proportion of resources should be devoted to the audit of applications under development rather than to the testing of operational systems and what proportion of the auditor's time can be devoted to 'value for money' at the expense of regularity audits. The following guide may be helpful in initially allocating time though individual organisations will need to tailor these figures to their own needs.

	Initial Review/ Assessment	Testing
Management of computing resources	30%	10%
Acquisition of IT	5%	5%
Installation controls	20%	10%
Application controls	40%	50%
Value for money exercises	5%	25%

When planning an audit of a computerised environment, the auditor must have regard to the element of risk. As organisations become more dependent upon IT to satisfy their needs so the risk of the loss or corruption of data and the consequential damage to business confidence becomes more acute. The auditor must weigh up the financial and other consequences of a loss of an IT service and take this into account in planning the audit. This will be particularly important as organisations devolve their computing down to departments where experience of traditional control mechanisms over computer processing may be less evident.

2.2.1   Computer Audit Coverage

Where an organisation uses IT facilities the auditor has three broad areas to consider: those aspects relating to management of IT, those concerning the overall controls over the IT facilities and those controls relating to each application which makes use of those facilities.

As more concern is expressed about the value for money from IT investment so audit needs to devote resources to exploring how the benefits from IT have been realised. This will involve attention being given to the strategic direction of IT throughout the organisation and to such issues as the acquisition procedures, methods of costing and charging and measuring the performance of the IT service.

In reviewing the overall controls over IT throughout the organisation the auditor will need to address:

- the standards, controls and procedures which ensure the safe and efficient day-to-day operation of the facilities;

- the procedures which the organisation adopts when determining the need for and acquisition of computing facilities; and

- the arrangements made by management to ensure that the facilities are used effectively and efficiently.

All those aspects are concerned with controls and procedures of a general or managerial nature. They relate to the administrative and organisational features which must be installed and applied by IT management and which provide the framework for the safeguards governing specific applications.

As far as the individual applications processed within the IT environment, the auditor will review:

- the controls and procedures which govern the day-to-day processing of each system;

- the controls and procedures which are incorporated into each system during its various stages of development; and

- the standards and procedures adopted by the organisation for managing the development of computerised systems.

When reviewing the adequacy of controls within any one system the auditor will rely to a greater or lesser extent upon the general standard of controls and safeguards which exist within the computing facilities as a whole because it is difficult to form a rounded view of the adequacy of controls of any particular application without having a sound knowledge of the environment within which it operates.

2.2.2   Relations with IT Management

Although all auditors strive for the co-operation and understanding of those they audit, the auditors' dependence on the IT department for technical information and support makes the achievement of these ideals of particular importance. It is therefore crucial for the auditor to act professionally on all occasions, and display an awareness of the practical problems and considerations which arise in running an IT department. The auditor should take care to explain the role of audit to all levels of IT staff and management, and to listen to any suggestions or criticisms that may be made.

Auditors should be competent and constructive, balancing the requirements of control against the demands of rigid work schedules and remembering never to confuse independence with insularity.

2.4

2.2.3   Relations with User Management

As with all auditing, it is important to establish effective working arrangements with the customers of audit services. When auditing in a computerised environment, the auditor has to have regard to the fact that the owner of the data may not necessarily be its custodian. Technology may provide both the link and the barrier between the user of the data and so when planning an audit, attention must be given to any concerns of the data owners over the control of their data.

2.3   Computer Audit Documentation

This publication continually stresses the importance of good standards of documentation for IT, but audit too must be scrupulous in maintaining high documentation standards. It is not for these Guidelines to dictate what form audit documentation and files ought to take as there will be large variations from one organisation to another. These will depend on a range of factors, not least being the size and nature of the computing service subject to audit. Nevertheless some broad guidance may be useful:

–   There should be an installation file for each IT centre subject to audit even for relatively small mini or micro based installations. Apart from the usual sections for audit reports and working papers, there should be an information section containing details of hardware, software, staffing, basic administrative procedures and controls. This section, which may include separate installation manuals, should be kept up-to-date from whatever sources are available, as the information contained therein relates to all computer audits being carried out based at that installation.

–   There should be an application file for each computer application subject to audit. This file would benefit from a section giving a simple outline of the system, its important control features, facilities useful to auditors, and a non-technical description of the data held on the computer. The latter information is particularly useful to auditors in determining ways in which computer retrieval software can assist with general audit work.

–   All audit use of the computer through interrogation or any of the other computer assisted audit techniques should be documented properly and indexed so that a ready reference on the facilities available exists. Such documentation should include the relevant computer listings of programs or data and, where appropriate, a written description of the objectives of the exercise. Alternatively, retrieval program listings and associated job control language instructions may be held by audit within allocated work space on a computer. This has the advantage of reducing problems with updating, but restrictions on access need to be carefully controlled. Information on the changes required between one test and the next should be clearly identified to provide continuity and to avoid abortive runs.

Other information that is of use to the auditor, such as system specifications and user manuals, should be readily available from the IT or user departments and it would therefore create an unnecessary overhead in storage and maintenance if auditors retained their own copies of such information. Similarly, data listings and other working papers should be properly disposed of as soon as they have served their useful purpose. Auditors should be mindful of their responsibilities under the data protection legislation to protect their own and their organisation's information.

Files on computer applications and the related general audit files on such matters as fundamental systems should be cross referenced to ensure that both aspects of the audit are considered.

CHAPTER 3

RECRUITMENT AND TRAINING

Continued overleaf

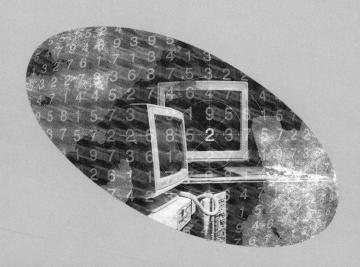

3.5 Management Issues   **3.8**

3.5.1 Costs of training computer auditors
3.5.2 Training of non-specialists
3.5.3 Career development for computer auditors
3.5.4 Isolation
3.5.5 Career development of general auditors
3.5.6 Retention of trained staff
3.5.7 Advanced training
3.5.8 Small organisations

3.1 Introduction

Auditing in a computerised environment demands of the audit manager an ability to assess the level of expertise required to give audit cover to computers and computer based systems, to identify the sources from which staff may need to be recruited and to identify the methods of training available for audit staff.

Understanding the developing IT scene is important because:

— The technology and its terminology can create a gap in communications between IT professionals and other members of an organisation including its auditors. Auditors must be able to close this gap to provide a full and proper audit service to management and users.

— The depth of knowledge required is unlikely to be commonly found amongst auditors.

— Computing is a continuously developing technology; training is therefore essential to keep abreast with it.

There is no single solution to these problems and managers need to determine the skills required within their audit team and then determine the most effective way of securing and maintaining that skill base.

3.2 Profile of Required Expertise

3.2.1   Overview

All audit staff should have an appreciation of IT irrespective of the amount of day-to-day contact that they may have with computers and computer based systems. The influence of IT is constantly expanding: as the boundaries of computer applications advance, more and more staff – including auditors – will rely upon computers to provide the means of performing their duties. Each organisation should attempt to give staff at the least an awareness and understanding of the basics of computing to enable them to cope with their environment.

Set out below are profiles of skills, classified as primary, intermediate and advanced, that would be expected from audit staff involved to differing degrees in computing. These range from the need for a basic appreciation of computing to the skills required from an experienced computer auditor. Within each class the skills and knowledge required are listed under basic audit skills, information technology, and computer audit. Primary skills should be regarded as the minimum that might be expected from auditors who only come across computer systems periodically, whilst those skills listed under advanced will allow auditors to cope with more complex areas.

3.2.2 Primary Skills

Audit

Auditors who periodically come into contact with computer systems would be expected to possess basic audit skills including an understanding of audit objectives, internal control, internal check and reporting, systems based auditing, communication and flowcharting skills.

Information technology

All audit staff should have an awareness and understanding of the basics of computers and computing. Skills should include the ability to use microcomputers and their operating systems and use software such as word-processing and spreadsheets.

Computer audit

Audit staff should have knowledge and understanding of the objectives and methods of computer audit and its relationship to general audit. Skills should include the ability to use simple enquiry languages and menu driven applications. Auditors should appreciate how and when to use computer assisted audit techniques and be able to specify requirements for the use of retrieval software.

3.2.3 Intermediate Skills

Audit

Audit staff should be able to communicate and report effectively, have practical experience of systems based auditing, flowcharting and analytical audit skills.

Information technology

An understanding of IT principles covering:

- Information technology management – the organisation of the IT department, liaison with corporate management and users, policy formulation, staffing.

- Business or systems analysis – the role of the analyst, the definition of user problems and the specification of computer based systems, communication and reporting.

- Programming – the duties of programmers and their relationship to systems analysts, and an understanding of programming languages.

- Operations – the organisation of operations including data capture and control techniques, an appreciation of operating systems, system software, databases, communications and networks.

Skills should include the ability to use macro facilities contained in menu driven packages and programming in simple languages such as BASIC or other appropriate microcomputer based programming languages.

Computer audit

Skills in computer audit should include experience and ability in reviewing and assessing the security of all types of IT centres, including user driven computing, the control of systems development, and the audit of computerised accounting systems including input, output and processing controls. The auditor should not only know when and how to use computer assisted audit techniques, but also be able to use retrieval software and interrogation techniques.

3.2.4   Advanced Skills

Audit

As well as the skills listed under 'intermediate' above, advanced computer audit skills include experience in planning and managing audits and supervising or managing staff.

Information technology

As for intermediate skills, plus a detailed knowledge and ideally experience of:

—   the use and coding of a major high level language, for example COBOL or fourth generation products such as ORACLE and INGRES, or structured query languages;

—   specific operating systems such as that used by the organisation;

—   database techniques;

—   networking and transaction processing systems;

—   access control software products;

—   personal computing and distributed processing methods;

—   strategies for IT and the management of computer resources.

Computer audit

Ideally an experienced computer auditor should be able to review and assess security and controls in any computing environment, eg:

—   centralised and departmental computing;

—   networking and other distributed computing;

  — micro-computing; and

  — batch, on-line and real time processing.

  The auditor should also be able to review the management of computer resources including the review of IT strategies and costing and charging for computer services.

  The attributes listed above provide a profile against which the suitability of candidates for computer audit posts may be measured. It may be that not all of them will be required. Not all computer auditors will necessarily need all the skills and experience specified.

3.3 Recruitment

3.3.1 Factors Affecting Recruitment Decisions

Organisations are often subject to severe constraints on grades and salaries, and market forces may dictate how and where staff are recruited and the level of training and development that can be provided.

  A job description is essential and should be related to the level of IT activity in the organisation and to internal audit policy regarding the expected roles of general and specialist audit staff. Typically, the job description would cover the following areas:

  — Description of the purpose of the post

  — Required qualifications and experience.

  — Details of the main areas of responsibilities.

  — Relationships.

3.3.2 Sources of Recruitment

Computer auditors may be recruited from a number of sources:

Finance

Staff from a financial background should present no problems regarding integration into an audit office and should be at least aware of the objectives of internal audit. Depending on their previous job experience and professional status, it may be necessary to supplement their knowledge of internal audit procedures.

  A background in finance provides a good basis for reviewing computer systems as the most important of these remain financially based applications. However, the auditor recruited from a

3.4

finance background may lack expertise in IT, which will lead to immediate pressure for training. The precise need can only be assessed in individual cases but managers should bear in mind that formal training tends to be expensive and it is unrealistic to expect those recently trained to be immediately effective.

Through a structured programme of work, finance staff new to computer audit can extend their knowledge and contribution without risking loss of credibility with IT staff. There is, of course, the option to recruit an accountant who can also demonstrate the required degree of computer expertise and the application of this through computer audit. Because of the salary that such an individual can command that option, with all the advantages that it brings, may be open only to larger organisations.

Information technology staff

Staff recruited from IT departments should have the technical knowledge required and if recruited from internal sources would also have the benefit of familiarity with the facilities and procedures of the organisation. However, care must still be exercised when recruiting from this source because:

— Such individuals may not be experienced in audit and may not, therefore, be able to apply their IT skills and knowledge in the manner expected of an auditor. Training in basic audit objectives and principles and short secondments to general audit teams to do non-computer audit work may overcome this.

— Auditors who were formerly IT staff may also retain an undue sympathy with their colleagues in IT. It may be difficult for such an auditor to appreciate why internal audit needs to be involved in certain areas and to be objective.

— A computer auditor is expected to be knowledgeable in the areas of business and systems analysis, programming and operations. It should not be assumed that staff recruited from IT will automatically have experience in all three areas. Some training may therefore be required where the necessary breadth of experience is lacking.

References should, of course, always be taken and it may be advisable to invite a representative of IT management to sit-in on job interviews so that their reaction to applicants can be assessed.

Experienced computer audit recruits

Computer auditors recruited from other organisations should possess a high degree of experience and expertise, but may still require further training. Management needs to consider both audit and IT issues. From the audit point of view the recruit will need as a minimum, some instruction on the procedures that are peculiar to the recruiting organisation such as local statements of audit objectives, organisation of the audit department, standing orders and financial regulations and reporting procedures.

On the IT side, existing skills will need to be compared with the needs of the organisation and any deficiencies made good through training. Even if the applicant comes from a site which uses the same supplier, the recruit should be made aware of any significant differences in approach. Formal training may not be required in such circumstances, the necessary information being obtained through discussion with IT staff or by 'on the job' training.

Other sources

Candidates from other backgrounds may be valuable, particularly if they have been engaged in analytical or investigative work. In such cases qualifications as well as previous work experience will be important. Such candidates will almost certainly require extensive training and a great deal of support in the early stages. Their particular merit could be a fresh and unaffected approach to the task motivated and enhanced by the newness of the situation.

If it is decided to engage staff on short fixed term contracts then clearly only fully experienced and well-qualified persons should be considered. The same considerations also apply of course to contracting out the work. There will of course still be a learning curve for such persons, at least regarding the organisation itself and its objectives, strategy and procedures.

3.3.3 Personal Attributes

Irrespective of the source of recruitment, management needs to consider the specific behavioural and inter-personal skills the computer auditor should possess.

Auditors are expected to identify difficulties and weaknesses and express them in terms that lay persons can understand. Any auditor who reviews the work of professional staff will know they may be sensitive to questions about how they apply their professional skills and techniques. IT is particularly prone to this problem with its jargon and the mystique the profession enjoys. The need for tact is obvious but a computer auditor must also appreciate when to admit ignorance of technical areas and seek additional explanation.

Computer auditors deal with a wide range of staff including managers, users, IT staff and other auditors and need to be personable, mature and authoritative. Management needs to give such attributes due weight in assessing applicants.

3.4 Methods of Training

For convenience, the available methods of training have been categorised into three sections covering professional examinations, shorter, less prolonged, methods of training and suggestions on keeping up-to-date with current developments.

3.4.1   Professional Examinations

Professional accountancy qualifications

A professional training course may provide an individual with a better appreciation of the working environment, and a recognised qualification which may be of assistance in career progression. The employer may also subsequently have greater confidence in the individual's abilities to discharge responsibilities in a competent and professional manner.

However, professional accountancy courses, which take up to three or more years to complete, devote only a small proportion to computing and computer audit and are more likely to be appropriate for staff seeking a wider career in auditing and accountancy than in the narrower discipline of computer auditing.

Other professional qualifications

An alternative to accountancy qualifications is the availability of specific qualification in computer auditing. A number of courses are available leading to the award of qualifications by recognised bodies such as the EDP Auditors Association or the Institute of Internal Auditors.

Some professional institutes and higher education bodies conduct examinations and award qualifications in computing which may be of benefit to auditors. They are of course vocational in nature and essentially technical but may contain material on the management of IT. The associated periods of study are lengthy, demanding and expensive, but a person qualifying may be expected to have considerable theoretical knowledge or practical skills in computing.

3.4.2   Short-Duration Training Methods

Programming courses

If a computer auditor has to acquire a working knowledge of a programming language then attendance at a programming course affords the opportunity to gain the required technical knowledge relatively quickly. As more users become familiar with microcomputer-based programming languages so there is an increasing opportunity for auditors to learn and use programming languages more readily.

Computer audit courses

Professional bodies and commercial businesses offer a variety of courses designed to cater for computer auditors or auditors interested in taking up computer auditing. The cost of such courses varies widely, depending upon location and length of course, but they offer a comparatively cheap means of acquiring knowledge. They are generally well documented and usually of short duration; the majority taking less than one week to complete.

The disadvantage with this type of training is that there may be difficulty in finding courses offering advanced computer audit training. Careful selection of the courses may alleviate this problem.

In-house courses

Internally organised training courses offer the opportunity to tailor the training closely to identified needs. For organisations which lack the necessary resources for running audit courses a variety of computer audit training packages are available at relatively low cost. On-the-job training provided by senior staff is another relatively low cost method of training which can be very closely tailored to needs. All internal training, by whatever means it is provided, does require there to be staff available who have the requisite knowledge and experience coupled with adequate training skills.

Seminars, lectures etc

Such events are organised by most professional bodies and provide a cheap and effective method of acquiring additional knowledge. Staff time involved is often one day or less, and such events may provide the opportunity to react quickly to recent changes in the field of computer auditing.

Computer audit groups

Most audit and accountancy bodies have associated computer audit groups based on common mainframe or software products. In some cases such groups are sponsored or supported by the manufacturers and suppliers. They may also be regionally based.

The primary purpose of such groups is to meet informally for discussions on common problems and the exchange of ideas. Personal contact at such meetings may lead to exchange visits between computer auditors of similar organisations allowing discussions to be concentrated on common problems. Some groups also undertake research and produce papers for circulation.

Books, articles and publications

There is a vast array of reading material available on subjects relating to computing and computer auditing, enabling the auditor to gain background knowledge and to keep abreast of current developments. In addition, manuals and system documentation produced within an organisation enable the auditor quickly to acquire knowledge of systems in the working environment.

3.5 Management Issues

There will be a continuing need for computer audit expertise to cope with the more sophisticated and complex aspects of IT and to enable audit to keep pace with future developments of the technology. However, computer awareness and computing skills should also be maintained and developed amongst auditors generally. To meet this requirement, senior management and audit managers must address certain issues which otherwise will act as constraints.

3.5.1 Costs of Training Computer Auditors

The cost of training computer auditors is inevitably greater than that for auditors generally for two reasons.

- Firstly, to be fully effective, the computer auditor requires the same managerial and basic audit skills in regularity and VFM audit as are required by the non-specialist in addition to specialist skills.

  Secondly, the costs of specialist training are often greater than those of non-specialist training.

Such training is essential for the computer auditor to be fully effective and maintain the credibility required for dealing with computing professionals.

3.5.2 Training of Non-Specialists

The issues to be faced by managers are that:

- auditors generally need training in computer awareness and the basics of computer auditing if they are to be able to audit effectively in a computerised environment; and,

- auditors generally should be trained in the use of computers for practical reasons and to improve the efficiency of audit;

but

- such training should be appropriate to the operational tasks of individual auditors; and

- only auditors with the appropriate aptitudes should receive such training.

It is necessary therefore to define clearly and carefully the roles and audit tasks of individual post holders, to identify their training needs and to assess their capabilities and aptitudes.

3.5.3 Career Development for Computer Auditors

Audit management should be aware that a specialism within audit can prove to be a 'cul-de-sac', and may be viewed as a hindrance to future career development. It is essential to be aware of this problem, and have a positive approach to avoiding its impact if staff of the right calibre are to be recruited and if the organisation is to retain the knowledge and experience of its computer auditor.

The expectations of computer auditors or prospective computer auditors are likely to differ

3.9

according to their background, experience and qualifications and of course their personality. The individuals may usefully be broadly categorised as follows:

Auditors

They are likely to require assurances about future job progression in the audit department, and whether their computer audit experience may fit them for management posts in the future. Alternatively they may be concerned about rewards in the form of status and remuneration for special responsibilities or progression based on the development of their skills. They may also be concerned with the permanency of their position.

Qualified accountants

They will commonly require assurances about future job progression in the finance department and about the way in which their computer audit experience will be valued by senior management. Their qualifications give them the advantage of choice and mobility, and they are likely to see computer audit as one stage in their development. Such a post holder is likely to be influenced by such matters as the flexibility of the organisation in creating career development opportunities, and their approach to the training of staff in advance of career development moves.

Non-qualified finance staff

Such staff may view a computer audit post as a fresh opportunity and like existing professional auditors be concerned about career progression in audit – probably directing their view towards audit management. Alternatively they may be looking to specialise to enhance their status and earning power, and be strongly influenced by the opportunities that computer audit affords.

IT staff

Typically, such individuals will look for two avenues of advancement, firstly within audit leading to audit management and, secondly, after an appropriate period, back into a senior post with IT. The latter path may become difficult if the individual remains within audit for more than about two years, as specialist knowledge may quickly become out-dated in this field. Attitudes will be determined by management's' approach to training and keeping computer auditors up-to-date in IT.

These problems will tend to be far less serious where individuals are committed to looking for career development within computer audit by moving from one organisation to another, often in and out of the public sector. Individual organisations will find it difficult to replace such staff, as their movements are influenced by factors outside the control of the employing organisation. There is also a danger of such a person being regarded as 'mercenary' and never becoming properly integrated into the audit department.

The issue for management is to ensure that procedures for recruitment, staff management and staff appraisal ensure that the aspirations and expectations of staff are identified and taken into account in making appointments to avoid subsequent disappointments.

3.5.4 Isolation

There is a risk that other audit staff will view the computer auditor as an outsider. The computer auditor will have normally undertaken more formal training than other members of the audit section and will be less reliant upon the IT department for technical advice and assistance. Other auditors may view with suspicion any close relationship established with the IT department. The dangers of isolation may be increased if the computer auditor came from an IT and not an accounting background.

Audit managers should be aware of the dangers and should take positive steps to ensure that the computer auditor becomes, and remains, an accepted member of the audit section. This may be achieved through integration of general and computer audit work on specific audits and through emphasis and use of the service provided to audit as a whole by the computer auditor.

3.5.5 Career Development of General Auditors

General auditors may look upon computer training as a means of acquiring additional skills, and as an indication of their personal flexibility in reacting to a changing environment. They will therefore expect enhanced career opportunities within the finance department. Occasionally an auditor may wish to undertake further training with a view to making a career move into computer auditing. Opportunities can normally be created to satisfy this demand. The issue for management is to determine a policy for career development generally and ensure that staff are aware of it.

3.5.6 Retention of Trained Staff

The indications are that there are more vacancies than experienced computer auditors able to fill them, and this exerts an upward pressure on computer audit salaries. An organisation may risk losing a highly trained computer auditor if it does not increase the payment attracted by that post. The re-grading of a computer audit post can, however, lead to the disruption of an established and accepted salary structure within a department, which may lead to further complications later.

There are no easy solutions to the problem. Arguably, auditors who have undertaken specialist computer audit training and proved successful show ambition, flexibility and ability that warrants their favourable consideration for promotion. Failure to promote able staff in an attempt to retain their skills within audit, may result in the organisation losing very able and skilful staff because they will look outside the organisation for better career prospects. Promotion may however itself entail movement and the loss of the individual's skills to computer audit.

The pragmatic response is to recognise and accept that good staff are likely to move on eventually. The issue for management is to ensure that it is geared to recruitment and that not only

3.11

are the terms and conditions of service the best that they can make them but also that the functions of a computer auditor make the post itself an attractive and satisfying one. An alternative is for the organisation to adopt a policy of fixed term contracts ensuring some degree of certainty.

3.5.7 Advanced Training

In the context of this chapter, the phrase 'advanced training' refers to both computing and computer audit training as relevant to the audit approach to more complex systems and to the training necessary to permit the computer auditor to understand fully and use the more complex computer audit techniques.

The problem often encountered in these areas is the difficulty of finding appropriate training courses or material. Computer suppliers and others provide computing courses, although these are rarely designed for the benefit of auditors. The supply of suitable courses is extremely limited and worthwhile written material only a little easier to come by.

Besides the difficulty of obtaining suitable 'advanced' training, there is the problem of gaining practical experience following such training. Very often the computer auditor will be isolated and able only to seek advice from those he is auditing. Management should not permit this to become the normal practice, and should encourage their computer auditors to meet opposite numbers from other organisations.

The computer auditor is therefore recommended to attend computer manufacturers' courses covering specific areas. Skilful auditors should be able to apply their knowledge of audit in conjunction with newly acquired technical expertise.

3.5.8 Small Organisations

Small organisations face additional problems when attempting to recruit, develop and retain computer audit expertise. These may be summarised as follows:

- Individuals may be unable to devote sufficient time to training, without having an unacceptable effect on the audit coverage of the organisation.

- The organisation may lack sufficient expertise to organise and run the necessary in-house training.

- The IT section may lack sufficient staff resources to offer any worthwhile assistance to the auditor, and there may be insufficient hardware resources to run audit work. Because of insufficient staff resources the system documentation may be poorer than is acceptable at other organisations, and there may be a lack of formal standards.

- The organisation may be unable to offer an attractive salary if it wishes to recruit expertise.

3.12

— There may be a lack of readily available interrogation packages which can be run on the organisation's computer. This will result in an additional training need so that the auditor may access data.

— Many small organisations share computer facilities with larger organisations. There will be a need to clearly establish the auditor's responsibilities.

There are no easy solutions to the problems of the smaller organisations but the following possibilities should be considered:

— Use the computer audit resources of other organisations including firms of auditors. In some parts of the country, organisations have made local arrangements whereby the services of the computer auditor of another organisation are made available for a short period and recharged at cost. This provides a relatively cheap and professional service but loses the advantages of continuity. Many external auditors will provide this sort of service as well as the cover necessary to comply with statutory responsibilities. Extra fees may be charged for this and again the advantages of continuity are lost.

— There are a number of areas of computer audit which demand less technical skill but are nevertheless important to the organisation. Internal audit, if short of resources and technical expertise, should attempt to maximise its impact by identifying areas where they may apply audit principles without the need for an in-depth understanding of computing.

— Some in-roads to technical areas can be made with minimal investment in training. For example, the ability to use some of the more user-friendly fourth generation languages, or the use of microcomputer packages, or retrieval software may allow internal audit to use the computer for its own purposes and simultaneously gain an appreciation of the principles of programming.

— Careful consideration of training methods can often identify an effective but inexpensive alternative, for example, a short term secondment to IT specifically to work in a particular area.

CIPFA

COMPUTER AUDIT GUIDELINES

THE MANAGEMENT OF IT

4 MANAGEMENT OF INFORMATION TECHNOLOGY RESOURCES

5 ACQUISITION OF INFORMATION TECHNOLOGY

CHAPTER 4

MANAGEMENT OF INFORMATION TECHNOLOGY RESOURCES

4

Continued overleaf

4.1 Introduction

4.1.1 Responsibilities

The extent of today's investment in IT demands that management addresses the key issues of obtaining best value for money from that investment, and ensures that the benefits from IT are fully achieved. Whilst management is responsible for providing the means to achieve the effective and efficient use of all IT resources, the auditor is concerned with determining whether or not management arrangements and procedures achieve their objectives.

This chapter addresses the resources and activities that require the attention of management such as hardware, software, staff, data and development, and considers the management approach adopted to maximise benefits and reduce costs.

4.1.2 Audit Objectives

The IT resources of an organisation are wide-ranging, and any overall measurement of their effective and efficient use will not be a self-contained or straightforward task. Indeed, it will be very unlikely that IT management or audit would consider a full review of IT resources as a specific project because of the difficulties in defining precise objectives and of having sufficient experienced staff to undertake such reviews. While management has a continuing commitment to ensure that best use is made of the assets of the organisation, a review of a specific area or activity may be prompted by a number of factors, such as complaints that output is late, recurrent faults in peripheral equipment and networks, failures or malfunctions of data preparation equipment, or the adoption of new programming techniques and the introduction of programming software.

Some of the more complex aspects of information technology, such as the efficiency of the central processor, the best mix of terminal and batch jobs, networks and communication links, are subjects which require computing expertise. That is not to say, though, that audit is unable to make any contribution in reviewing the best use of hardware and software. Where the audit section has an auditor with computer experience, a joint exercise with computer staff can often prove to be of mutual advantage because of the auditor's knowledge of the organisation and its procedures.

In reviewing the use of resources, the auditor may be involved in 'across the board' rather than service or application based activities but audit, like management, is often faced with the difficulty of trying to assess the use of resources without the aid of comparative costs or standard measures for the IT industry. The absence of standard measures does not absolve management or audit from their respective responsibilities, and audit will need to satisfy itself that management has an effective mechanism for monitoring the use of IT resources.

The task has become more difficult with the fragmentation of computing brought about by user driven computing and office automation in particular. Such developments not only lead to hidden costs but also in the absence of central control greatly increase the potential for wasteful use of resources, inefficiencies and duplication of activities if not worse. The situation serves to emphasise the importance of management constantly reviewing the arrangements for achieving value for money.

This chapter considers, therefore, the following aspects of the management of IT resources:

- the strategy for the acquisition and use of IT facilities throughout the organisation, including facilities management arrangements;

- the control over the development of applications;

- monitoring the performance of IT facilities; and

- the costs of providing IT facilities and charging users for those services.

Priority should be given to a review of policies and management arrangements and controls in order to produce an independent appraisal of the IT department as a whole, and an assessment of the value for money it offers to all its users. This consideration of value for money should be continued through the subsequent review of general controls or application controls. Consideration may then be given to whether current procedures could be improved to promote a more effective or efficient service.

Much of the review will call for a clear understanding of the organisation's IT philosophy and of IT itself. Although the prime responsibility for monitoring performance and reviewing arrangements lies with management, audit has a part to play. It may be that neither audit nor management have the requisite skills, and consideration should be given to the use of external assistance, for example from independent consultants, the IT department itself, or even suppliers of computing facilities.

4.2 Management of IT

4.2.1 Overview

Developments in IT have already resulted in dramatic changes in the application of that technology such as a change to user-driven computing, where users are given the facilities to develop and maintain their own system. Such facilities may be provided by on-line links to a mainframe, by independent microcomputers or by networks. IT may not necessarily be provided by a central computer resource: it certainly is no longer the exclusive preserve of any one department, and may even be provided by a third party outside the organisation.

In reviewing the management arrangements and strategy for the use of IT resources, auditors should have regard to:

— the involvement of management in directing policy;

— the impact of developments in computer and telecommunications technology on the organisation;

— the establishment of and adherence to standards and a corporate security policy within the overall strategy;

— staff resources within the IT and user departments; and

— alternative methods of service provision, eg facilities management.

4.2.2   Management Involvement

A clearly defined information systems and information technology strategy is essential for any organisation seeking to ensure that it gets maximum benefit from its investment in IT efficiently and effectively. It is equally important that while ultimate responsibility for the organisation's IT strategy rests at the highest level, all levels of management who will be responsible for its implementation should be actively involved in the definition of the strategy. That strategy should form part of the organisation's overall business strategy so that the IT plan is seen as an integral part of the corporate business plan of the whole organisation.

4.2.3   Impact of Technology

Continuing developments in IT provide a wide choice of technical and technological solutions for managers but also create difficulties for them in planning and seeking to maximise benefit and minimise cost. The automated office brings to the manager's desk a considerable range of technologies, and through the technology of local area networks, it is possible to link word processing, view-data, micro computing, telephone systems and electronic mail to each other and to central mainframes. This convergence of voice, text and data processing provides a far wider range of options for automating office procedures than has ever been previously available. (The implications of networks are considered in chapter 12.)

Further important developments include the rapid growth of open systems such as those based on UNIX and the spread of electronic data interchange (EDI) facilities. Such options present management with the need to determine whether a strategy for central corporate IT departments and centres should give way to a strategy for a number of discrete independent IT centres.

4.2.4   Standards

The benefits to an organisation of devising and adhering to standards for IT activity are discussed in more detail in chapters 6, 7, 8 and 9 but there can be little doubt that the existence and application of standards promote both efficiency and effectiveness in any long term activity.

Major computer systems take several months to design and even longer to program and install. After installation, most computer systems can be expected to have an effective life of several years and it is likely that the system will be maintained by different personnel at different times. An effective means of communication should therefore exist between different generations of staff to ensure that they do not waste rediscovering the purpose and capabilities of the system. Documentation which is comprehensive and in a standard format is the key to effective communication, and it is essential to produce and maintain documentation conscientiously so that time spent on maintenance is kept to a minimum.

The absence of programming standards is also to be deplored because programmers are left to design programs according to their own preference and previous experience. This results in an amalgam of conventions and techniques which cannot readily be understood by any one programmer. Different programming techniques such as structured programming should be evaluated, and if it is decided to adopt a new technique then adequate training must be arranged and the new procedures closely monitored.

Standards within an IT department are designed to reflect levels of attainment and achieve uniformity of approach over a long time scale. It is advisable therefore to formalise these standards in a written document with sections for each discipline, eg system development, operations, data preparation and data control, and network support.

User departments with immediate access to IT facilities should also implement standards to ensure that their use of computing is secure, efficient and economic. The IT department in view of their experience in organising computing use should be able to prepare such standards for users. This would have the advantage of ensuring the adoption of best practices and co-ordinated use of IT facilities.

People at different points and different levels in an organisation will each have their own perception of security and efficiency and effectiveness. There is a need for a common awareness and appreciation of both and therefore a need for education tailored to satisfy different perceptions. The range of CIPFA publications under the generic title of 'Computer Survival Guides' addresses these key issues and may satisfy the educational need.

4.2.5   Staff Resources

Staff employed in the IT department are a significant corporate and specialised resource which demands careful and effective management. This is particularly so because of the pace of change of information technology and recurrent shortfalls in some specialisms particularly at the 'leading edge'. To make optimum use of this resource management must ensure that staff are adequately trained, properly graded and fully deployed through a planned development programme of work. The number of IT staff should be appropriate to the size of the organisation, computer configuration and the development and maintenance programme. Overall, management should aim to strike a balance between workload, numbers of staff and the expertise available so that efficient and effective use is made of staff resources.

The shift towards user-driven computing inevitably leads to an increase in the number of persons engaged in computing activities but, because they are not part of a central IT department, they may not be recognised as part of the total IT resource and be omitted from training schemes. It will become increasingly important for the same staff management considerations applied to IT departments to be applied to user departments to ensure efficient and effective use of the total IT resources.

Management will in any event need to evaluate the quality of its IT staff and assess their capabilities based on observations, intuition and reports from user departments. As a minimum, one would expect that monthly records are kept of the total complement of staff, actual available personnel each month, and time lost to sickness, leave and training compared with time allocated to functions and projects. More detailed measures may however be employed for each discipline.

Data preparation

There are various factors to be taken into account in measuring data preparation. For example it is claimed that the speed and accuracy of data preparation increase significantly because validation is handled by the key to disc equipment rather than the mainframe. The attributes of the data itself affects productivity; for example pure numeric data is easier and quicker to key and verify than a mixture of alpha numeric characters. The poor quality of the data itself may slow down operations because it will be rejected at entry by validation routines. Comparative statistics may be obtained from computing bodies and publications.

The workload of a data preparation section will inevitably peak and trough so sufficient in-house equipment should be provided for the normal requirements of the organisation, with standby arrangements with a bureau for abnormal demands.

Operations

The impact of modern operating systems on the operations staff will be significant since job satisfaction may be reduced if operators are reduced to the role of machine minders or expected to work unsocial hours. Management should always review working arrangements on the introduction of new facilities and software.

The computer operations staff will tend to be judged by the incidence of operational problems

4.5

and their cause, eg:

- — inefficiency or mistakes in the operations control section;

- — weakness or faults in the operating systems or applications; and

- — lack of resources in the operations section.

Management should monitor failed or aborted jobs including such details as the number of job re-submissions, incidence of duplicate submission or processing of data. It should then seek to identify whether the causes of such problems lie in the operating or control areas or the software.

Where shift working is in operation some comparison between shifts may be possible, but regard must be had to the type of work handled by each shift. Much of the day shift's workload may for example consist of servicing terminal requests whereas the night shift may be scheduling and processing batch jobs. Comparisons of staffing and accommodation with other similar installations may also be possible but should allow for differences in circumstances.

The continuous reduction in the amount of operator intervention required may bring about the possibility of unmanned operations. Where this is seen as a viable option, it is important to ensure that the whole range of potential risks, from single system failures leading to lost processing time to security or fire risks is fully evaluated before management adopts such a practice for cost reduction purposes.

4.2.6   Alternative Methods of Service Delivery

The earlier sections of this chapter have considered the management of IT resources from the standpoint of an 'in-house' service. However, in seeking the best value for money from its IT facilities, management should actively consider alternative options for service delivery.

Facilities management

Facilities management (FM) entails the organisation's IT service being handed over to a third party. The arrangement may apply to the whole information technology and systems functions or selected parts such as operations or system development. The FM business may take over the information systems and run them from the organisation's site or from a site owned by the FM business with the contracting organisation having access to the systems through communication links. The service may provide for the FM business to take existing staff into its employ. FM could also be used as a temporary measure during a period of major change to provide continuity of service.

Whatever the reason for or nature of the arrangement there are two key points:

- — any move to FM should accord with the IT strategy;

— there must be a clear definition of IT requirements and the levels of service needed.

The longer term strategy for after the period of the FM contract will also need to be considered.

A wide range of factors needs to be taken into account before a policy decision is taken to adopt FM for the provision of IT services or facilities. An FM project team with contract negotiating skills should be formed to identify the key issues, produce a specification, identify potential FM providers, evaluate tenders, and establish contract monitoring procedures. This team should ensure that alternative means of providing the service are considered.

The tendering and selection process should follow good practice as described in chapter 5, and the contract should cover:

— ownership of hardware;

— ownership of software copyright;

— maintenance and support in the event of a collapse or withdrawal of the FM contractor;

— procedures for enhancements and changes to existing systems;

— minimum acceptable performance levels;

— interim review dates for management reports;

— responsibility for tactical management of the communications network;

— respective responsibilities concerning accommodation provided, costs of cleaning, heating, power etc;

— insurance;

— payments; and

— the rights of access for internal and external auditors to data files and programs and facilities.

There needs to be a clear provision for the organisation to monitor performance of the FM service against defined response times, down-times, maintenance times, etc. Payments due to the service provider should be linked to the achievement of defined targets.

Considerable care therefore needs to be exercised before placing the organisation's IT facilities in the hands of a third party to ensure that the investment in the use of IT is adequately protected. IT is such an integral part of day-to-day process of most organisations that a failure of the IT function could result in a failure of the organisation itself.

Consortium arrangements

For smaller organisations another possible means of achieving a more cost-effective IT service can be to join with other similar organisations to create a computing consortium. Such arrangements

4.7

are however not without their own difficulties particularly when the IT strategies of the partners diverge. The most common problems are:

- differences in priorities;

- reaching agreement on common systems;

- different levels of funding available; and

- personality clashes.

Any organisation considering moving towards a computing consortium arrangement will need to weigh these possible difficulties against the projected gains in the provision of IT facilities and value for money. The approach required is comparable to that employed for FM.

Use of consultants and contract staff

If there are shortages of IT skills or staff recruitment problems, short term contract staff or consultants can often be an effective means of solving specific problems subject to suitable contracts being drawn up. Developments in telecommunications provide the option of teleworking to provide a solution to local shortages of skills or the immobilty of people.

In brief, management needs to consider the whole range of possible methods of service delivery when seeking to obtain the best value for money.

4.3 Application Systems Development

4.3.1   Overview

By far the largest proportion of IT staff resources and a substantial proportion of machine resources are devoted to the development and maintenance of applications. The development of applications should therefore have a high priority in the list of management concerns.

The standards and procedures for system development are addressed in chapter 8 but the management issues considered here are the development programme, efficiency of processing, clerical support and quality assurance.

Development programme

Efficient and effective use of IT resources for the development of applications is unlikely to be achieved without a development plan. A major element in determining the viability of the plan is the availability of staff in numbers and the skills and experience required for the task. The task of determining the numbers and appropriate skills required and the most effective and efficient way of employing them should be assigned to a project management team created to co-ordinate all requirements for developments. The team should advise the management body responsible for approving the development plan of the implications of any decisions affecting the deployment of staff in the execution of the plan.

The methodologies used in development should be considered including the use of fourth generation languages and techniques such as computer aided systems engineering (CASE) to improve productivity.

IT trends

Current trends are towards users being provided with software tools to enable them to develop their own systems. The arguments in favour of this approach are that it reduces the development time scale and the user produces precisely what is required. The effect of user driven computing on the corporate IT policy needs careful consideration. The risks and consequences are the loss of integrated or compatible systems, the additional costs of providing equipment at each user site, and the duplication of development at each separate site.

Management approach

Management and the auditor in turn should review development procedures regularly to assess whether or not:

  – the expectations of system performance have materialised in practice;

  – the applications architecture and facilities are appropriate to the current user environment; and

  – the applications provide adequate and proper management information.

The above factors are indicators or measures of the effectiveness of development procedures in producing the right products. Attention also needs to be given to the methodologies employed for cost/benefit analyses of systems to be able to determine cost effectiveness.

4.3.2   Processing Efficiency

Optimising software

Measures taken to maximise the efficiency of programs are essentially detective in nature and may employ one of two approaches. The first is investigative aimed at identifying the likely causes of poor performance of programs evidenced in operation. The second is preventive involving the systematic examination of program code.

The investigative approach involves the examination of the costs associated with processing; this may reveal specific programs or procedures that appear to absorb a disproportionate amount of machine resource and, therefore, merit investigation.

4.9

The alternative is either the independent and systematic review of the coding by an experienced programmer to identify poor programming techniques and inefficient coding or to use of specialised software packages known as software monitors. The software is usually loaded into the processor while the program to be optimised is running and, depending on the particular type of monitor, it may identify program instructions which are rarely used and which may, therefore, indicate redundant coding. It may also identify the number of times each program instruction is used so that consideration may be given to using different instructions to achieve the same ends, but with more effective use of the computer's resources. (See also 4.4.4 for further information on the use of software monitors.)

There are conflicting views about the merits of software optimisation. Where the organisation adopts structured programming techniques, then piecemeal optimisations may affect the structure of the program and make it less rather than more efficient. It is also said that the reducing hardware costs, coupled with the increasing performance and storage capabilities, make it more cost effective to acquire additional memory than to devote more expensive resources to optimising applications software.

Performance measures

Most operating systems have facilities available to log details of software performance but other job accounting software may be available to analyse such aspects as the resources used by each program. Such information can then be used to identify application programs with apparently high demands on the peripherals or the processor.

In seeking to provide a measure of programming performance management may refer to the failure rate of programs rather than say the speed of development, and could record the number of compilations necessary to produce a workable program. The number of workable lines of program source code produced has been suggested as one unit of measure, but this may depend on the type of programming language used and the programming standards applicable within the installation, and the complexity or technical innovations of the program's objective.

Other areas worthy of examination may include:

- the extent of requests for system amendments;

- external factors affecting system performance;

- the need for supportive clerical systems;

- documentation quality; and

- user and management satisfaction with the system.

4.10

4.3.3 Clerical Support

The costs determined for clerical support of a system should be subject to examination. This entails the further analysis of costs into their constituent elements, preferably relating the analysis to system requirements and grades of staff involved. For example, a preliminary analysis might consider data capture, resubmission of rejections and output management. In some organisations, the support of management services staff may be required to undertake this task successfully.

4.3.4 Quality Assurance

To meet user requirements is the ultimate test of a good system. IT departments are often criticised by their users for failing to complete projects within the estimated time scale, or even for being unable to start projects within a time scale acceptable to the user. Unless joint agreement is reached management problems will arise. If users are greatly dissatisfied and have sufficient resources then they can turn away from central computing facilities and cause a substantial resource to be under utilised. User satisfaction is important but unless there are well-defined procedures for monitoring the degree of satisfaction, then potential problems may not be identified sufficiently quickly.

Increasingly there is a wider understanding of the benefits of improving the quality of the production process to minimise errors and consequential costs of correction. European standards have been devised and promoted widely and are increasingly being adopted by organisations.

Users' responsibilities

User satisfaction is generally greater when the users have been involved throughout the development process, allowing difficulties to be resolved at the earliest opportunity. Users should therefore have definite responsibilities regarding the systems being developed for them to ensure that they are satisfied that their requirements are fully known to the IT department and, equally, they are aware of the approach they propose to use to satisfy those needs. They must also recognise that there will be a demand upon their own resources during development, and will need to take this into account when making a bid for IT facilities.

4.4 Hardware

4.4.1 Overview

Hardware performance is a subject which calls for technical knowledge and experience, and it is unlikely that many organisations have the resources to monitor, measure, and improve the performance of their processor and peripherals, without the assistance of the supplier or specialist organisations.

Nevertheless, if management wishes to satisfy itself that it is getting the claimed benefits from the equipment, some measures of the hardware's performance will be necessary if only to support any claims the organisation may wish to make against the supplier for poor performance.

Several techniques can be adopted to provide data for analysis of the workload and capabilities of each item of hardware eg:

- physical measurements;

- system journals and logs;

- software monitors; and

- hardware monitors.

4.4.2 Physical Measurements

Physical observation and measurement can easily provide management with information on:

Measures of throughput

- number of jobs processed in a shift; and

- number of units of processor time used.

Utilisation of hardware

- number of tape decks in use;

- number of disc drives in use; and

- time used by printers.

System response times

- time waiting for jobs.

Indications of possible excess capacity

- time lost in correcting faults; and

- time lost in re-running program failures.

Some information may be obtained from operators' manual logs though it is likely that most organisations would need to define the information they require and then arrange for the appropriate staff to log the details during a specified period.

Another source of information of hardware failures is the engineer's log which may either be manually maintained by on-site engineers or logged and reported by the operating system. While this information is primarily for use by the suppliers' engineers in maintaining the equipment, arrangements may be made for users to be kept informed of data so recorded. It should be said, however, that the installation's operators would probably know about faults in equipment.

4.4.3   System Journals

Most operating systems log details of the resources used by the system and while the potential range of data that can be logged is considerable, there are few facilities provided by suppliers for retrieving and analysing the data.

The sheer volume of data that can be logged and the consequential demand for disc space requires the data to be stored in condensed form and this exacerbates the difficulties in searching for specific data and tabulating reports. Computer-assisted audit techniques can often be employed, though, to extract and re-present information from system logs so that key information can be identified for a review of performance.

Information on performance which may be available from system logs and journals includes:

— processor usage;

— core occupancy;

— multi-programming loading;

— terminal activity;

— disc and tape transfers and failures; and

— volume of input and output records.

It should also be noted that the volume of information logged is under the control of the system programmer who may vary the type of data recorded from time to time. Care should be taken, therefore, to compare like with like.

4.4.4   Software and Hardware Monitors

A software monitor is a program which resides in a computer and collects information about the way the system is being used over a period. Two broad types of such monitors are available: the program monitor and the system monitor.

The program monitor reports on processor utilisation of individual programs by counting the number of times a routine is entered during a program run. It may produce a histogram of the

4.13

frequency with which every instruction is obeyed, and conduct activity sampling to determine the amount of time spent in each instruction or routine.

A system monitor collects information on the performance of the system as a whole by collecting data maintained by the operating system, and then reporting on the utilisation of various hardware components over time and core usage. An operating system's accounting routine is an example of such a monitor.

The advantages of software monitors are that they are cheaper than most hardware monitors and they provide comprehensive data and are easy to use. Against this it is argued that they impose an overhead on the system since they depend upon the facilities of the operating system and they may, to a greater or lesser degree, distort the resources they measure.

A hardware monitor is an electronic device which is physically connected to the computer and measures and records its activity. For the monitor to produce useful and meaningful statistics it is essential that the user knows what they are measuring and thus how they connect the monitor. These devices are powerful and accurate; they incur little overhead or degradation of performance but they are expensive.

4.4.5   Sizing Hardware Needs

The acquisition of IT facilities is dealt with in chapter 5 but one particular aspect which impinges on the use of IT resources is the sizing of hardware needs. Measuring anticipated capacity over say a five or seven year period is a difficult task particularly for installations servicing many different departments, all with different needs and priorities. Deciding when to upgrade to a new computer model is a decision which has significant pitfalls:

- upgrading too soon may waste money;

- upgrading too late may disrupt the organisation's computer development policy;

- upgrading to the wrong model may mean long term problems at high cost.

Sizing the hardware needs will thus demand identification of current space capacity and hardware bottle-necks to try to make better use of existing resources rather than automatically increasing the capacity of the hardware.

Additional considerations are the capabilities of mini and micro computers and the opportunity they provide to satisfy additional demands for processing power without affecting the loading of the mainframe.

4.14

4.5 IT Costs

4.5.1 Overview

The management of any organisation which depends upon information technology to support its business needs to know the costs of IT. The growing demands for competitiveness and accountability place an even greater emphasis on the need to know all the elements of the cost of the service being provided. The need for costing information also applies when computing has been distributed across the organisation.

CIPFA has developed and issued recommendations on the standard form of accounts to promote a consistent basis for published statistical information. The information paper 'Knowing What IT Costs' published by the Audit Commission (1990) also discusses the principles and alternative methods of dealing with IT costs and charging.

It is to be expected, of course, that the detailed system of accounting and costing adopted will depend on a number of factors such as:

- the size and complexity of the operations;

- the extent of outside use; and

- the organisation's policy on charging.

Nevertheless, certain principles capable of common application can be identified and summarised as:

- the identification and operation of cost centres;

- the full allocation of all costs to those cost centres, including overheads, and a charge for capital assets based on current value;

- the estimation and collection of meaningful and productive resource units for each cost centre as a basis for charging;

- the calculation of unit costs; and

- the allocation of cost centre expenditure to individual jobs on a realistic and practical basis that properly reflects the resources required by those jobs.

4.5.2 Objectives of Costing

There are many benefits of full and accurate accounting. Most of them arise from the improved information available to management which provides a better basis for decision taking. The objectives of costing and accounting may be summarised as follows:

Preparation of accounts

At the lowest level the accounting system must enable the final accounts to be prepared. This is, of course, self evident, but the final accounts must pass the auditor's certificate of 'present fairly' or 'true and fair view', and there have been occasions on which an auditor has commented adversely on the accounting system for IT costs.

Reporting/accountability

There has been a considerable interest in recent years in performance measurement in the public sector, and this has rightly lent increasing emphasis to accountability and financial reporting.

It is essential to be seen to be in control of costs, and to be able to demonstrate efficiency. This in turn depends on an effective accounting and costing system, providing the right information for management.

Budgetary control

Budgetary control requires an effective accounting system. Budgetary control should be exercised at the level of each cost centre in the first instance, and performance measured by comparing expenditure with achievement of pre-determined targets.

Planning and budgeting

Full and detailed knowledge of the costs of the different sections of the IT department is necessary, both for budget preparation and for effective longer-term planning of resource allocation.

Financial evaluation of applications

An appropriate costing system should be used to measure the continuing cost-effectiveness of the current live applications, and this need for management information exists independently of the policy adopted for charging. Evaluations of the costs and benefits of possible new developments should also be undertaken, within the same financial framework.

Information for charging

The information necessary for allocating costs and charging users should be available as a by-product of the costing system. This is not to say that the accounting costs should simply be charged out to the user; that will be a policy decision. In drawing up its policy, however, management must be aware of how much each application is costing so that the cost or benefit of adopting a different charging policy can be readily assessed. This is especially important where the policy is other than simply cost recovery. The accuracy of the costing information will largely determine the financial outcome for the computer unit at the year end.

Cost centres

For purposes of budgetary control and allocation of costs it is recommended that the IT department

4.16

be divided into a number of distinct cost centres. These cost centres, which together will cover the entire expenditure attributable to the unit, should reflect its organisation, indicating the boundaries of responsibility and accountability.

The number of cost centres established will depend on the size of the installation and the range of its operations. Examples of appropriate cost or centres of responsibility would include:

Functional cost centres

— data preparation;

— control;

— central operations;

— data communications;

— development; and

— support.

Holding accounts

— administration; and

— others as required (eg research and general development, equipment financing).

4.5.3   Accounting Software

Many operating systems provide facilities to log details of all jobs run and the IT resources used but the nature of these facilities varies considerably.

Most accounting software uses the job name as the identifier for the task, and then usually logs all peripheral activity, eg the number of units of data transferred to and from magnetic disk, and the number of lines printed on the line printer, on to a separate disk file. Software may then be available to read this disk file and using a predetermined table of costs for each element of processing calculate the total cost of the job. The costing algorithm can be quite complex depending upon the requirements of both computer management and users on the one hand, and the operating system's accounting facilities on the other.

Such an algorithm may include costs for such activities as:

— disk file transfers;

— occupancy of main memory;

— on-line printing;

— off-line printing;

4.17

—   terminal connect time; and

—   processor mill time.

Alternatively, the IT department may adopt a less complex method of costing by merely taking the total costs of the department, and then calculating a unit cost, based on the number of time units available for the year, according to the shifts operated. The cost of each job would then be based on the machine time used, irrespective of the specific processing resources used.

Most accounting routines allow the IT department to allocate budgets to users   when a job is presented for running the system checks that the budget has not been exhausted and, provided a balance is available, allows the job to be run. At the end of the job, the cost is calculated and deducted from the budget.

Where budgets are allocated to users, and a user exhausts his budget before the end of the financial year, the organisation may choose to refresh the budget (for the primary financial applications, for example) but may deny facilities to other users or penalise them in some way.

Management approach

The issue for management is to determine the objectives of a costing system and how it may best be established and maintained and used to good purpose.

The first question is what is the costing mechanism intended to cover and what it is to be used for? Is it intended, for example, to identify all costs of the IT department and apportion them over all jobs? If so, what of the computing initiated from say workstations owned by a user department? Are the rentals for such equipment charged in turn to the computer department? Management needs to be quite clear firstly as to the purpose of costing and the uses to which it will be put.

Management should also consider the mechanics of the system. For example job identifiers are needed to distinguish between live processing of applications and development work which may use the same programs and operating system accounting routines are dependent upon the job name to allocate the associated costs. The integrity of the job names will therefore be significant and management needs to consider the need for enforced standards.

Where the IT department is seen as a service unit for other departments, from whom the full costs must be recouped, the organisation may well impose higher charges for external bodies. Alternatively the organisation may negotiate a fixed charge with the customer but variances from the actual cost should be identified and the charge reassessed if it is markedly different.

Finally management should ensure that charges are regularly reviewed to take account of changed circumstances and should comment critically on the perceived effects of that policy, be they adverse or favourable.

4.6 Audit Approach

The IT resources of an organisation are wide ranging and it is unlikely that IT management or audit would consider an overall review of the use of resources as a single project because of the difficulties in defining precise objectives and the lack of resources to carry out such an all embracing review.

Although auditors should be able to break the job down into a series of manageable tasks it is more likely that audit will be alerted to specific matters requiring attention while reviewing the administrative and procedural controls of an organisation which may cause it to direct its energies to a specific value for money exercise.

Alternatively management may ask audit to review a specific area because of:

— complaints from users of the failure to produce output within previously agreed time scales;

— recurrent faults in peripheral equipment;

— adoption of new programming techniques; and

— acquisition of specialised software as an aid to program development.

It is unlikely that audit will have the resources or technical ability to make technical evaluations of many aspects of computer processing and such matters as sizing or capacity planning; such matters would require the services of an external consultant. However the auditor should be capable of making a judgement on the adequacy or otherwise of management arrangements for use of IT by using the criteria for good management set out in previous parts of this chapter. Similarly an auditor should be able to determine where and when the services of a consultant or specialist are required to assist audit.

An auditor with experience of computer operations could usefully undertake a joint exercise with a member of the IT department which could be of mutual benefit. Examples of such reviews may include examining:

— the efficiency and effectiveness of the organisation's computer development programme;

— the use made of error-reporting and monitoring to assess the efficiency of particular applications;

— the results of any post-implementation reviews to assess if they indicate objectives that are largely being achieved or frequently not being attained;

— the effectiveness of the IT department in supervising the purchasing of micros and microcomputer software by user departments;

4.19

–   the method used to assess the costs and benefits which might accrue before deciding to proceed with requests for changes to systems;

–   the use made of reports provided by the IT department for users of particular system;

–   the supervision and advice that the IT department provides to users (eg on security, access control and the need for clerical back-up systems); or

–   the assessment of centralised IT facilities against the benefits and/or disadvantages of decentralised computing.

4.20

CHAPTER 5

ACQUISITION OF IT FACILITIES

5

Continued overleaf

5.1 Introduction

5.1.1 Audit Objectives

For most organisations IT is essential to the effective delivery of services. They consequently incur significant amounts of expenditure not only on acquisitions but also on the support and maintenance of the information services that depend on IT facilities. Management should ensure that acquisitions of all IT facilities and services meet the business needs of the organisation in a cost effective manner. Audit should determine:

- whether or not the management arrangements and procedures for such acquisitions will meet the objectives of management; and

- whether the arrangements and procedures have been applied in practice.

The auditor is also concerned with whether or not the organisation has complied with the requirements of European Community (EC) legislation for public sector bodies to implement open systems and make greater use of competitive tendering.

Areas of interest

The term *IT facilities* covers hardware, software and services at central and departmental levels. Hardware acquisition may include the:

- central mainframe processors;

- departmental minicomputers;

- micro computers;

- networking facilities;

- peripherals such as printers; and

- dedicated equipment such as word processors and other facilities used for office automation.

Such acquisitions may be new, but are often replacements or enhancements of existing hardware.

Software acquisition is often linked to hardware acquisition because new software is frequently needed to support the new hardware. However, software may also be acquired independently. Software may include:

- operating systems;

- other system software;

- application program packages; and,

    — general purpose packages such as word-processing and spreadsheets.

The justification for audit interest in the acquisition process is two-fold.

    — The impact of IT upon the functions of the organisation is likely to be considerable. The scale of the organisation's IT budget, however large, is unlikely to reflect the full impact of investment in technology upon the day-to-day workings of that body. The investment of time, expertise and financial resources in the acquisition of IT resources needs careful assessment. Mistakes have long-term effects on the efficiency and effectiveness of the organisation so it is an essential part of the audit function to ensure that adequate procedures exist to minimise the risk of such mistakes.

    — It is essential for audit to be aware of the nature of any changes and the alterations in control procedures that may occur following the acquisition of new facilities.

The actual procedures to be followed will depend on the complexity of the hardware or software to be installed, the cost and time scale of the acquisition, and the extent of its effect on users outside the IT department. The principles behind the control and management of acquisition are the same, regardless of the complexities of the process.

In the following sections, acquisition has been broken down into seven stages. These are:

    — IT policy and strategy;

    — establishing the need for the hardware and software;

    — the preparation and presentation of a feasibility study containing a recommendation and calling for a decision;

    — the implementation of that decision by specifying precisely the requirements for the hardware, software or services which reflect the needs of the organisation itself as well as any relevant legislation;

    — the appraisal of the prospective suppliers' products and a decision on which to adopt;

    — the installation of the product and its handover to the user after testing;

    — a post-implementation review to determine whether the anticipated benefits have been realised within the time and costs specified.

5.2　IT Strategy

5.2.1　Overview

A clearly defined information systems and technology strategy is a pre-requisite for any organisation seeking to ensure effective IT acquisition procedures. Organisations have a wide range of options for satisfying their IT requirements, ranging from large central mainframe installations to a plethora of personal microcomputers. Similarly, the modes of operation may range from simple batch processing through to on-line enquiry, transaction processing and other interactive operations.

The choice of options, however, should be dictated by the needs and resources of the organisation: what is acquired should satisfy existing and anticipated business needs and be within the capability of the organisation to resource and utilise. If an organisation is to satisfy its requirements properly, it should clearly define and adhere to an IT strategy that articulates those requirements and predicts how they may change in future. For such a policy to be established and implemented, management needs to appreciate the potential of IT to satisfy business needs, and evaluate requirements and determine the ways and means of satisfying them, but most of all they must be able to analyse current needs and predict future ones. The strategy should be regularly reviewed to reflect changing requirements.

5.2.2 Responsibility

Ultimate responsibility for the IT strategy of any organisation should rest at the highest level. In practice, responsibilities are delegated to a person or management team employed within the organisation to determine amongst other things the needs of the organisation and to formulate a policy or policies for approval by the superior body.

In some organisations there may be a permanently appointed management team with responsibility for implementing the overall IT policy, which reports to a board or committee. Alternatively, such a team may be formed only when the need arises. Such a team should represent all affected divisions or departments of the organisation. For example, if it consisted only of the IT manager and head of finance, it would be unlikely fully to represent the views of the departments and may be accused of bias. Similar considerations apply to the team responsible for controlling implementation and in practice a single team may perform the two functions of formulating and implementing policies.

Whatever the organisational structure, the important points to be made are:

– The persons responsible for formulating policy should take account of all the requirements of the organisation to produce a corporate strategy. The needs of individual departments can then be assessed in the context of corporate priorities.

– Areas of responsibility and delegated powers should be clearly defined.

– The arrangements should be appropriate to the size and structure of the organisation.

– Significant acquisitions should always be treated as projects and a project control team formed and be responsible for implementing the decisions of the management team.

It is clearly desirable to avoid conflicting policies such as the IT department actively promoting the development of large central IT resource whilst the organisation's management services division encourages users to acquire their own small, dedicated computers. The consequent fragmentary IT development would have long-term adverse effects on the organisation. Any IT strategy must therefore have a corporate view and be enforced assiduously.

The auditor needs to identify the organisation's development policy and review how it is applied. The auditor should consider how the policy was formulated and assess how effective it is likely to be.

5.2.3   The Decision Making Process

If an organisation is to obtain full benefit from its investment in IT, it is essential that an appropriate management structure is in place to monitor and control each stage of the acquisition process.

Each stage in the process of acquiring IT facilities should be marked by a decision whether or not to go on to the next stage, or approval of a given course of action. The first of these decisions ought to be the determination of an IT strategy according to an agreed corporate policy.

The objective of the auditor, and indeed that of management, is to be satisfied that decisions are taken by the right persons and that the arrangements for taking such decisions are satisfactory.

Matters for consideration under this aspect of procedures include:

— identification of the decisions to be taken and who is to take them;

— the availability of skills to advise on these decisions;

— the co-ordination of computer plans; and

— the allocation of terms of reference and responsibilities.

The decisions

The principal matters requiring decisions are:

— whether there is a need for acquisition and whether such an acquisition is feasible;

— which suppliers should be short-listed and which supplier is to be preferred;

— whether the specifications conform with EC requirements concerning open systems interconnectivity (OSI) and tendering;

— whether contracts are acceptable and suppliers have met their obligations; and

— whether the acquisition was successful and met the needs of the organisation.

Arrangements should ensure impartiality and the avoidance of conflicts of interests, and the application of the appropriate skills and knowledge. They should ensure that individuals do not avoid the responsibilities proper to their position. A suitably high level committee or board should be responsible for budgeting and approval of decisions. The end users should be responsible for making their case for the use of IT facilities and specifying their consequent requirements. The IT manager has a responsibility to provide technical advice on the potential of computing facilities and alternative solutions in addition to contributing to long-term planning. An independent person should be responsible for co-ordinating needs and proposed solutions.

Other matters to be considered are:

— the timing of the decisions;

— the requirements, if any, for consultation with bodies such as staff associations and auditors;

— control over involvement of suppliers in the decision- making process.

Availability of skills

The successful implementation of an IT strategy depends on expert knowledge being available to those taking and those implementing the decisions.

It may be advisable for some organisations to employ specialists not only to advise on solutions and evaluate suppliers' proposals, but also to manage an acquisition project on behalf of the organisation, including installation of the hardware or software. This is especially relevant to organisations which have limited resources, but also applies to specialist skills in technical evaluation, negotiation and legal advice on contracts.

Co-ordination

Clear and specific allocation of duties and responsibilities should serve to prevent confusion and conflict between users and the IT department. Some matters by their very nature call for co-ordination of activities. The first of these is the relative priority of users' requests for facilities and in turn the time scale for IT planning. The second matter is the respective roles of networks, mainframes, minis, micros and word processors within the organisation and, in turn, the plans for centralised hardware and software against the plans for distributed or independent facilities.

Terms of reference

The particular points which should concern the auditor and management alike are the delegated powers for certain aspects or activities of the process of acquisition. These are:

— the IT expenditure budgets;

— approving short and long term plans;

— approving major acquisitions;

5.5

- examining and approving technical aspects of acquisition;

- examining and approving financial aspects of acquisitions; and

- examining and approving the areas where IT techniques should be applied.

Finally, if management control is to be effective, then they should give clear instructions on the form and frequency of reports and on their presentation to the appropriate body or person at all stages of the acquisition.

5.3 Establishing the Need

5.3.1 Overview

Establishing the need is a crucial stage in the acquisition process. There is a risk that any feasibility study will be undertaken in an atmosphere that precludes any alternative to acquiring the resource. It is only by the process of thorough investigation and a system of reporting that both managers and users can demonstrate the need for further action leading to acquisition. Without this investigation to establish the need, it is all too easy to rely on 'gut-reactions' and for misconceptions about the reasons for poor performance or unsatisfactory service to lead to ill-advised and costly decisions.

In some circumstances a detailed examination of the situation may not be necessary: the size of the proposed solution and the probable cost of a feasibility study may militate against it. A costly feasibility study should not be undertaken without prior approval. However, reasons for the acquisition, whether self evident or not, should still be formally presented for a decision.

5.3.2 Identifying the Need

It is vital to undertake a needs analysis, firstly to define the need in broad terms and then to determine whether it has arisen because of problems or because of the general requirement to enhance facilities so that an adequate service can be maintained.

For example, consistent delays in processing or poor terminal response times may be caused by:

- overloading of the computer;

- computer malfunctions;

- inefficient program design;

- staff shortages; or

- poor staff performance in particular areas such as operations or development.

It may be found that a combination of these factors causes a delay, and only when all factors are identified is it possible to consider all the alternative solutions to the problem. Poor machine performance would warrant an examination, not only of the computer itself and associated activities, but also of the applications run on the computer.

As staff costs represent a considerable and increasing proportion of the IT budget, many organisations consider increasing their productivity with high level languages and software development aids. Indeed, some organisations are dispersing their programming capability by providing users with the facility to develop their own expertise in the use of user- friendly development software. This relieves the IT department of the burden of developing programs for the ad hoc enquiries that they receive and, at the same time, ensures that they can direct their specialist skills at more demanding work. Making better use of existing staff resources is clearly better than increasing staffing levels within the IT department.

It is important to remember that the IT resource of an organisation is not just the hardware installed, but the total contribution of hardware, software and staff. The performance of any one of these cannot be considered in isolation because of the contribution made by the other two factors. The performance of any one of the factors can be improved by acquiring more of the scarce resources, but perhaps more effectively by improving the contribution of the other factors.

5.4 Feasibility Study

5.4.1 Overview

Effective procedures for managing IT acquisition are vital to avoid wasting the organisation's resources.

For major procurement or enhancement of IT facilities, it is important that management's decision is based on a thorough examination and evaluation of the alternatives available. This review, or feasibility study, should normally culminate in a formally prepared written report.

There are three fundamental elements of control relating to the consideration and evaluation of IT procurement or enhancement which are of interest to the auditor:

- the existence of a formal set of procedures to be followed during a feasibility study which is consistently enforced by management;

- the existence and use of standard documentation in all such evaluations; and

- a clear management decision.

While all the formal procedures discussed in this section should be applied wherever possible, less formality may be acceptable for small scale projects. The measurement of scale is based on a combination of value, importance and impact and should be determined by management.

5.4.2   Elements of Control

Formal procedures

It is important that a formal system exists which is followed for every significant procurement or enhancement of IT facilities. Not only does this lead to a more controlled and secure approach for the organisation, but also serves to protect involved members of staff, especially computer staff, from any undue pressure from within the organisation, which can occur even in the best run organisations.

Clearly, if management is to make the best decision on behalf of the organisation, based upon a written appraisal of alternatives, it is essential that the document includes all valid points. There should be a mechanism to ensure that all interested parties are given the opportunity of commenting upon a proposed course of action before the management decision is taken.

Documentation

Organisations should adopt a standard format for the documentation upon which to base a decision. This document, the 'feasibility study report', should include the following sections:

Statement of Objectives

This will clearly inform management of both the need for and the objective of the proposed changes; not in any technical sense, but in terms of the functions of the organisation.

Existing Arrangements

All relevant information about current systems and procedures affected by the proposals should be included in the document, highlighting any existing or anticipated problem areas.

Alternative Solutions

Wherever possible the report should discuss solutions other than those being recommended. It should evaluate these and make the reasons for rejecting them clear. A detailed cost benefit evaluation of any alternative is not, itself, cost justified if that option is excluded for another major reason.

Proposed Course of Action

The report to management must contain an outline of the proposed course of action, note any implications that would be of interest to management, such as any resulting reorganisation of staff or accommodation, training requirements, the effect upon operational schedules, insurance aspects and trades union consultation.

Security and Audit

All significant implications for security and any audit comments should be included in the proposal. It will normally be the investigating team's responsibility to consult with staff who have audit and security responsibilities where appropriate, and to include any relevant matters.

Finance

The report should provide best estimates of all costs accruing from a management decision to proceed with the proposal, together with information, if appropriate, on methods of financing the project. The financial analysis should include direct and indirect costs, both capital and revenue.

Along with the costs of hardware and software acquisitions themselves, the report should present:

- the cost of staffing and training;
- the cost of installation; and
- the life cycle costs of the facilities, including maintenance and the disposal of obsolete or replaced equipment.

Marginal capital costing is not sufficient – management should be aware of the full financial impact of computerisation, including the effect on annual computer revenue budgets.

In addition, all benefits to the organisation from the proposal should be identified and wherever possible quantified.

Schedule of Implementation

The proposal should include an outline schedule of implementation, although it is accepted that more detailed working schedules will often only be possible at a later stage.

Management decision

Having evaluated the costs and benefits set down in the study, the team will then have to determine whether further resources should be devoted to the project. Acceptance of the proposal will lead to the next phase in the procurement process – the detailed specification of requirements.

5.5 Specifying the Requirement

5.5.1 Overview

If the IT needs of an organisation are an operational requirement then the feasibility study is the formal expression of that requirement. In turn, the specification for the supply, enhancement or replacement of IT facilities is the translation of that requirement into a technical document which forms the basis of the formal invitation to prospective suppliers to tender for the contract. If current and future requirements are properly considered in the feasibility study, then much of the information in the report will contribute naturally and directly to the specification of requirements.

As the specification will form the basis of a legal agreement it must be precise and large sections will therefore need to be expressed in technical terms. The specification must be comprehensive and reflect accurately the operational requirements of the organisation as agreed during the feasibility study stage.

5.5.2 Responsibility

Responsibility for small enhancements to existing IT facilities will often be delegated to the IT manager. This delegation should be subject to the usual controls over capital expenditure and there should be a financial limit to the expenditure which can be incurred in this way.

User departments may also be given delegated purchasing power for the acquisition of office equipment including microcomputers. In such circumstances it is essential that a mechanism exists for the IT department to be advised and indeed to approve specific equipment models to ensure compatibility with existing facilities. It is unlikely that such small acquisitions will be supported by a detailed feasibility study involving a meticulous consideration of alternatives, although evidence should exist to justify the purchase.

The selection of a corporate network is a major task in any organisation and will have a considerable impact on all departments. So that all relevant issues are considered during the investigations leading to the specification of requirements, it will be necessary to establish responsibilities to deal with technical and financial matters. An approach adopted by many organisations is to establish two major groups – one at senior management level to guide and monitor developments (the project management team), and one at a lower level to undertake the spadework of research and to suggest priorities (the project control team). As much of the work of the project control team will be of a technical nature, it is desirable that senior IT management is represented as well as sufficient departmental involvement.

All findings and recommendations of the control team should be channelled through the project management team to the decision making body for ratification and approval.

5.5.3 Specification Details

Contents

The specification of requirements will be the first formal document used by potential suppliers and should, therefore, state requirements concisely and precisely.

Although it is possible that existing suppliers of computer equipment will have been consulted during the preliminary investigations, it is important that the specification is phrased so that no supplier has an undue advantage. Therefore, the specification should address broad areas of computing in terms of computing power, throughput and communications, rather than the means of achieving those requirements.

For the sake of clarity, it is desirable that the specification is split into sections, each one dealing with a different aspect of the acquisition. Although all of these sections should be included in the specifications when tenders are being sought for a new computer or major enhancement to an existing one they may not all be necessary when enhancements of a minor nature are being considered.

In the case of an enhancement, however, details of the existing workload could significantly influence, or be affected by the proposal should be carefully considered and be included if necessary in the specification. Without that there is a danger that suppliers may propose a product that is not compatible with existing facilities. That could be a costly mistake for the organisation, because it could lead to the abandonment of the project or additional enhancements at a later date.

Existing and future applications

This section should summarise the operational workload and include information on

- file sizes;

- volumes of throughput;

- turn-round time;

- scheduling; and

- frequency of run and back-up requirements.

Where relevant, details of existing workloads and any possible future enhancements which materially affect any of these factors should be included. Finally, the specification should highlight any limitations of existing equipment that militate against the achievement of these objectives, so that alternative proposals may be evaluated.

Hardware

Having evaluated the demand for computing power from all current and planned applications, the specification should define the total workloads in terms of input, processing, data storage and output.

A crucial factor in this calculation is the scheduling of processing. The hardware must have the capability of responding to demands at peak times and should have sufficient in reserve to allow for a certain amount of growth. In this context, it is desirable that hardware supplied is 'upwardly compatible' so that further enhancements may be made later if considered necessary.

Where existing equipment or facilities are to continue in use, details of their specifications and use should be included, so that suppliers have the opportunity to assess their compatibility.

Software

The evaluation of existing computer applications will highlight the software products used by the organisation which belong either to the supplier of the existing equipment or to some other body.

Such software products can be classified in one of two ways. First, and most important, are the products without which the hardware could not function. Under this category would fall such software as operating systems, file handling software, communication software, compilers and sort routines. All of these are major programs that are unlikely to be developed with the limited resources available to each organisation. In the second category are applications packages and third party system software, (eg security packages and performance review software). All software should be specified so that alternatives, including in-house development in the case of applications, may be considered. As with hardware, it will be necessary to consider security features that should be incorporated in each software product and to define a minimum level of acceptance.

Modes of operation

Three characteristics of the application for which the purchase is being made will influence the type of hardware and software bought. These are the mode of operation, the work environment and the principal programming languages employed. Such matters will normally be the subject of detailed discussions between potential suppliers and the organisation. However, the specification should indicate the mix of batch and on-line operations, the working conditions under which operations will be conducted, the response times required including speed of operations, and a precise description of the programming languages to be employed. All these factors will help determine the architecture and operational capabilities required of the equipment.

Compliance with EC requirements for OSI

It is also important to ensure that the specifications give due consideration to compliance with European Community (EC) directives and decisions on public sector and government procurement where these apply. In particular, EC Decision 87/95 requires the move to open system interconnection (OSI) and places a mandatory requirement on all public bodies to conform to these standards.

The aim of the directive is to achieve common usage of European and/or international standards within the Community thus giving organisations the freedom to exploit the benefits of standardisation. However, it should be noted that these benefits also carry potential further costs because sound technical knowledge and specialist skills may be necessary to evaluate properly any proposal.

There are a limited number of exclusions from this directive available to organisations but it should be noted that reason for the use of the exclusion has to be recorded if possible within the initial tender documents, and always in the organisation's internal documentation.

All affected organisations must make suitable provision for compliance with EC directives. Where an immediate movement towards implementing OSI is not possible or practical, organisations should produce at least a strategy document or long term plan, which explains why they are unable to comply and indicates a commitment to the future introduction of OSI standards. This basic information should also be included in all tenders or requests for quotations for IT equipment, to avoid potential suppliers questioning the organisation's intentions regarding OSI or compliance with EC directives.

Conditions of supply

Apart from hardware and software, both of which will be specified in some detail by the organisation, there will also be a number of related matters on which the organisation will require assurances.

Most mainframe suppliers provide a considerable amount of support for a conversion task. This support consists of a combination of software to assist in the conversion of programs, and personnel to assist with re-training of staff and with program conversion itself.

A measured amount of free testing facilities may be provided by the supplier prior to the installation of the mainframe. Again, it will be necessary to ascertain the extent of this facility.

An important element in the running of a computer installation is the maintenance of the computer. Appropriate engineering cover, both for regular and emergency maintenance, should be specified.

In the event of total breakdown, it will usually be necessary to arrange back-up facilities at another site. Suppliers may propose other compatible sites and arrange the necessary introductions. Some suppliers have their own recovery facilities, and may offer the use of them as part of their package. It is important to 'unbundle' such offerings from contract bids so that the purchaser can compare tenders on an equal basis.

Certain computer equipment requires particular environmental conditions. Where applicable, the supplier's specification for these conditions should be sought and its implications evaluated.

Finally, matters common to any major contract such as delivery, implementation dates, financial constraints and penalty clauses should be included in the specification.

5.5.4   Tendering Procedures (including EC requirements)

The administrative procedures to be adopted will vary from one organisation to the next, but should be contained within the regulations of each organisation. The regulations should provide for variations in procedure in special circumstances such as small-scale procurements.

If the enhancement is of a minor nature (perhaps a small increase in memory) it is neither practicable nor economic to opt for a system of full open tendering. Indeed, many such transactions are conducted directly with the original supplier without any competitive tendering. What is important is that the IT manager is aware of other suppliers of the same or compatible equipment and of the potential savings that may justify the cost of a more elaborate system of tendering.

It is also vital that those public bodies affected by EC Directive 88/295 on tendering arrangements ensure that their IT acquisition procedures comply fully with its requirements. EC Directive 88/295 seeks to increase competition within the Community and provides for the prosecution of organisations which allow unfair competition or biased tendering criteria in their IT acquisition procedures. The EC has defined three forms of tender: negotiated tender, restricted tender and open tender. The 'open tender' is the preferred method, but in recognising the existence of single tenders, and to limit their use, it has created the 'negotiated procedure', only to be used in exceptional circumstances. The 'negotiated tender' allows authorities to consult suppliers of their choice and negotiate terms of contract with one or more of them. Although the directive allows for the use of the negotiated procedure without prior advertisement, the circumstances where this may be invoked are limited.

Organisations may award contracts using the restricted tender method, only if justified by 'a need to maintain a balance between contract value and procedural costs' and by 'the specific nature of the products to be procured'. Otherwise contracts must be awarded by open tender.

To avoid the possibility of contravention of EC directives leading to penalties or suspension of the tenders in question organisations must ensure that they fully consider the requirements of EC legislation at an early stage in the IT acquisition process. To achieve this, it is crucial to ensure that all staff involved in the acquisition process are made aware of the requirements.

Further details regarding the EC directives are set out in chapter 14.

5.6 Appraisal of Tenders

5.6.1   Overview

The appraisal of tenders continues the work done during the feasibility study and specification stages. It involves evaluating the proposals of the different suppliers against the organisation's criteria and results in a recommendation of acceptance.

There are a number of aspects to be considered in the process of selecting a supplier and its facilities.

5.6.2   Technical Appraisal

The overall objective of this appraisal is to ensure that potential suppliers' proposals meet the requirements of the specification and that the claims made in the proposal are justifiable. Because of the close link between hardware and software considerations, it is desirable that the project control team acts as a unit, with the appropriate computer expert given particular responsibility for his speciality.

Methods

Two methods of appraisal which organisations may consider are the use of benchmarks and comparisons with other users.

Bench marking involves running a representative sample of the total workload on the proposed computer and measuring throughput for comparison. Large mainframe computers may have to cope with a job mix of batch, real-time and time-sharing systems, and devising the sample may prove to be a formidable task. However, where a dedicated minicomputer is under consideration, the benchmark technique may be simpler to apply and provide a good measure of the machine's performance.

Existing users of the equipment or software, particularly those similar in size, job mix and information requirements, are an invaluable source of information in assessing equipment or software performance. Attempts should be made to examine other users' performance records, especially if a major conversion is required, and discussions should be held to identify particular conversion problems. Existing clients of the supplier will also have had first hand experience of the support and training provided and therefore will be in a good position to comment on the quality of such support.

Product suppliers usually welcome the opportunity to make the necessary introduction to other users to help sell their products and full use should be made of this method of appraisal. When the supplier is either reluctant to adopt this approach, or is unable to because the product is yet to be released generally, it is advisable to proceed with caution and consider the supplier's past record of reliability and thoroughness.

An organisation may also wish to make its own contacts, by contacting the appropriate user group, as the supplier's list of sites may not be typical of the experiences of all buyers.

Reports

The technical appraisal should result in a report that contains a clear recommendation based solely on technical considerations. The report should be supported by appendices containing details of the research undertaken and comments of other users.

The technical appraisal is concerned with comparing rival products as much as establishing the authenticity of each proposal. To achieve this in a methodical and rational way, the factors should be ranked in order of importance and weights attached to each factor according to its importance. Thus, a final weighted score for each proposal may be produced which determines the final decision of the project control team.

The scoring system and weightings should be devised at the conclusion of the feasibility study and approved by the project management team.

The requirements of EC Directive 88/295 may also be relevant at this stage. Organisations have to set down how they are going to evaluate tenders within the EC advertisement, and they need to ensure that the EC is advised about the award of a contract. Where an organisation has used negotiated or restricted tenders, they are required to produce a report stating their reason for so doing. This may be required by the EC or may be used as evidence where a supplier questions the tender.

5.6.3   Business Appraisal

The options open to organisations to finance the acquisition of capital purchases are well documented in other CIPFA publications. This section describes some of the problems peculiar to a business appraisal of computer products.

Obsolescence and useful life

Because of the speed of IT hardware and software development, obsolescence may come much faster than originally anticipated, thus reducing the effective life of the product. This potential shortening of useful life can have a significant effect when making the decision to lease or purchase. The appraisal should take this into account.

'Bundling' and 'unbundling'

Some suppliers tender on the basis of a 'bundled cost'. This is the total cost of all specified hardware and named software packages. The software cost is an integral part of the contract sum and is not identified separately by the supplier.

Others tender on the basis of 'unbundled' cost. They quote separate prices for hardware and software items, and purchasers are at liberty to choose from the software packages offered, thereby reducing total costs. A further complication is that software may be proposed on a separate tender with options to rent or lease only. In order to compare different tenders, it will be necessary to cost each proposal over the entire life of the machine. To do this effectively will require estimates of the life of the machine and the software.

Incidental costs

Another area of costs that complicates a financial appraisal is referred to as 'incidental' costs. Although incidental, these costs could be sufficient to completely reverse the results of an appraisal, so they must be considered carefully.

For example, the preparation of the site to house a computer will form a significant part of the incidental costs, and, as the requirements of different suppliers may differ, it will be necessary to produce separate costings for each. False floors and ceilings, power supply, air conditioning and size of accommodation are four of the features that may vary.

The training or re-training of staff is perhaps the most important single incidental cost to be considered. Whereas one proposal may require minimal re-training, another might require a complete change of direction, with a great deal of training before staff become productive again.

Stability of supplier

A final, but important, area for appraisal concerns the stability of each product supplier. This will be of particular concern where the hardware or software is being sought from smaller or specialised suppliers.

Such information can be obtained from trade journals and computer bodies as well as from the supplier. If possible, an undertaking should be obtained from the supplier concerning the maintenance of the product and its compatibility with any developments of hardware or software that are known to be imminent.

In the case of software, access to source code should be available in case the supplier ceases to trade or to support the product.

5.6.4   Comparison of Tenders

The comparison of competitive tenders should be conducted as a separate exercise after completion of technical and financial appraisals of individual tenders. A crucial factor is the method of comparison (in particular the means employed, such as weighting) so that like is compared with like. Whatever the means employed, they should be determined by persons other than those who make the actual comparison. They should not be made known to the prospective suppliers. The method of comparison used, together with any other factors to be taken into account, should be identified and approved at a high level.

5.17

5.6.5   Contract Appraisal

Because of the complexity of agreements for the provision of IT facilities, it may be necessary for a legal specialist to scrutinise the contract documents.

As described earlier, the decision to choose a particular product is based on much investigation and assurances provided by suppliers. It is important that these assurances are fully documented and that they form part of the contract itself.

This is particularly important because many contracts contain clauses restricting the supplier's commitments. When a product is being purchased jointly by more than one organisation there should be a separate contract between the organisations concerned, containing agreements on ownership of hardware and software and defining specific responsibilities for maintenance and development, appointment of staff and apportionment of costs.

5.6.6   Decision and Recommendation

Because of the long-term implications of the decision, it is probable that the appraisal of the technical team will carry most weight. Indeed, because of the far-reaching implications and uncertainties of computer products, the proposed tender may not be the cheapest.

It will be the responsibility of the project management team to evaluate the recommendations and propose the acceptance of one particular tender. It will then be for the members or board, to debate and ratify the recommendation.

5.7   Installation of Facilities

5.7.1   Overview

Management's aim in the installation of the newly acquired hardware or software should be to ensure that delivery schedules are adhered to and, in the case of hardware, that structural, environmental and electrical requirements are met. All areas affected by the installation need to be identified. The installation of workstations in user departments, for example, may require structural changes to offices and additional electrical supplies which will be outside the IT manager's responsibility. Software installation too may affect more than just the department installing it. For example, output from a new application may feed a system in another department. Any problems with installation could affect that second department.

Planning the installation programme

Various management techniques can be applied for establishing and monitoring the programme for the installation of new products. Network analysis, for example, can help to ensure that the primary acquisition, together with associated equipment or activities, can be planned to become operational by the agreed date.

The installation programme should take account of existing systems, whether clerical or computerised, and the amount of conversion to the new procedures which will be necessary. This conversion may well require a substantial clerical effort and may, therefore, be time consuming and affect the installation timetable. The user department will need to provide for those responsible for planning the installation a reliable estimate of the conversion time scale.

Where the organisation owns existing equipment, arrangements may have to be made for its disposal. Its market value may be minimal though, if it can no longer be maintained by the supplier.

Acceptance of the facilities

Circumstances will vary according to the terms of the supply of the facilities but the supplier should, if possible, test on site before handing it over to the customer. During or immediately after this phase, the supplier may provide some time for the customer's staff to test out the hardware or software.

During this period the customer may not be able to fully test the new acquisition (as the installation may not be operating under normal conditions), but users should nevertheless seek to confirm that the primary claims of new hardware and software are met. Once users accept the product from the supplier they will be committing their organisation to paying for it and should ensure that such payments can be authorised.

Maintenance and insurance

It is likely that suppliers of all products will provide maintenance and support services: for example, training, product documentation and advice. Such services may not be free of charge and the user may have to pay a fixed annual charge in addition to the acquisition costs of the product. Maintenance charges will probably increase with the age of the product particularly if it is an item of hardware. In time, this may be high enough to make continued use uneconomic.

A supplier may also withdraw support for their product and leave customers with the options of upgrading to a new version, of trying to maintain the product without the supplier's support, or of joining with other users and mutually trying to maintain the product without the supplier's support. With software, however, the customer cannot undertake their own maintenance unless the source code is available. Changes in the hardware may determine the life of the software and the organisation may be forced to look for a replacement for the software.

Additional insurance cover may be necessary when new equipment is installed. When hardware is rented or leased the terms of insurance may be dictated by the owner of the equipment rather than by the user. Even where software is rented, users may be obliged to provide insurance cover to protect themselves against claims for misuse of the product (such as allowing unauthorised use or copying of the software).

Where replaced equipment is to be disposed of then any maintenance and insurance agreements should be terminated.

Staffing

Staffing is a matter directly affected by acquisitions and calls for good co-ordination. Therefore, recruitment and training of staff should be closely associated with the procedure for the acquisition of computer facilities. The primary concern is to ensure that staff are available and trained in good time, not only to operate but also to make use of the facilities.

Another aspect of staffing to be taken into account when planning implementation is the reorganisation or re-deployment of staff that may follow the acquisition of computer facilities. The effects may extend to restructuring whole sections or departments and re-allocating duties and responsibilities. Such operations should also be co-ordinated with the computer development plans.

5.8 Post Implementation Review

5.8.1 Overview

Having gone through the detailed process of evaluating proposals, specifying requirements and installation, management should, after a reasonable time, satisfy itself that the costs and benefits promised in return for the acquisition have been realised.

It is important to measure the actual costs of the acquisition and compare them with the estimated costs specified in the feasibility study, and to identify the benefits which were anticipated and determine whether in fact they have been realised. This may help to identify weaknesses in the sizing and costing procedures or highlight areas of poor performance, and thus sharpen management's decision-making process for the future.

5.8.2 Extent of Review

The timing of the review will be significant. An attempt to measure costs and benefits before sufficient time has elapsed to allow teething problems to be resolved will be unsatisfactory, unwelcome, and probably draw invalid conclusions. On the other hand, a review long after the implementation may prevent any remedy against the suppliers, if any problems are directly attributable to them.

The timing of the post implementation review should be considered before the installation stage, and an estimated starting date fixed for the exercise. The precise timing will be determined by the nature of the acquisition, but it is unlikely that the study will be conducted until three months or more after the handover date.

Definition of, responsibility for, and objectives of the study

The management team should be responsible for directing the study although it may be carried out by those who requested the acquisition. The need for a review team to be formed and its precise membership will be governed by the size and effect of the procurement or enhancement. For a major project, the team should comprise a representative from the IT department, user department and, perhaps, from a management services section. For a minor project, which may only have an immediate effect on one department, the review will probably only be conducted by a member of that department.

Internal audit should not normally be responsible for conducting such reviews, nor should they be members of any review team. It may be, however, that management requires an independent view, and feels that audit is best placed to assist in such a review. Auditors should make it clear in such circumstances that this function is not provided as an audit duty, and is without prejudice to later audit opinion.

The effect of hardware changes

To measure the benefits claimed for hardware the review team will probably at first turn to the supplier's tenders, and details of the product's performance. In discussion with the IT department they should determine whether the equipment is performing satisfactorily. There should in any event be monitoring of equipment where the supplier has maintenance responsibilities. Where hardware is not under the immediate control of the computer department, such as computing facilities in a user department, the review team will wish to ensure that a satisfactory procedure exists for monitoring the performance of the equipment.

In an organisation heavily dependent upon on-line systems 'down-time' and the length of response times may be critical and should be monitored. Where the existing system software does not provide adequate facilities for performance monitoring, the review team may wish to initiate a clerical system to record for each workstation the times it was unavailable and the reason for the 'down-time', eg mainframe unavailable, communications link broken, terminal equipment failure.

The effect of software changes

As with hardware, the extent of the post-implementation review of the acquisition of software will depend largely upon the impact of the procurement on user departments. Where application

5.21

software has been acquired, the review team will wish to ensure that the requirements of the user have been fully realised and that the system has performed as promised. Where a modification to the package by the supplier is subsequently requested, the team will wish to determine whether this could or should have been anticipated at the specification stage and whether the responsibility lies with the supplier.

The measurement of actual costs

A post implementation review of the actual costs of the acquisition may at first sight appear to be a straightforward exercise. Where the item of hardware or software is easily identifiable, and its effect on those outside the IT department negligible, that may be the case. However, most applications will also affect the users, and the review team will need to identify such costs as those of additional staff in user departments or additional training required but not anticipated, and any 'hidden' costs in having to support the manual and computerised systems during the development period.

Assessment of user satisfaction

User satisfaction may prove difficult to assess. Users' opinions will be subjective and influenced by their expectations which may have been misplaced. However, both management and audit should attempt to verify the expressed views by reference to such facts as are available. To this end, users should be encouraged to keep records of performance and incidents.

The review team should discuss day-to-day operations with those actively involved in the new procedures, to identify, for example, whether the incidence of errors has diminished, whether working conditions have improved and whether the improvements promised in the feasibility study have been realised.

Reporting on the review

Having undertaken the review, the team should produce a report for the project management team or a nominated senior individual in the IT and user departments. The report should state:

- whether the costs were held within the approved estimate;

- whether the benefits claimed for the procurement or enhancement did in fact accrue.

Shortfalls in either of these areas should be identified, the reasons stated and an assessment made of the action deemed necessary to correct the problems and prevent their recurring in future acquisitions.

5.9 Microcomputers

5.9.1 Overview

Because of the relatively low cost and easy availability of microcomputers and the software and related equipment such as printers, many users may feel disinclined to embark upon detailed acquisition procedures. Nevertheless the principles already defined for acquisitions are still relevant; it is merely their application which calls for the exercise of discretion.

5.9.2 Procedures

The organisation should have a structured procedure for small-scale acquisitions. The procedure should cover:

- Specification of requirement – details of the system(s) should be provided including data volumes and any system constraints. An attempt should be made to demonstrate that a microcomputer is the best choice from alternative methods.

- Justification for acquisition – there should be a clear link with data processing policy or a statement showing why a variance from strategy is required. The acquisition should as far as possible be shown to be cost effective or to achieve benefits otherwise denied to the users.

- Market search – with so many microcomputers available an assessment should be made as to which microcomputer to buy. This will include an evaluation of:

    - supplier reliability;

    - compatibility;

    - ease of upgrade;

    - peripherals;

    - maintenance; and

    - compliance with hardware and software standards.

The whole process should adhere to the organisation's rules for tendering and purchase of goods and services.

5.9.3 Software Packages

While the acquisition of microcomputers may be subject to overall acquisition procedures it is less likely that individual items of software will be so strictly controlled because of the relatively low cost of such packages.

However, the IT department should advise user departments of the packages it is willing and able to support. If users choose to acquire other software then they should not expect to receive assistance from the IT department in installing and providing support. These issues should be clearly laid down in policy statements or strategy documents within the organisation. Departments wishing to buy non-standard packages should evaluate the resource and service implications of support. The IT department should also lead or contribute to the production of procedures for the evaluation and acquisition of software packages. Key issues to be addressed in any such guidelines would include:

- ensuring that the package meets the functional requirements of the user;

- evaluation of the integrity of the package in relation to the completeness and accuracy of input, processing and output;

- reliability of the package for backup, recovery and security of files, data and programs;

- compatibility with existing hardware, operating systems and other systems;

- performance of the package in terms of ease of use, flexibility and efficiency of operation;

- subsequent support and maintenance;

- achieving a competitive price, balanced against ensuring adequate security, reliability and support.

A further consideration which must be addressed by organisations acquiring software packages is compliance with copyright law (Copyright, Designs and Patents Act 1988, see chapter 15), and ensuring users within the organisation do not take and use illegal copies of software. There should be procedures to inform microcomputer users of the requirement to acquire software through the official procedures, and to monitor compliance with this throughout the organisation.

5.10 Audit Approach

5.10.1 Overview

The auditor's role is not to make the decisions or even to advise on the best course of action. It is rather to examine the structure and procedures adopted in the acquisition of resources, in order to comment on their effectiveness in providing management with the complete facts. There is a tendency to believe that any change of IT resources is an exclusively technical exercise to which non-technical staff cannot usefully contribute. There are many features in the acquisition of IT facilities, however, that bear a close resemblance to the acquisition of any other equipment of a capital nature.

When standing orders or financial regulations exist to control the acquisition, the auditor should comment on the extent to which they have been observed. It is worth noting that even when financial regulations exist they are likely to be phrased in general terms, allocating large areas of responsibility to various groups. It is unlikely that they will be so rigid as to stipulate the precise responsibilities of each group involved or the research and reporting that should accompany each acquisition. This will clearly depend on the scale and nature of the acquisition, and therefore much must be left to the discretion of management in determining what is, or is not, an acceptable level of control.

The auditor must accept that for smaller acquisitions, such as the purchase of microcomputer software, managers may exercise their professional skill and judgement in assessing the benefits, without necessarily considering and quantifying every possible effect of their decision. Provided there is evidence that internal check exists, for example that senior IT staff have been consulted in the decision making process, the auditor should be satisfied that smaller acquisitions do not require an elaborate exercise in cost benefit analysis.

5.10.2 Audit Procedure

Familiarisation

The auditor should begin by identifying the IT policy of the organisation. Standing orders and financial regulations may or may not be relevant to an acquisition, but the auditor should look also for a formal policy which allocates or restricts the responsibilities of the management team, IT manager, or user departments. Without this to provide a structure, there is a danger that the development of computing in the organisation will be haphazard and fragmented. Where a policy does not exist, the auditor should recommend that the management team develop one. Such a policy provides a yardstick for both auditors and management against which proposals for development can be measured. It will also serve as a reminder to all staff of their responsibilities and the limits to their authority.

Communication

It is highly desirable for auditors to establish a channel of communication with the IT department so that they are kept informed of new developments, in time to take effective audit action. Minutes of the meetings of the management team are perhaps the best source by which an auditor can be kept informed. If the auditor is satisfied with the procedure for acquiring facilities, then it may be sufficient to review only the larger purchases such as a major enhancement of the computer, or the purchase of a major item of financial software.

Acquisition recommendation

The first formal step is likely to be a report by the IT manager to the management team. Depending on local circumstances, this report may take one of two forms. It either analyses the problem in some detail and then recommends what is required to solve it, or it discusses the problem and presents the management team with a series of alternatives to be considered. The difference between the two approaches is one of internal check.

In the former case, there is an implicit acceptance that there is only one solution to the problem, whereas the latter case requests management to consider alternatives and commission a feasibility study. The auditor must be watchful that where only a single solution is recommended, other alternatives have been fully considered.

The auditor should confirm that all interested parties were consulted during the feasibility study, and that the results of those discussions have been properly documented. Minutes of meetings and other formal reports should be circulated to all represented parties for confirmation and approval.

When all discussions and evaluations have been completed, and the feasibility study report prepared, the auditor should check the report for completeness and accuracy and ensure that it contains all the points discussed above, in the section on the feasibility study.

The auditor should also ensure that running expenses are considered in each alternative considered, in addition to the capital sums involved. It is common for running expenses over three to five years to be greatly in excess of the capital sum. These should therefore be analysed under itemised headings such as accommodation, staff and other incidental costs.

Specification of requirements

The specification of requirements is the formal tender document presented to suppliers. One of the auditor's main responsibilities in this area is to ensure that the specification is a true reflection of the requirement contained in the feasibility study report and management's chosen course of action. The specification should be phrased in such a way as not to give any one supplier an unfair advantage.

Negotiations

There will be many cases where there is no scope for obtaining tenders from more than one such, such as for a new operating system. For that reason the auditor should be careful in seeking the enforcement of standing orders related to tendering, and should consider each case on its merits. However, the number of prospective suppliers of computer hardware and software is increasing, and the auditor should therefore ensure that alternatives to the monopoly supplier have been considered.

Suppliers will almost certainly need to spend a considerable time at the organisation clarifying points in the specification and presenting their product. For larger purchases, the supplier may demonstrate the product by taking those responsible for the technical appraisal to other locations where the product is installed. The auditor should be watchful that judgement and impartiality of the decision-makers are not jeopardised through acceptance of hospitality prior to the formulation of the specification.

As a result of the presentations from competing suppliers, variations to the original specification may be deemed necessary. The auditor should ensure that these are formally documented, form an integral part of the specification, and that they do not diverge from the original objectives of the management team.

All other procedures for the submissions and receipt of tenders should conform to the standing orders and financial regulations of the organisation, that are designed to control contracts in general.

Installation of facilities

The auditor should assess the adequacy of the programme for testing the acceptability of the hardware or software delivered. Application packages will, of course, call for a subsequent systems audit.

Where the new facility replaces existing ones, the auditor should check that there are proper arrangements for the prompt and efficient disposal of the redundant facility. It will also be necessary to check that the insurance arrangement on the replaced product is terminated, and that insurance, maintenance arrangements and contingency plans have been brought up to date.

Where the new product is self-contained, the auditor should check that it is brought into the inventory.

Post-implementation

The final stage of the process is the post-implementation review. The auditor should ensure that this review is conducted after a suitable interval and that the results conform to the expectations of the organisation and the promises of the supplier. In practice, this is an exercise that is often overlooked unless specific problems arise. Where this is the case, the auditor should recommend that such an exercise is conducted. Unless this is done, there is no measure of performance against original objectives and no evidence that the best course of action had been followed.

Microcomputers

Particular issues need to be considered by audit regarding microcomputing.

The auditor may not have the necessary knowledge of the microcomputer market to assess the particular piece of machinery acquired. However, the IT department should be aware of developments in the marketplace and should have laid down certain recommendations for microcomputers, their operating systems, communication networks and communication protocols

5.27

that they require. In this way, exceptions to the rule are easily recognised and reasons for the variance can be sought.

Audit evaluation of software packages

The following checklist covers the auditor's main concerns regarding software packages.

— Specification

Whether the user's requirements are properly defined and whether the package, when compared with the specification, matches and meets those requirements.

— Integrity

The auditor may not be able to examine validation routines and other internal controls directly. It should be possible however to test or check the range or relevance by reference to the documentation that should accompany the package and the printed or screen control output of errors, exceptions and control totals. The auditor should test control totals for completeness and accuracy and ensure that they provide for reconciliation of any accounting process. It may also be possible for the auditor to participate in acceptance testing during implementation.

— Reliability and Security

The facilities for back-up and procedures for recovery should be checked. Alternative measures should have be set up if the new hardware or software does not provide them. The same considerations apply to security of files and programs, in particular the security of access and the extent to which users or operators may determine the order and sequence of processing.

— Compatibility

The operating procedures and functioning of the package should be compared with the procedures and requirements of existing hardware and software to establish whether or not there are discrepancies, anomalies or other adverse conditions for which new procedures will need to be developed.

— Performance

The actual performance of the package should be compared with specifications for response times, volumes and time taken in processing. The package should be assessed for flexibility and ease of use by reference to such facilities as menu driven and parameter driven functions and report generators.

— Acquisition procedures

The purchaser should have considered the status, reputation and resources of the supplier and the user base of the package.

   — Support and Maintenance

The auditor should review the terms of the licence and the conditions governing amendments to the package; the availability of the source or object programs to the users in case the supplier ceases to support the package or goes out of business; and the availability of support to ensure that the package remains in working order.

   — Implementation

The auditor should ensure that arrangements for testing the package before acceptance, training of staff, documentation of the package and its use, amendments to the clerical, office and operating procedures to accommodate the package, were all appropriately performed.

The overall approach to the evaluation of a software package must be comprehensive and all the above should be considered key areas.

5.10.3 Conclusions

The stages in the process of acquiring IT facilities described in this chapter will often overlap or merge into one another. It is common for there to be only one formal submission for approval, which in effect contains the original requirement, feasibility study, tender and proffered solution, contained in one document. There are two important points to be made. The first is that whilst such a procedure may be acceptable management should recognise that it is giving approval to a number of decisions. The second is that the auditor is concerned not only with the existence of a procedure but also whether or not it embodies all the principles, elements and factors discussed in this section of the guidelines and that they are effective in practice.

Finally, it is worth restating the role of the auditor. The primary audit role is to ensure that a sound structure exists to produce a proper analysis of the IT requirements of the organisation, that procedures are effective in producing a viable IT policy and strategy, and that the process of evaluation and selection ensure that the requirements of the organisation are properly met in the most effective and efficient way. However, although auditors may comment and advise on procedures, it is not their duty to guarantee the propriety of the final decision. That is clearly a function of management.

CIPFA

COMPUTER
AUDIT
GUIDELINES

INSTALLATION
CONTROLS

**6 GENERAL
CONTROLS**

**7 USER DRIVEN
COMPUTING**

CHAPTER 6

GENERAL CONTROLS

6

Continued overleaf

6.1 Introduction to General Controls

6.1.1 Audit Objectives

The objectives of an audit review of general controls are:

'To establish the controls and procedures governing the organisation of staff, operational functions, access to data and software files, workstation activity and general environmental protection, and verify that they provide secure, effective and efficient day to day operation of the computer installation'.

The term 'computer installation' implies any computer and its working environment, from the largest of mainframe installations down to a stand-alone microcomputer. The computer's physical environment may vary from a purpose-built air-conditioned computer room to a normal office environment.

This chapter considers the control techniques that govern the secure, effective and efficient day-to-day operation of any computer installation, whether large or small. Although the principles are relevant to all types of computer installations, the auditor will need to take care when dealing with particularly large or small installations to ensure that the application of those principles is sensible and relevant. Chapter 7 *User Driven Computing* discusses additional issues that arise with small computer systems.

Many of the control techniques described are well established, having been developed for large mainframe installations many years ago when central IT departments serviced all the needs of user departments and the emphasis was on batch processing and central data preparation. The changes which began with the move towards on-line systems have accelerated recently with the growth of distributed computing and minicomputers and microcomputers within user departments. The basic principles, however, remain the same; controls should be cost effective and appropriate to the level of risk. A stand-alone microcomputer processing low-risk administrative applications may require limited controls, but if the organisation's payroll were to be processed on such a machine clearly a higher level of control would be needed. Similarly, if that microcomputer were to be linked to a large computer installation, access controls would assume greater significance. In all cases, auditors should consider the 'computer installation' in context and give due regard to the potential risk and the appropriateness of the control techniques they recommend.

The need for adequate general controls has been reinforced by the requirements of the 1984 Data Protection Act. Under the Act, all data users must ensure that appropriate security measures are taken against unauthorised access to, or alteration, disclosure, or destruction of, personal data and against accidental loss or destruction of personal data. Further details about data protection legislation can be found in chapter 14.

General controls are discussed below under five headings:

— Organisational Control:

dealing with the organisation and responsibilities of all involved in the computer process and the standards established for their efficient working.

— Operational Control:

relating to those aspects of data preparation, data control and operating which are common to all applications within the installation.

— File Control:

governing the access to and protection of all files and to the data contained on them both by way of software controls and physical controls.

— Network Control:

governing the access to and processing performed on networks.

— Environmental Control:

dealing with the risks of fire, flood, vandalism, sabotage and theft, and the adequacy of insurance cover.

The control techniques are relevant to all organisations, but should be reviewed bearing in mind the size of the installation concerned. Additional problems that are sometimes experienced with microcomputers and departmental computers are considered separately in chapter 7 *User Driven Computing*.

6.1.2   Audit Approach

Initial preparation

General controls operate across the environment as a whole but specific controls will also be implemented for each application being processed. An overall assessment of the security and control mechanisms in an organisation will need, therefore, a review of both general and application controls. In installations which are dedicated to a single application, the two may be audited simultaneously. In installations handling several applications, though, the two topics are usually reviewed separately. There are benefits to an auditor in first concentrating on the general controls because:

— The auditor should gain an appreciation of the overall workings of the computing environment. Such a review will provide the auditor with a good insight into the standard of controls and procedures wherever IT facilities are used, thereby influencing the study

6.2

of the adequacy of those controls and procedures within user departments.

- Particular procedures that are applicable to specific systems and adhered to for historical rather than for current practical reasons can be more readily identified.

- Having made contact with staff in the IT department, an opportunity exists for the auditor to be kept informed of developments both in hardware and software.

- Weaknesses in general controls jeopardise all the applications processed by the installation.

The auditor will need to understand the technical background to some of the control techniques which are in place: particularly those for file and software control. The auditor will therefore require some technical knowledge. It is essential to have a sound appreciation of the particular computer equipment and software used by the organisation and to ensure that the audit approach always reflects the current state of the technology in use.

Planning the review

The audit plan for the review of general controls should embrace the identification of the computer facilities, the assessment of risks and then the identification and evaluation of the general controls.

IDENTIFICATION OF THE COMPUTING FACILITIES

Hardware

The auditor needs to gather information about the present and planned facilities, including:

- whether any IT facilities and services are provided through facilities management or other external arrangements;

- the machine supplier(s);

- the nature of file store facilities (whether large volume fixed disks or exchangeable disks, for example);

- the method of any central data preparation;

- the number and types of workstations connected to the central processor or networks and their locations;

- the number and types of microcomputers, their locations and whether they can be linked to a network or to other computers within the organisation.

Software

Closely related to the identification of hardware will be the compilation of a schedule of software, including:

6.3

- the operating systems for the machines;

- other system software such as that used for providing on-line processing systems; and for database management systems;

- programming software used for business systems;

- retrieval software; and

- financial application packages.

Staffing

The auditor should obtain details of the organisation of IT, including the posts and the responsibilities of staff. This research must take into account the possible presence of development and operations staff in user departments with their own computer facilities.

The Range of IT services

The auditor should prepare or obtain a schedule of user departments and external organisations for whom IT services are provided and the nature of those services.

ASSESSMENT OF RISK

The auditor should be aware that most business activities rely on IT. The purpose of this part of the review is to determine the degree of dependence up information systems for the primary business activities, and assess the risk to the organisation of any loss, error, delay, disruption or disclosure.

The auditor should conduct this risk assessment before engaging upon any review of general controls so that the absence of and necessity for any controls and safeguards can be related directly to a positive risk. The auditor will be able to present a stronger case for improvements in procedures to management if the risk to the day-to-day business activities of the organisation can be identified.

ASSESSING GENERAL CONTROLS

The remainder of this chapter discusses general controls under the five headings listed above. Each section identifies specific control techniques and outlines an audit approach.

6.2 Organisational Control

6.2.1 Audit Objectives

The auditor should ensure that the procedures adopted within the computer installation provide a good separation of the various disciplines and comprehensive written standards. Unless both these aspects have been given due attention, it is unlikely that internal control will be generally good in the other operational areas. The auditor needs to tailor the approach to fit the scale of operation being reviewed. Staffing and operating a small installation may lead to reduced scope for separation of duties, for example, and the auditor will have to ensure that compensating controls are in place to remedy the weaknesses this causes.

6.2.2 Areas of Control

Separation of duties

The duties of staff should be organised so that the work of one person acts as a check on that of another. A clear separation of duties is fundamental to internal control within any organisation. To achieve a satisfactory separation of duties within the computer installation requires the preparation of and compliance with job descriptions, and the establishment of a chain of command.

Standards

Adoption of and adherence to written standards should help to promote efficiency and effectiveness, support operational work and help in the education of new staff.

6.2.3 Control Techniques

Separation of duties

JOB DESCRIPTION

Written job descriptions should define the duties and responsibilities of all staff engaged in the IT department and

- clearly define the separation of duties;
- avoid any ambiguity in the precise roles of each of the disciplines within the IT department;
- define and detail the various control activities; and

— facilitate the setting of standards

Model job descriptions may be found in several publications dealing with the organisation of IT departments such as the 'Computer Users Yearbook' and National Computing Centre publications.

CHAIN OF COMMAND

Managerial responsibility for security should be clearly defined. Within the IT department itself there should be proper chains of command for development and operations. These should clearly determine who has responsibility for duties such as data preparation, data control and operating, and for development and maintenance. In an IT department, separation of duties should provide for:

— a clear differentiation between designing and writing systems on the one hand and testing them on the other;

— operators responsible for processing data not being allowed to correct errors in rejected data nor to override error conditions unless specifically authorised to do so; and

— the handling of source documents being restricted to data control and data preparation staff.

The ability to apply and enforce separation of duties depends very much on the scale of computer activities and number of computing staff employed. The small IT department with few staff or the service department with its own facilities may be unable to separate fully the responsibilities of the various IT disciplines. For example:

— The officer with overall responsibility for IT may be involved in systems analysis and programming work, assisting in the development and maintenance of systems, operating the computer or performing data control functions.

— The duties of systems analysis and programming may be combined and the designing and testing of the system may, therefore, be in the hands of the person who also does the programming.

— Programmers may be expected to operate the computer, to perform their own system testing and to provide support for day-to-day operating.

— End users who are able to initiate computer processing may also operate and program the computer, and will probably also carry out data entry and data control functions.

In those circumstances there is greater risk of inaccurate or improper processing and a greater need for IT management and users to satisfy themselves that systems are properly tested and compiled. In the case of systems developed by users separation of duties and responsibilities may be completely absent and additional risks incurred.

Standards

Management should establish and maintain standards for the full range of IT disciplines.   For example:

— operating procedures;

— standby facilities;

— personnel recruitment and vetting;

— training;

— file access;

— care and maintenance of magnetic tapes and disks;

— procedure for developing new systems;

— documentation for software and data files; and

— network and terminal connection procedures.

Such standards may be based upon international agreements (eg ECMA), professional organisations' statements (eg British Computer Society) or on 'model' standards issued by such bodies as the National Computing Centre.

Standards will carry more weight if they have been committed to writing.   Standards communicated orally are susceptible to misinterpretation and the time of experienced staff is taken up instructing newcomers in the accepted unwritten procedures that are to be followed.

An increasing number of user departments have facilities to develop programs, initiate their own processing and hold their own programs and data on local devices. It is therefore important for standards to be established for non-IT department staff. To be effective, however, these must be tailored to the needs of remote users who may wish to be self-sufficient. They should encourage users to adopt fundamental procedures and safeguards to protect local processing as well as that of the organisation.

The issuing of standards is unlikely in itself to be sufficient and consideration should be given to the provision of short training sessions to encourage users to recognise the advantages of adhering to a disciplined approach to program writing and data custody.

6.3 File Control

6.3.1   Audit Objectives

The auditor should ensure that controls and procedures adequately safeguard files against loss, misuse, theft, damage, unauthorised disclosure and accidental or deliberate corruption, and provide for the recovery of information held on files.

Physical media exist in different forms, according to the hardware available. Common examples are floppy and hard disks, disk cartridges, magnetic tape and CD-ROM. These will hold what may be called *logical* files: the programs and data used by the computer and its applications. A logical file may exist on several volumes of a physical medium, or a number of files may be stored on a single volume. Some media are *fixed,* and may not be taken from the computer or related peripherals. Others will be *removable*, and therefore capable of being stored away from the main computer, as well as use in other sites.

6.3.2   Areas of Control

There are three primary areas of control of interest to the auditor:

   —   physical file custody;

   —   software access control; and

   —   back-up and archive routines.

6.3.3   Control Techniques

Physical file custody

Staff responsible for physical file custody must be able to provide the appropriate file at the right time, in a suitable condition for use, and must protect and safeguard the media from damage, contamination, corruption and unauthorised use. Functions will include control over the movement and storage of portable media such as magnetic tapes and removable disk packs and the management of on-line media such as fixed system disks. In smaller installations, particularly on stand-alone or networked microcomputers, controls may only need to be exercised over disks or data on a file server.

The size and scale of the installation will determine whether members of staff will be appointed specifically to custodial and data management functions. Where specific appointments are not made, the duties may be performed by a data control section or operations staff, sometimes in conjunction with system programmers. They may be aided by a librarian system or other software aids.

The duties of those involved in physical file custody include:

— storing and labelling physical files;

— controlling the issue and return of files in accordance with installation procedures;

— the maintenance of files both physically and logically; and

— reuse of media, taking into account the retention period of logical files thereon.

Larger installations usually need much more storage space for removable media than smaller ones. Often, a separate area is set aside as a media store or file library. This may be simply a room next to the computer room to which operators have access, or it may be a separate room controlled by a file librarian. However, *file librarianship* is a function that exists regardless of the size of installation or the precise disposition of duties, as described above.

Storage of files

Labelling and recording the use of magnetic files is particularly important for small machines where the software may be limited in its ability to recognise particular files such as different generations of the same files, or reel and disk volume numbers. Organising and labelling files is also important when data is held locally by users. Suppliers' maintenance engineers who have access to the computing area should be denied access to the media store. If files are located in the computer room then operations staff should be in attendance to ensure the safe-keeping of all files.

Media storage should be sufficiently secure to prevent damage caused by fire, flood and other contamination and to prevent loss caused by theft and accidental or deliberate corruption. It should be lockable and only accessible to authorised staff, with primary copies of files being located separately from the computer processing area. Where processing is performed outside normal working hours, arrangements may be necessary to allow for physical files to be issued to operators or users beforehand, avoiding the need for unauthorised staff to have uncontrolled access to the store.

Some installations may use remote stores with fireproof safes or strong rooms to store data essential for recreating original files. The files held in such stores should be kept up-to-date and always be capable of being read by the installation's equipment. Access to the store must always be restricted to authorised personnel whilst file storage requirements should be the same as those that apply to the primary file library.

Secure storage facilities should be provided for printed records. These should preferably be lockable cabinets, and may need to be fireproof depending on the availability of other copies of the information and the ease with which they can be recreated or reconstructed. Confidential data should always be locked away when not in use and access strictly controlled.

Issue and return of files

The issue and return of files will involve keeping manual records or the use of file librarian software. File librarian software makes use of information held on the media itself such as:

- the serial number of a tape or disk;

- dates used;

- the run number of a program file;

- the identity of the file or its owner;

- generation number;

- file status, ie usable or non-usable;

- retention criteria based on days or date or number of generations);

- physical constraints such as the length or number of usable tracks of a tape; and

- logical constraints such as the number of free tracks on a disk.

Maintenance of files

It is a file librarian function to ensure that all files, particularly those to be retained for some time, should be maintained in readable condition. Back up copies of files should be read immediately after creation and periodic checks should be made to confirm the readability of critical files such as the back up copy of the operating system. Such checks should include files held in remote store.

File retention

It is inefficient and wasteful to retain out-of-date files for longer than is necessary. In determining the retention period due regard should be paid to:

- the information needs of the users;

- internal audit requirements;

- external audit requirements;

- statutory requirements;

- other forms in which the data may be available eg original documents; and

- the risk of media deterioration.

Master files such as those from which the figures for the final accounts are derived, need to be retained for a longer period than transaction files. Where master files are held on a generation basis for the purposes of recovery, the appropriate control and transaction files should also be held on the same basis.

If data must be held on magnetic files for a very long time, then due regard must be had to the need to retain supporting documentation and the requirement for facilities such as general purpose file handling programs which can read files in outmoded forms. Special software aids may also be needed to read files that have become corrupted with the passage of time.

The need to retain files should be continually re-assessed. Out-of-date files, whether on disk or tape, should be deleted and the storage media released for other use. If the data is thought to be confidential then more secure facilities may be required to erase the data from the file.

System software files

The increased need for magnetic files to be permanently loaded for on-line services means that greater use must be made of the operating system and associated system software for file control.

System software (which is dealt with in chapters 10, 11 and 12) includes:

— The operating system for controlling the computer.

— General purpose utility programs for relieving the installation's own staff of routine tasks such as sorting and printing.

— Job control language instructions devised by the installation's own staff.

— Special purpose software such as communications and network systems, database management systems, file librarian packages and retrieval software.

The importance of the software is:

— firstly, that it is crucial to the operation, control and efficient and effective use of a computer processor and associated equipment; and

— secondly, that it may be used to alter and amend data and program files.

Not only is the software vital, but its potential misuse is probably the most serious security risk all to computing operations and activities. System software programs, like data and application programs, are held on computer files and access to them and the use of them must be strictly controlled, monitored and properly authorised. Back up copies should be held in secure locations and maintained and kept up to date. In addition an inventory of such software should be maintained indicating the source of the software and the support and maintenance procedures required and available.

Back-up and archive routines

The accidental or deliberate loss of an organisation's data through hardware, software, data or operator actions may have major consequences if secondary copies of the files are not available or cannot be readily reconstituted. An adequate number of back-up files must be maintained and facilities must be available to ensure that any interim updates of master files, made since the

6.11

appropriate back-up copies were taken, can be conveniently reprocessed. This is particularly important in on-line systems where a system failure could cause major disruption for users as well as the need to re-input large volumes of data. Software should provide facilities for reconstitution of files so that there is no loss of data and its integrity is preserved.

Back-up copies of the application program files, operating system files and other system software files should be tested periodically, on both the main and back-up sites. Access to security copies of files must be restricted and personnel should not routinely have access to both the current and the security copies of files.

6.4 Operational Control

6.4.1 Audit Objectives

The auditor should ensure that operational controls provide the discipline and uniformity necessary to ensure the completeness, reliability and timeliness of all aspects of the day-to-day running of production systems, from the reception of prime data through data conversion and processing to distribution of the final output and provide safeguard against the misuse of programs and unauthorised processing of data and use of programs. Controls in this area may be different for different applications. Where this is so, the auditor should refer to chapter 9, *Audit of Application Systems*, which covers similar ground for a single application.

6.4.2 Areas of Control

The areas of control fall into three major categories:

- receipt and conversion of data;

- control of data during processing; and

- operations procedures.

Although it is desirable for data preparation, data control and operations to be discharged by different individuals, the extent to which this separation of duties is achievable will depend largely on the size of installation, workload and resources available, and the nature of the computer applications processed within the installation. For small installations, separation of these functions may not be possible, and the auditor should look for compensating controls. Chapter 7, *User-driven Computing*, addresses these problems.

Receipt and conversion of data

The function of data preparation is to convert authorised prime data into computer readable form.

This task is achieved with greater efficiency, accuracy and promptness if attention is paid to the following areas of internal control:

- authenticity of prime data;

- recording the movement of documents;

- verifying data which can materially affect the accuracy of processing; and

- special controls over data prepared by other bodies.

Auditors should remember that users often undertake data preparation and conversion, with a consequential loss of the centralised control typically obtained in a central data preparation section.

Responsibility of the data control section

As user departments take on responsibility for the conversion of data and for controlling its processing, so the role of the central data control section will diminish. Their responsibilities are then likely to pass to the user. In any case, the following responsibilities should be addressed:

- to ensure that input data is complete, received in time to enable processing to take place and authorised by the appropriate user;

- to see that computer operators are provided with accurate and sufficient information so that correct programs and data files are used in processing and that delay is avoided; and

- to examine output for both quality and quantity and ensure that it is distributed promptly to authorised personnel.

Operations procedures

The main responsibility of computer operators in a mainframe installation should be to run production programs and other software according to instructions with data supplied by the data control section. In larger installations it may be possible to make this their only responsibility whereas smaller organisations may involve operators in many of the control functions such as completeness of input, file control and checking of output.

As operating is the only discipline with prolonged and regular physical access to the computer, then for physical security to be effective adequate controls should exist to cover operating procedures in the computer room and provide a record of computer activity. Operations will be greatly influenced by the presence of operating system software which:

- minimises operator intervention during the processing of any job by taking on the burden of:

  - scheduling tasks,

> > – making required resources available to each task, and
>
> > – satisfying all requests emanating from jobs during processing;
>
> – provides operating instructions written in a job control language;
>
> – controls access to files by the provision of file librarian facilities;
>
> – provides various levels of protection over files accessed by users from workstations; and
>
> – provides detailed listings of the progress of each job.

This subject is discussed further in chapter 10, *Operating Systems and Systems Software*.

6.4.3   Control Techniques

Receipt and conversion of data

In the early days of computing, IT tended to be centralised, and users submitted batches of documents to the IT department or bureau for conversion to input data. This arrangement provided several opportunities for implementing effective controls:

- Batches of documents could be counted, and key fields totalled within the batch. The batches themselves would be numbered.

- The document count could be used to help ensure that items had not been lost or added to the batch. The batch totals could be used as control totals over data entry and processing, to ensure that entry and conversion were correct.

- There would be several changes of possession of the data in document form, and later in the form of magnetic media. This allowed for internal check at the end of each key stage in the processes of data entry and conversion.

- The batches could each bear a signature which would simultaneously authenticate the batch and act as an authorisation to process it.

Although modern computing has devolved many of the processes of computing from the central IT area to the users, many of the control techniques are still available: batching is such a one. This section outlines a number of controls which were developed when computing tended to be centralised, but which are capable of being adapted to modern situations. Further guidance on user-driven computing is in chapter 7, and controls within applications are discussed in chapter 9.

AUTHENTICITY OF PRIME DATA

Where data is forwarded to an IT department or a computer operator for processing, the persons appointed to receive it should be able to establish the authenticity of the documents and the identity of the deliverer. This is often achieved through maintaining a record of authorised signatories for each system, both for the authorisation of processing and for the delivery of data. This record should contain the person's name and post together with a specimen signature. Prime data should be batched by the user and carry a batch header. Authenticity will usually be verified by an examination of the signature on the batch header.

MOVEMENT OF DOCUMENTS

Control of data should be established as closely as possible to the point and time of origin by the user.

A register of all data received by a central IT department should be maintained by the data control function and the information recorded should be sufficient to identify the batches of data and trace their movement. Both the deliverer and the recipient of the prime data should sign.

User departments should not be permitted to submit or amend data in such a way as to by-pass registration procedures and special care should be taken to ensure that this rule is observed when errors are being corrected. In larger organisations with separate data reception and data preparation sections, it may be advisable to implement a similar system of registration for documents passing between the two sections.

All batch header documents should provide for certification by the person(s) who enter and verify the data. An important purpose of these certifications is to provide the necessary trail in the movement of documents.

VERIFICATION

Data items that would materially affect the result of processing should be checked, or 'verified', on entry, to reduce the chance of significant error to an acceptable minimum. For example, fields such as hours worked on a time-sheet, creditor reference numbers and amounts of invoices might be verified at the time of entry.

In large installations with data preparation departments, verification entails re-entering information from the prime documents to detect errors made at initial entry, such as misreading of documents. In on-line systems, 'answer-back' techniques may be used in place of verification. These work by requiring the operator to confirm certain detail, before it is accepted by the application. For example, entry of a creditor reference number might cause the computer to display the relevant creditor's name and address and ask the operator for confirmation.

6.15

VALIDATION

Validation consists of programming the computer to check that data is of the correct type, and appearance, and within likely ranges. Where an organisation uses data preparation equipment, they should consider having the equipment programmed to perform validation checks during data entry. This reinforces the principle that controls are best implemented as early as possible in any system. As validation is generally a function of the application system, there is more discussion of this topic in chapter 9, *Application Controls*. With on-line applications it is still possible and relevant to have controls over input using batching techniques as a check against errors. Such applications should also test the validity of data prior to acceptance. A comprehensive monitoring system to ensure that all terminal activity is authorised and recorded should also be implemented, and exception reports from such a system should always be examined independently.

All the foregoing controls are just as important when a third party is contracted to do data entry or processing – for example, when a computer bureau is used. Contracts for external IT services should specify security and control requirements as part of the conditions of contract.

Data control functions

Data control is another function which had a separate existence in the days of centralised mainframe computing. The work still exists, especially when one part of the organisation has responsibility to another for data processing.

SCHEDULING

So that both users and computer operations staff are aware of processing deadlines and that effective and efficient use is made of computer resources, it is advisable to prepare long and short-term plans for scheduling processing.

A long-term plan will vary in time scale according to the needs of the organisation but may be prepared annually for each system and should in any event be formally agreed between the operations manager and user department. This plan should timetable each cycle of the system and should be split over the various stages of the process such as submission of input, data preparation, validation and error report, error re-submission and production of final output.

Apart from assisting management in its task of forecasting future resource requirements, the long-term plan will form the basis from which the short-term plan will be prepared.

The short-term plan may then be drawn up. It will provide details of the systems to be run on the computer during the following period. It should also provide some indication of the time of day or shift during which each system is to be run. This plan is designed primarily as an internal working document with the operations section and, provided dates and times specified in the long-term plan are met, a degree of flexibility in this plan is acceptable. However, the short-term plan is an important document because it serves as a reminder to data control staff to collate operating instructions and parameters for the running of jobs by the operators and to ensure that the appropriate magnetic files are made available.

Although this form of planning is most appropriate to larger installations, it can be useful to others. For example:

- Regular long print runs on a network printer can be scheduled so that other users can time their printing needs around them;

- Processor-intensive jobs in departmental minicomputer installations can be programmed to run outside normal hours;

- Users sharing a microcomputer can arrange a schedule of work which will prevent their having to queue.

SYSTEMS PROCEDURES AND REQUIREMENTS

If process scheduling is to be performed effectively, there should be sufficient information on each system to identify the processes and input requirements and to predict, with a reasonable degree of accuracy, the run times and output volumes expected. Standard forms, designed specifically to impart this information in a succinct yet comprehensive manner, greatly improve the efficiency and smooth running of computer operations.

For each application, the data control section should be able to supply the operator with the required information and check that the output corresponds with estimates.

Operational Procedures

Some computer installations operate a shift system of working. During the night shift the only persons in the building may be computer operators and if staffing allows there should be at least two operators per shift to provide an internal check. This would offer individual operators some protection from the dangers present when working with machinery and at the same time safeguard the interests of the organisation. The shift of duty operators should be rotated regularly and frequently so that unauthorised use of the computer by operators cannot take place without collusion on a large scale.

Many large sites are now moving to unattended operations, using system software to perform all major operator functions.

RECORD OF COMPUTER ACTIVITY

Many operating systems provide a system journal which records the processing time for each job run, analysed over the different activities and peripherals used in the job. The information is usually held on file by the operating system, and the onus is usually on the organisation to use this information effectively. For reasons of efficiency, the system journal may be erased or overwritten at regular intervals. It is important, therefore, that selected control information on the system journal is either printed out immediately or backed up on magnetic media for future use.

Logging and journal facilities may however be optionally switched on or off, or classes of recorded data modified in various ways; audit must be aware of the consequent risks of suppression of important management information.

Operators should maintain a record of any malfunctioning either in the hardware or in the software. Unexpected and excessive run times for programs and systems should also be recorded. Engineers' reports, either computer produced or manually prepared, may also provide useful information on system performance for management and the auditor.

6.5 Networking and Terminal Control

6.5.1 Audit Objectives

Network management and audit are discussed in chapter 12. However, the auditor must also examine the use and controls over terminals on the network. Those aspects which relate to general controls are discussed below. The auditor should ensure that all activity at workstations connected to the network is properly authorised and controlled, that unauthorised or improper use of such workstations is prevented and that inaccurate and inefficient processing are minimised.

6.5.2 Areas of Control

Workstation facilities

Because of the range and diversity of workstation facilities, control techniques will vary according to the internal organisation and networking facilities. Workstations range from dumb terminals linked directly to a central processor, to micro computers on a network which may be linked to a central mainframe.

With that in mind, three primary areas of control can be defined:

- controls exercised by means of physical restrictions;

- controls provided by software; and

- facilities for recording terminal activity.

CONTROLS BY PHYSICAL RESTRICTIONS

The primary purpose of restricting access to a workstation, or terminal, is to prevent unauthorised access and use of the equipment itself. The auditor must therefore consider how people are authorised to use workstations, the location of the workstation, whether physical locking devices are used, and how the terminal is connected to the network or mainframe. Controls will also be necessary where workstations have facilities for local processing.

CONTROLS BY SOFTWARE

The capabilities of the workstation depend on the facilities afforded by system software. In addition to physical restrictions, therefore, controls also need to be exercised in this area. Depending on the characteristics of the workstation and its related software, it may be possible to adopt a structured approach to restricting access and subsequent processing by requiring identification of the workstation, the user, the job and the files required. It is possible to ensure that users are allowed access only from nominated workstations. It may also be desirable to restrict the time allocated to each workstation task, provide for an automatic log-off for inactive workstations and to encrypt data if it is regarded as sensitive and confidential.

System software may also be able provide a log of workstation activity or jobs run.

6.5.3   Control Techniques

Physical restrictions on access

Physical access control for workstations may involve:

- authority to use the workstation;
- suitable location of the workstation;
- the provision of locks and identification devices; and
- secure methods of connection to the network.

Only individuals who are authorised to use a workstation should be allowed to do so. Physical access may be restricted through supervision of workstation locations or by controlling access to the rooms where workstations are located.

Some processing may demand special safeguards. Cash receipting terminals, for example, may be housed in a separate, lockable room or within a controlled environment. Separate locations provide the opportunity to restrict access to authorised users by issuing a key to the locked room housing the workstation.

The use of keyboard locks, badge readers or other personal identification devices may be thought worthwhile to provide additional restrictions over physical access. The value of these features will be determined by the adequacy of control over the issue and custody of keys.

Workstations may be connected by direct wiring when they are located within a single site up to a distance of about 1000m. Where further distances are involved or lines need to cross roads, leased or public lines using the telephone network may be used. Various types of line connections are available from this service and the appropriate line will be determined by the processing being undertaken and the type and numbers of workstations to be connected to the available lines.

In some installations, operators of the host computer may make the connection after satisfying themselves that they recognise the user by applying a question and answer routine. However, where several workstations require access at irregular times, automatic connection equipment is usually employed to allocate free lines on request. A useful control over automatic connections can be simply the changing of telephone numbers periodically, especially following breaches of security or staff changes.

Software restrictions on access

The opportunity to impose effective controls will be governed by the software facilities available and the effort which must be provided by the organisation in designing, implementing and maintaining such controls. Software may offer the means of:

- identifying the workstation;
- identifying the user;
- identifying the files required;
- imposing time restrictions on activity; and
- encrypting data passed through the network and communications lines.

IDENTIFYING THE WORKSTATION

The system software may be able to identify each workstation but this may depend on the methods of connection to the network. A portable device by its very nature will not be located in a fixed place and may use an ordinary public telephone line. However, even here the software may be able to identify the modem or port through which access is made.

IDENTIFYING THE USER

The most widely used technique for identifying users is the password. This requires an identification code which may be associated uniquely with:

— the user;

— the file area, file or group of files the user wishes to access; or

— the particular task the user wishes to perform eg updating a master file.

Other available methods of identification include magnetically coded identity cards, hand-prints, fingerprints and voice recognition. These are likely to be used only for more sensitive applications or locations.

Further controls may be available to supplement the use of passwords. It may be possible, for example, for the system software to monitor the number of occasions invalid passwords are submitted and then to report such activity to a security administrator or lock out the offending workstation after allowing, say, three attempts. It may also be able to disconnect the offending workstation from the system until a satisfactory explanation is found. Having received a valid password, the system could obtain further identification by requiring the user to provide an answer to a specific question.

Much reliance is placed on the password system but its value as a control mechanism depends on:

— the procedures for designing and issuing passwords;

— the quality of passwords used, for example their ability to be easily remembered but difficult to guess;

— the frequency of changing passwords;

— the user's interest in safeguarding their password;

— the ability of the system to inhibit the displaying of the password; and

— the secure safeguarding of passwords within the file system.

Whatever method is adopted for devising and issuing passwords, users will be responsible for protecting their password from unauthorised use. If passwords are written down and posted by users next to their workstations their value is negated. Similarly, if passwords are printed on logs or displayed on a screen then precautions should be taken to ensure that the log is stored securely and that the password is not left displayed on a screen.

Facilities may also be available to ensure that users can only operate from nominated workstations so that, for example, access to payroll files can be denied to a stores area workstation, even if password security is breached.

The subject of password controls is discussed more fully in chapter 10

TIME RESTRICTION

Two types of time-related controls may be available to limit or control workstation use:

- A time-out facility may be available. Depending on the system software, this may disconnect the terminal and log out the user, or merely blank the screen to prevent so-called 'burn-in'. If the time-out requires the user to re-enter a password to reconnect, this can be an effective control against the risk of a workstation being left connected to the system while unattended.

- Set times may also be allocated to workstation users over the processing period to avoid demands from all users at certain peak times. While this method of granting 'time slots' affords a means of restricting the processing of certain tasks to specific periods, it also helps to identify access taking place outside normal times.

ENCRYPTION

Where data is thought to be of a confidential nature, encryption may be available to encode data during its transmission to and from the host computer. This minimises the impact of unauthorised tapping of communication lines.

6.6 Environmental Control

6.6.1   Audit Objectives

The audit objective is two-fold; firstly to be satisfied that there is adequate protection against accidental or deliberate damage that would impair or prevent the provision of a regular and reliable IT service to the organisation; and secondly, that arrangements exist to minimise the effect upon the organisation of a failure of the IT service, whether partial or complete. The protection and arrangements should apply to staff, computer equipment and premises, data and software files and documentation.

All organisations which rely heavily on the availability of their IT facilities need an adequate and effective disaster recovery plan that can be brought into effect as soon as any of the key preventative measures described in this chapter fail. Without effective recovery procedures, failure of systems can very easily lead to a failure of the organisation itself.

Areas of loss

If potential threats materialise, it is possible that the organisation will incur:

- direct financial loss;

— indirect financial loss;

— loss of control; and

— embarrassment to the organisation.

DIRECT FINANCIAL LOSS

These are the most immediate and obvious consequences of an interruption of the computer service. The main areas of loss will be the physical destruction of hardware, plant and equipment, and loss of income.

INDIRECT FINANCIAL LOSS

These are the secondary consequences of the computer centre being out of operation for a prolonged period. Examples are:

— the organisation will have to make extra payments to staff, perhaps to perform manually for a period tasks that have been previously carried out by the computer;

— delays occur in the collection of income, and irrecoverable debts arise;

— the organisation incurs fines or damages: this is particularly likely if they process work for third parties and it can be proven that they were negligent in the execution of that processing;

— there is always a cost attached to the process of recovery.

LOSS OF CONTROL

The loss of control over operations may result in increased potential for error or fraud. Once a system's basic controls and safeguards have been disabled or by-passed, then any data subsequently entered into the system must be treated with doubt and suspicion until the system has been fully restored and checked through.

The possibility of undetected fraud should also be considered whenever any of these threats materialise. Many of the manual and computerised checks and safeguards built into an organisation's operating procedures may have to be temporarily abandoned or by-passed to get essential work done on time, and this provides the ideal opportunity for various kinds of fraud.

6.23

EMBARRASSMENT TO THE ORGANISATION

Unfavourable media exposure may result from an organisation neglecting certain control procedures resulting in some form of breakdown of computer processing. What is more important, the organisation may project a poor public image as a result of the interruption of computer processing.

6.6.2   Areas of Control

A computer installation may suffer from a variety of hazards both accidental and deliberate.

Accidental damage may result from:

- natural disasters such as fire and flood;
- local disasters caused by the proximity of adjoining risk areas; and
- disruption of essential services such as a breakdown in the power supply.

Deliberate damage may be caused by:

- vandalism and sabotage;
- theft;
- fraud;
- unauthorised use of facilities; and
- withdrawal of facilities, for example through strikes or disputes with FM suppliers.

Environmental controls relate primarily to measures taken to provide physical security and physical safeguards. Such measures apply equally to central and departmental computer installations, and to workstations and terminals attached to them. Countermeasures against these hazards need to be commensurate with the risk and the likely impact if the threats materialised. Smaller installations such as office environments may therefore have smaller-scale controls. The auditor should consider whether the controls are adequate to protect not just the software and hardware, but the data, the system, the building and the staff.

Fire, smoke and flood

Every organisation using computer systems should be protected against hazards such as fire and flood. Arrangements should be implemented to reduce risk and to minimise the damage and effect upon the organisation should fire or flooding occur. Advice should be sought from the fire service and specialist organisations.

One of the keys to the prevention of fire or flood is in the design and type of premises in which the computing facility and networking equipment are located. They should not be located, for example, in a basement or near plant or machinery used to service the building, as the risk of fire and flood will be increased. Fire resistant materials should be incorporated in walls, ceilings, floors and furnishings.

The provision of good fire detection and fire fighting equipment is essential if outbreaks are to be contained and their effect minimised. Modern smoke and heat detectors should be installed together with an appropriate combination of manual and automatic extinguishing systems. Detection and fire fighting equipment should be regularly serviced and maintained.

Steps should be taken to reduce the risk of fire occurring. All staff should receive adequate instructions and training in fire prevention as well as in evacuation procedures. Fire prevention rules should be strictly enforced. Procedures will include the regular cleaning of all areas of the computer room, including under-floor cavities, to remove any waste paper or dust that may have accumulated. Where practicable, all paper material and printers should be removed from the computer room or immediate vicinity of the processing area.

Smoke is often the main cause of damage when a fire occurs. The use of extractor fans and filters in and around the computer room provides a safeguard against contamination by smoke.

The effect of water damage can be serious depending on the particular equipment affected, and on any impurities that may be present in the flood water. If the water is relatively clean, many electronic parts can be cleaned by engineers and returned to service. If the equipment has been badly contaminated, with chemicals or sewage for example, then it may be worthless. Mechanical units such as disk drives and air conditioning are likely to be worse affected than purely electronic components.

The controls in operation against flooding or water damage will vary in complexity depending on the size of the computer installation. Particular attention should be paid to the location of water pipes and storage tanks and, where flooding is a possibility, an adequate flood warning system should exist. In some locations it may be necessary to install pumping equipment.

There is a risk that fire, smoke or flood may spread to the computer room from adjacent rooms or buildings, and upstairs or downstairs in a building. It is necessary therefore to review controls in the immediate locality of the computer room.

The organisation must have a practical contingency plan which may call upon standby and recovery arrangements should the fire, smoke or flood damage require it.

Location

The threat posed by the choice of poor site or the wrong type of building for housing a large computer centre can pose long term problems for an organisation. It is important therefore that detailed and comprehensive planning is undertaken before a site is chosen. The risks posed from adjoining buildings, for example, can be high, depending on the design and nature of their use.

Essential services

The main services necessary for the effective continuation of computer processing are the power supply, telecommunications and for water cooled mainframe computers the water supply. When significant computer 'down time' is unacceptable to an organisation, standby electrical power supplies must be made available, not only for the computer itself, but also for ancillary equipment such as the air conditioning plant, and lighting. The alternative power supply may be provided by generators or powerful batteries or a combination of these. The back-up power source should be regularly maintained, inspected and tested.

Where flooding is a serious problem and water pumps have been installed, an alternative power supply should be considered for this equipment.

Where the maintenance of permanent telecommunications is essential to an organisation it may be necessary to install duplicate or alternative telecommunication links. The two sets of lines should be physically separate and, if possible, use different exchanges.

Standby facilities

If preventative measures fail and the hardware malfunctions, then the implementation of standby or recovery arrangements will be necessary. Procedures for invoking these procedures should be clearly laid down, identifying who has the final responsibility for making decisions. There should be a properly documented recovery plan that is understood by the staff responsible for its implementation. The recovery plan should cover all aspects of standby and recovery, for example:

- the commencement of standby procedures;
- operating at the standby installation;
- the movement of staff and data;
- alternative data preparation procedures;
- reconstituting data files; and
- implementing alternative manual systems.

Standby computing may be available on an informal basis between two similar installations, but it is recommended that these arrangements should be put in writing to protect both parties. The requirements for careful planning and regular testing of the re configured installation should not be overlooked. Arranging for standby facilities can present particular problems if the configuration, network or other characteristics of processing are unconventional. Here a greater reliance on the resilience of the hardware and configuration may be necessary.

It is possible that the damage to the organisation's installation may be so great that weeks or months may elapse before normal service can be resumed. If this possibility is unacceptable, then the organisation may enter into a 'cold restart' or 'warm restart' arrangement with an insurer,

6.26

computer manufacturer or other party. The arrangement involves the contractor keeping a site available for use following a disaster. A 'warm' site has a computer ready installed and staffed, for maximum response.

In any standby or recovery plan the importance of a high standard of security systems and program operations documentation should not be overlooked. All aspects of standby should be tested on a regular basis, probably at least annually and always following changes in hardware and system software.

Maintenance

Reliable functioning of computer hardware, plant and equipment will only be achieved when regular maintenance is carried out. For small computers located in office environments, maintenance may be considered too costly, as replacement is comparatively cheap. However, if a replacement policy is adopted, the organisation should make sure that replacements are available, and that the equipment in use is not obsolete.

A detailed log of breakdowns should be maintained and periodically examined to determine the extent of machine failure. It should be remembered that computer plant such as air conditioning, back-up generator and alternator should also be subject to high standards of protection and maintenance.

Vandalism and sabotage

The threat from vandalism covers all types of hardware, plant and equipment, and can come from internal or external sources. The internal threat can be minimised by the rigorous vetting of staff, good supervision and well-defined procedures, including those governing dismissals.

The external threat can be minimised by the careful siting of the installation and controls on physical access. The size and portability of small systems mean that simple theft is also a significant risk. Again, careful siting and basic physical controls (eg door locks or security marking) can reduce this risk. Basic recovery procedures, such as back-up copies of key files, help to contain the risk of loss, whether through theft or vandalism.

The risk of sabotage has increased over recent years and this, together with the growing dependence upon computers, requires preventative measures to be taken. Like many of the other threats, sabotage can take many different forms and can come from external or internal sources. The threat from external sources is difficult to control, and is designed to exploit the vulnerability and complexity of modern computer centres.

The principal defence against such forms of attack is tight physical security. This presupposes that the computer is located in a defensible site and not, for example, behind a plate glass window open to public view. Control over all entry into the building should be positive and effective. Ideally, a computer centre should be windowless and should not face either a perimeter road or car park. Strict identification procedures should always be enforced.

Equally destructive attacks can arise from within the computer installation. A disgruntled employee could cause serious damage to the computer centre, especially if the employee has specialised knowledge of the system and its vulnerabilities. In addition, the destruction or alteration of key data and program files may remain hidden until long after the guilty individual has departed. The internal threat can be minimised by rigorous vetting of staff, good supervision, and the immediate withdrawal of both physical and logical access rights from leavers.

Distributed processing and dependence upon telecommunications make installations more vulnerable to malicious acts, since the 'installation' is effectively spread over a wider area. Destruction of telecommunication switch gear can close down processing as effectively as destruction of the computer. Organisations nowadays cannot be complacent. Terrorist acts can affect buildings over a wide area, regardless of which building is targeted.

Insurance and inventories

Organisations using computer systems should assess the risks involved and make arrangements to insure against them. This assessment is often best achieved jointly with insurance company computer specialists. When the necessary insurance has been arranged, there should be a regular formal review, at least annually, of the scope and value of the policy.

The risks that should be considered in the assessment of insurance needs are as follows:

- damage to buildings, hardware and software;
- indemnity against malicious damage by staff to hardware, software or data;
- theft of equipment or software and losses caused by computer abuse;
- standby costs;
- consequential losses;
- reinstatement of lost data; and
- electrical or mechanical breakdown.

Particular attention should be paid to:

- the installation's responsibilities for buildings, hardware and software which are rented or leased;
- processing undertaken by a bureau and the cover for data both in transit to and from the bureau and whilst at the bureau;
- equipment located remotely from the computer centre;
- whether the cover is for full replacement costs including inflation cover;

6.28

—   whether indemnity cover is subject to a realistic limit bearing in mind the possible value of consequential loss; and

—   microcomputers and local area networks.

An inventory should be maintained of the installation's assets, recording details of all equipment owned, rented or leased, including its location and serial numbers.

Personnel policies

The existence of competent, contented and trustworthy employees in the computer environment reduces the level of risk posed to the computer processing procedures of the organisation. The threats posed by untrustworthy, inadequately trained or discontented employees are considerable, particularly when supervision and separation of duties are inadequate.

All applicants' qualifications, references and history should be checked and job definitions and conditions of employment should be reviewed regularly and kept up to date. When employees give notice of leaving, all their security responsibilities should be reassigned. Such employees should be redeployed outside the computer processing area for their period of notice. Once the employees have left, passwords and similar security devices including door keypads should be changed.

6.6.3   Control Techniques

Control techniques to assist in meeting the previously stated objectives can apply both at the computer application level and to the whole installation. Those referred to below exclude many that are better explained in other sections of these guidelines. The techniques described will follow approximately the same sequence as the points made previously under 'Areas of Control'.

Fire, smoke and flood

—   A contingency plan should be available in case of a fire or flood, and all relevant staff should be fully conversant with it.

—   The computer room should not be located near water tanks, or stores of combustible materials.

—   If a computer installation is located in a basement, extra precautions are necessary to prevent fire or flooding.

—   Advice of the local fire brigade should be sought to ensure optimal preventive and defensive arrangements.

—   Within a large computer room, fire resisting screens should be used.

—   Fittings and fixtures in the installation should be made of fire resistant materials wherever possible.

— A 'No Smoking' rule should apply throughout the installation.

— Rules should be enforced to ensure that all combustible material is stored tidily and removed from the installation as soon as possible.

— The cavity beneath the false floor of a mainframe installation should be periodically cleaned to remove any combustible waste.

— Precautions should be taken to protect important documentation in case of fire.

— Staff should be thoroughly acquainted with all the procedures and controls relating to fire, flood and smoke and should be clear as to their role. Training in the use of fire-fighting equipment should be undertaken.

— Smoke and heat detectors should be linked into the fire alarm system.

— Switches for cutting off water, electricity and gas supplies should be easily accessible.

— Portable fire extinguishers should be available for staff to use against small fires. Adequate staff training should be undertaken.

— Where water flooding is a serious possibility, water pumps should be available.

— Staff should be fully aware of and regularly practise the installation's fire and flood emergency procedures. New members of staff must be made aware of these procedures when taking up their appointments.

— All mechanical and electrical fire detection and extinguishing systems should be regularly checked.

— If the computer is housed in a large building, fire, smoke and flood controls should be reviewed throughout the building, in case fire or flood starts externally and spreads to the computer area.

Essential services

— Install standby electricity generators or uninterruptible power supplies adequate to support the computer and all the necessary ancillary equipment.

— Arrange with the electricity board to be notified of impending power reductions or withdrawals.

— Install an alternator in the power supply circuit to smooth out any fluctuations in the supply current.

— Ensure the equipment functions adequately, by testing it periodically.

— Review the need for alternative telecommunication links. If necessary, ensure that they

6.30

are housed separately.

Hardware, plant and equipment

— A maintenance agreement should exist to provide regular maintenance for the computer hardware according to the standards recommended by the computer supplier. As an alternative for small or cheap items, adequate replacements should be assured.

— Periodic and planned maintenance of ancillary equipment, such as the air conditioning plant, should also be carried out.

— Where justified by the importance of a reliable computer service to the organisation, standby air conditioning equipment should be available.

— Air conditioning plant and standby generators should be afforded the same degree of protection from hazards as the computer itself.

— The air intakes for air conditioning plant should be as unobtrusive and as inaccessible as possible, to minimise the risk of external damage or the introduction of contaminating gases.

— Contamination in mainframe computer rooms and data preparation areas should be minimised using:

   (a) tacky mats at all entrances;

   (b) air lock entrances;

   (c) prohibition of smoking, eating and drinking in the computer room; and

   (d) supervision of all cleaning materials.

— A detailed log of all machine and mechanical breakdowns should be maintained.

— Account should be taken of hardware and plant located away from the normal processing area when deciding on maintenance and standards of conduct.

Location and physical access

The control techniques that are available to regulate physical access are numerous enough to allow each organisation to select the right combination of measures to be effective for their needs, and yet to be within a reasonable cost limit when related to the risks involved.

— Wherever possible, design characteristics of the building housing the secure area should be used to improve access control:

   (a) The number of windows should be minimal and those present should be protected with wire mesh.

    (b) Make rest room facilities available within the secure area to reduce the number of entries and exits.

– Take all reasonable measures to reduce the number of entries and exits to the secure area.

– Maintain a log of all visitors to the secure area and issue them with visitors' identity cards (the issue of which should be strictly controlled).

– Make arrangements to maintain security should any mechanical or electronic control system fail.

– Do not overlook risks arising from access by office maintenance staff such as cleaners.

– Appoint a security officer or receptionist to vet the authority of everyone requiring access to the secure area.

– All visitors should be escorted at all times when in the secure area.

– All cases and bags taken in or out should be inspected.

– Employ an appropriate locking mechanism to control access:

    (a) Lock and key – note that a normal locking system may be abused if the number of entries and exits is high (for instance, the latch may be taped open).

    (b) Card operated locks, with or without a keyboard for the insertion of a password code. The password code should be changed regularly.

    (c) An electronic transmitter issued to each authorised employee which automatically unlocks and opens the door when the holder approaches.

– A problem associated with many locking systems is the risk of an unauthorised person entering the secure area by closely following an authorised person's legitimate entry. Staff should be encouraged to challenge unauthorised visitors.

– Install detectors to identify when unauthorised access to the secure area has been made:

    (a) Closed circuit television.

    (b) Burglar alarms on windows and doors.

    (c) Body heat, vibration or movement detectors .

    (d) Regular security checks.

Standby / recovery arrangements

– The standby and recovery plans should be thoroughly documented.

– All affected staff must understand their roles in such a plan.

- Wherever possible, a formal standby agreement should be entered into with one or more concerns.

- The standby agreement should be reviewed periodically to ensure that the computing capabilities of each party remain compatible.

- Reliable arrangements should exist to keep parties to a standby agreement informed of any relevant hardware or software changes.

- Acceptable levels of security and control should apply to any applications run on a standby site.

- It should be clear whether applications running on the standby site are to be run under the 'foreign' operating system, or the 'home' operating system is to be loaded onto the standby machine.

- Standby arrangements should be tested from time to time in circumstances as near as possible to those that would prevail in a real emergency.

- Plans should be available that will ensure the organisation can continue to discharge its responsibilities in the event of a prolonged loss of computing services.

Insurance and inventories

- An organisation should regularly reassess its insurance cover for risk arising from using computer systems and from abuse of or damage to them.

- A procedure should exist to notify the person responsible for insurance arrangements of all new acquisitions of hardware and equipment so that insurance records can be kept up to date.

- An inventory of the computer installation assets should be maintained showing the details of all equipment owned, rented or leased together with its location and serial number.

Personnel

- Job applicants' qualifications, references and history should always be thoroughly checked.

- Conditions of employment, job descriptions and security status of employees should be the subject of periodic review and if necessary updated.

- Management should make itself aware of staff morale by regular contact and meetings, to reduce the threat of industrial action, strikes and sabotage by disaffected staff.

- Any employees giving notice of termination of employment should, as soon as possible, be moved from the computer processing area, and made to return any identity or security devices they hold.

6.33

— The reasons for any employee leaving should be determined. Passwords or any other similar security devices should be changed as a matter of routine.

Contingency planning

Management should develop and maintain an up-to-date contingency plan for all significant eventualities, such as fire, flood, key staff loss, power cut, equipment failure and system corruption. The contingency plan should be in detail sufficient to define precise responsibilities, actions and sequences of action to restore any desired standard of service to a given timetable. Development and maintenance of such a plan can be very time-consuming but are increasingly necessary as organisations become more dependent upon computer processing for their continued and effective operation. Contingency plans should be regularly tested under simulated conditions to ensure that they are comprehensive and workable.

6.7 Audit Review

6.7.1 Organisational Control

Research shows that human error accounts for most of the problems in computer processing. Insufficient attention to good practice and standards, and lack of management and supervision invariably result in mistakes being made.

Discussions with the operations manager on operational controls will determine whether operating standards are adopted and whether operators are instructed not to accept oral instructions. In discussion with the IT manager, the auditor may well establish the presence of standards and the overall responsibility for the IT department's organisation but he will identify the completeness, effectiveness and extent of adherence to these controls and procedures when dealing with the other areas of control.

For audit reviews of installations outside the control of an IT department the auditor will need to obtain this information from the relevant officers.

Adequacy of separation of duties

The auditor should identify who has overall responsibility for IT and who has day-to-day management responsibilities. The risks of inadequate division of duties should be emphasised to management. Where the installation carries out work for another organisation on a bureau basis or as a member of a consortium, there should be a steering group that reflects the interests of all users. The auditor should obtain or create an organisation chart showing key IT personnel, and identify from this whether separation of duties is adequate. If it is not, the auditor will need to look for compensating controls such as more testing by users or direct supervision of staff involved in IT duties.

Job descriptions

Auditors need to examine job descriptions and satisfy themselves that they are comprehensive, up-to-date and reflect the current staffing structure.

If there are no job descriptions, this should be noted. The auditor should then try to find an alternative specification of responsibilities. If there is none, the auditor should point out to management the benefits of written job descriptions for IT functions.

Standards

The auditor should establish whether standards have been devised and committed to writing. Unwritten standards may be widely accepted in the organisation, and writing them down can take considerable staff time. However, the benefits of written standards for training, system maintenance and for ensuring compliance should be stressed by the auditor.

The auditor should find out whether staff are aware of standards that have been adopted, and see whether they are used in practice.

6.7.2   File Control

Responsibility for file control

To review file control effectively, the auditor will need to learn about the software mechanisms that are used to manage files. Auditors with existing expertise in IT can find this out from installation managers, software support or operators. Other auditors may need special training, or support from a computer auditor.

The auditor should identify the various types of media used, where they are kept and who is responsible for their custody and maintenance. Whilst in most cases magnetic disks and tapes will be permanently stored in the computer processing area there may be a remote file store.

The auditor should determine who has responsibility for the custody of physical files. The installation standards may highlight the responsibilities and duties of staff. The responsibility and duties relating to the management of media should be properly defined and brought to the attention of the relevant staff. This should extend to users of microcomputers and network workstations, who may have significant volumes of data stored on hard and floppy disks.

The auditor should confirm that staff are aware of their duties and that duties are being properly carried out by interviewing staff and checking compliance with what is known and documented.

Storage sites

Data storage sites should be inspected with regard to security and environmental hazard

6.35

protection. When examining physical file storage, the auditor must consider the controls over access and media handling out of normal office working hours when the appropriate staff may not be on duty. The arrangements for the night shift operators to gain access to back-up copies in the event of an emergency should be reviewed.

File librarianship

Where librarian records are maintained the auditor should determine whether they are up-to-date and contain sufficient information to identify when, by what and by whom the files were used, including files at remote locations.

Auditors will also have to consider file retention criteria. They must identify who is responsible for determining the media to be used and the length of time files are to be kept and the reasonableness of these decisions.

Auditors should remember that even when a file librarian has been designated, significant numbers of key files may be stored or copied locally by PC or workstation users.

File ownership

Consideration should be given to logical file ownership, especially where there is inadequate protection of files through physical or software controls. Auditors should establish the involvement and responsibility that users accept for their files and programs. Close attention should be paid to the control of input and output files as well as master files. For example, files holding details for a cheque printing run may be left on media, even on-line disk, for a considerable time before being printed on to cheque forms.

Access controls

Having identified the physical controls over files the auditor should focus on the restrictions on access provided by software. The auditor should discuss the control characteristics with the chief programmer or systems programmer. Software that controls access to files includes the operating system, communications software, specific file librarian packages and the application software.

The auditor will need to determine whether the controls and safeguards claimed by each of these complement or duplicate each other, to help ensure that files are safeguarded from unauthorised interference. This will best be determined by discussion with appropriate IT staff and by reference to suppliers' publications on the particular product. While an impressive range of control may be claimed for all of these software products, it is not certain that installations will have implemented all of the controls available. Indeed, varying levels of control will be appropriate according to the sensitivity and significance of the data. The auditor should be wary of demanding high levels of security for all files; IT management will appreciate and welcome a careful and balanced approach. The auditor should look for an approach that characterises files according to:

- contents, ie data or program;

- type, ie production or development; and

- level of risk, ie significant financial data or low risk non-financial data.

JCL and the operating system command line

The importance of control over operating system instructions cannot be over-emphasised. These may be accessed from a command line, when users are not guided into and out of applications by system controls; or through job control language (JCL) programs. It is within these high level commands that the files to be accessed and programs to be used are specified. A high level of security over programs will be of little consequence if access is freely available at JCL level to request a different file or program to be loaded. The auditor should also be aware of library maintenance software that allows quick and easy editing of source language files (both programs and JCL), and if such packages are in use in this installation, whether access to them can be controlled or their use automatically recorded.

Logging

The operating system may provide facilities for logging details of file access. This would provide the auditor with the opportunity to use software to search the log for details of access to particular files or by particular individuals. The extent of such facilities will vary according to operating system and supporting software and it is likely in some cases that such forms of access log will not be available.

Where logging facilities are being used the auditor must identify the scope for over-riding them; some features may provide just a warning message at the operator's screen to be noted and then ignored.

File reconstruction

In addition to reviewing file access controls, the auditor should ensure that the file reconstruction facilities are adequate. The procedures should be such that production files can be reconstituted completely and accurately by the retention of sufficient generations of files and the associated input and job submission data. Reports from the operating system or file librarian software, or clerical records can be examined by the auditor to determine whether sufficient previous generations of critical files are retained. As an initial step, however, the auditor should review the recovery procedures at the installation, to see whether management has properly considered the question.

6.7.3 Operational Control

Organisation

Before auditing the work of the operations section the auditor must understand its organisation and function. The operations manager or equivalent post holder will be the first point of contact for the auditor and will provide much useful information on the responsibilities and chain of command of individual members of staff.

The auditor should determine the split in responsibilities between the operations team and development staff and users. The information is needed to determine the audit approach: either to review operational controls in general, without reference to a particular system; or to consider a particular application such as payroll or creditors, which would also involve looking at the user department's arrangements.

Standards

Written standards, operating procedures manuals, job descriptions and processing schedules provide useful information for assessing the strengths and weaknesses of the section.

Having determined the standards that exist in the operations section, the auditor should identify and test the controls. These tests should be conducted methodically for each discipline within the section, ie data control, data preparation and operations.

Data control

In examining data control, the auditor should examine the procedures for receipt of input data to ascertain that all input data passes through appropriate control point, thereby formally transferring responsibility for input data from the user to IT staff. Clearly, this division of duties is not possible or necessary when users process their own input.

The auditor should ensure that users are not permitted to amend or add to batches of data after they have been registered. When it is necessary for changes to be made in input data prior to punching, it is preferable for the documents concerned to be formally booked out of the IT department back to the user.

Data preparation

The auditor should enquire into the controls exercised by the data preparation section or by users themselves and should be satisfied that they provide the required level of security, privacy and internal check.

The auditor must look for compensatory controls when data is input directly by users; and will need to assess these with the user department. In particular, verification and validation may be relaxed in these circumstances. User-driven computing is considered further in chapter 7.

Operating schedules

The auditor should examine operating schedules to ascertain that they are adequate for the purposes of anticipating run times and output volumes with a reasonable degree of accuracy.

JCL listings and accounting journals, produced as part of the operation cycle, may provide the

6.38

auditor with useful information on actual machine usage and will be the prime documents to be examined when attempting to identify unauthorised or excessive use of the computer.

Finally, the auditor may wish to examine computer usage and fault records to investigate the causes of certain failure and the remedial actions taken. Major or persistent failures in programs or systems would indicate that a full systems' investigation should be conducted in the near future. The treatment of failures by the IT staff may give the auditor an indication of their competence and the adequacy of the installation's procedures.

Emergencies

There will be occasions when, because of machine or program failure, emergencies will arise that require prompt and effective action. It is inevitable that internal control will be weakened when this occurs. Provided steps are taken to ensure that this weakening of control is no more than strictly necessary and that the occurrences are not too frequent, the auditor should recognise and accept the nature of the situation. Auditors should refer to a record of breakdowns, which should be maintained by computer management. The auditor must identify whether processing is undertaken outside normal hours and must review the level of staffing, separation of duties and other organisational and operational control during such periods.

6.7.4 Networking and Terminal Control

The controls required for networking will depend on the purpose and use of each workstation that is connected to the network. The capabilities of workstations will be determined by the application software and system software employed to control access. The auditor should therefore adopt the maxim that every workstation is a potential access point to financial data until they are able to satisfy themselves otherwise.

Location of equipment

The first task is to identify the location, type, capabilities and uses of each workstation connected to the organisation's mainframe or networks. That may not be a straightforward task since workstations may be located in many departments, and the responsibility for operational safeguards will be the responsibility of the client rather than the central department.

Access controls

Having located the workstations, the auditor should examine the procedures and safeguards that should prevent access by unauthorised persons. The auditor should visit the locations of workstations and study the normal operational arrangements. Where keyboard locks and similar devices are employed, the auditor should consider whether the control over the issue, custody and use of such equipment is satisfactory. The method of connection to the mainframe or network also deserves attention, particularly where public rather than dedicated or private lines are used.

Auditors should also refer to chapter 10, *Operating Systems and System Software*, and chapter 12, *Audit & Control of Networks*.

The auditor must evaluate the access control facilities provided by the operating system, telecommunications software and the application software itself.

Where a password system is employed the auditor should consider the adequacy of the arrangements for devising, issuing and changing passwords. They should also evaluate whether users take sufficient care to preserve the integrity of these and other identification codes, particularly where staffing changes frequently occur. The auditor should find out whether staff have sufficient guidance on choosing secure passwords.

Many systems can be instructed to report on such matters as the identity of workstations connected during a processing period and the jobs processed from such workstations as well as attempts at guessing passwords. Where software can monitor terminal activity and provide reports either automatically or on request, the auditor should take advantage of such facilities.

Standby procedures

The auditor should investigate the contingency arrangements made in case of the network becoming unavailable during the normal processing period. Where any workstation is essential to the system it must be possible to initiate manual procedures without loss of basic controls. However, the auditor should remember that weaknesses can be caused in workstation security procedures as a consequence of standby arrangements. For example, standby operators may be granted a wide range of access codes.

6.7.5   Environmental Control

When evaluating the adequacy of environmental controls, the auditor should remember that the computer assets may not necessarily be located in a single place. Equipment may be located in various departments each with their own facilities and file stores. The auditor will need to assess whether adequate precautions have been taken in all these areas and not confine attention to the computer itself.

A wide range of security and hazard protection products is available, and many bodies will provide consultancy services on the subject.

The auditor should be aware that insurance companies are becoming increasingly interested in their customers' levels of protection against risk and they may prove to be useful allies to the auditor in emphasising the need for adequate standards of protection. Indeed, high insurance premiums may arise from inadequate standards of protection.

Having reviewed the areas of control, the auditor will have to test that such controls are appropriate and are actioned. The auditor should become involved when the installation arranges tests of its own emergency procedures, such as a fire drill or visiting a standby computer site.

CHAPTER 7

USER DRIVEN COMPUTING

7

Continued overleaf

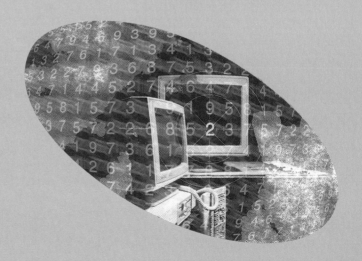

7.1 Introduction

The expression 'user driven computing' is used here to mean the use of computers which are not under the control and supervision of an IT department. Many user driven computing systems are based on microcomputers, but networks and minicomputer systems installed and managed at departmental level within the organisation are also used extensively in the same working environments. The term *microcomputer* has therefore been avoided in this chapter in favour of *small computer systems* or *user driven computer systems* in order to avoid the implication that the audit considerations under discussion are peculiar to micros.

Small computer systems can offer substantial positive contributions to the efficiency of the organisation. Computing at end user level encourages initiative and innovation and can, if applied properly, be a cost effective means of matching computing power with user requirements. It places the responsibility for processing in the hands of the users, it enables the organisation to benefit from computerisation of minor systems which might not otherwise figure as a high priority in IT department development plans, and it also spreads IT skills and the awareness of current technological developments.

7.2 Audit Objectives

7.2.1 Overview

The objective of an audit review of small computer systems is to assess whether the degree of control exercised by management is sufficient to protect the organisation's interests from losses or abuse through:

    — unauthorised acquisitions and development of systems;

    — incompatible or inappropriate hardware and software acquisitions;

    — insufficient user computer literacy;

    — deficiencies in general controls; and

    — inadequate or inaccurate computer produced information.

Where an organisation has both centralised and local computing facilities, audit management should consider them together in developing a strategy for IT audit. Audit coverage given to small computers and personal computing facilities should depend upon the relative significance and risk of the applications being run by end users on these systems.

Auditors should consider:

- the overall audit objectives for financial and non financial systems;

- the risks presented by such systems to the protection of and efficient use of the organisation's resources;

- the relative materiality or value of the applications running on those systems and the potential impact of loss, error or irregularity;

- the materiality of the resources expended in acquiring and using such facilities; and

- management policy on the development and use of such facilities.

Some of the risks arising from user driven computing have already been discussed. The controls discussed in the next section are not exhaustive and the auditor should not necessarily expect to find them present for every small computer system. They need only be implemented by management as necessary to provide a degree of control in a system consistent with its significance to the organisation and to efficient and effective use of the organisation's assets.

Risks

The uncontrolled growth and use of end user computing, can present the organisation with considerable risks. While organisations with centralised computer systems may have installed sophisticated procedures to protect them from damage or unauthorised access, such arrangements have often mistakenly been thought inappropriate with small computer systems. The user driven computer system is designed to work locally in a normal working environment and management with centralised systems may therefore overlook the need to control the development and use of smaller local systems. Similarly, organisations with no mainframe experience who acquire small computer systems for the first time may not appreciate the importance of basic controls in computing environments.

Management should be aware of the full extent of computing facilities in their organisation, the potential contribution that those facilities can make to better management and operational procedures and the possible risks which the presence and use of small computer systems can present.

Information is an important asset in any organisation. Small computer systems have the ability to store large quantities of information and manipulate that data in a variety of ways. This makes them, potentially, both a powerful tool and a serious control risk. The most common risks are discussed below.

Familiarity

Small computer systems are designed to appear attractive and to be relatively simple to operate. Management and users may therefore fail to appreciate their power and versatility and the potential dangers arising from misuse.

Hidden costs

It may be the case that purchased software packages cost more than the hardware. This can also be true of software developed in-house and management needs to be aware of the cost of fruitless or duplicate development time. Additional costs which are frequently not taken into account when acquisition decisions are made are those of peripherals such as data storage media, printers and modems, staff training and the cost of end user time in program development.

Cheapness

Suppliers and dealers often accept very low profit margins in order to sell small systems in large volumes but often without vital after-sales support. Organisations persuaded to purchase very cheaply or in large quantities to attract discounts thus forfeit support. Buyers should also consider the viability of such suppliers in a volatile market.

Location

Small computer systems are used in normal working environments, away from the strictly controlled environment of the computer room. Work locations may present many hazards such as:

- illegal access;
- the risk of theft of hardware and software from unsecured offices or workshops;
- accidental damage from spilled refreshments;
- static discharges from carpeting; and
- voltage spikes from power supplies.

Local disk storage

Local disks are a convenient, compact and versatile data storage medium, but they are also particularly susceptible to damage from deliberate or accidental maltreatment. The contents of floppy disks can be destroyed or made unreadable by exposure to strong magnetic fields, a source of heat such as a cup of hot coffee, or by bending. The consequences for an organisation dependent on such data can be catastrophic. Large quantities of data may present organisations with problems in backing up and the numbers of disks involved can be a disincentive to backing up at an appropriate frequency. Disks are easily removed from the workplace and this may present a security or confidentiality risk.

Proprietary software

Many user departments choose to avoid costly in-house programming with conventional languages by buying off-the-shelf program packages. There is a general belief that these will be tried and tested and therefore relatively free of bugs. This may not be the case, however, and no software should be purchased unless the user has taken the opportunity to test it thoroughly. Such packages are also designed to appeal to the widest possible market and users may need to tailor their working methods to suit the capabilities of the software. Often, packages require careful installation and optimising before the best benefit can be had of them but the cost of this is never apparent in sales literature for the software. Furthermore, since software controls add to development and processing time, there may be a tendency for suppliers to keep them to a minimum and not incorporate the full range of controls generally found in software for larger systems.

Compatibility

Users who are not expert in computing may buy incompatible or non-standard equipment or software which requires a specific hardware configuration which is not provided by their computer system.

Ease of programming and use

A wide variety of programming languages are available for small computer systems. In addition many utility packages such as spreadsheets are supplied with programming features such as 'macro' facilities whilst a large number of database products are effectively programming languages specifically geared to the creation of database systems. Users are often tempted by the suppliers' claims that such languages and macro facilities are easy to use and embark on the creation of complex application programs with them. The consequences of ill-trained staff writing critical applications are that:

- the programs may not be properly specified and may be subject to continuous refinement;
- the program is not properly documented;
- the program is not properly tested before use in a live context;
- the program code may be inefficient and may contain errors;
- the 'programmer' may in fact be paid more than an IT professional;
- several users may write programs which perform the same function but are written independently of each other thus wasting time and effort.

User friendly operating systems, interpretive programming languages and poor controls over access to the system and to data also make it easier for unauthorised users to interfere with small computer systems.

Interface with the network

Many small computer systems may be connected to a network and may be able to download data from a central machine into the local computer and use it for the end user's own purposes and for processing and updating the original file. Mainframe systems and databases are customarily subject to controls over access to and use of data but unless adequate safeguards are implemented it may be possible for the small computer system to be used as an intelligent workstation with unauthorised entry to the heart of the organisation's databases. Chapter 12 discusses networks and network security in more detail.

It is important therefore for management to appreciate both the contribution small computer systems can make to their organisation and the risks which can be posed to the integrity and security of its systems. A primary objective of management is therefore to enable the organisation to benefit from the application of end user computing through the use of small systems but in a controlled manner as to acquisition and operation.

7.3 Management of Small Computers

7.3.1 Management Policy

The introduction of small computing systems can have a dramatic impact on a wide variety of activities. They also increase the vulnerability of existing traditional systems and procedures and generate an entirely new category of risks. Management can however achieve the necessary degree of control without inhibiting creativity and innovation by adopting a policy on the use of small computer systems throughout the organisation which should be fully integrated with the organisation's overall strategies and policies for information and IT. The policy should extend to standards and procedures for the acquisition of new equipment and the manner of deployment, use and control of small computer systems including existing facilities. The policy should recognise the potential benefits of such facilities and take into account both their advantages and their drawbacks and stress the need for end user awareness of controls.

Small computer systems may have been introduced into the organisation with minimal advanced planning, or none at all. Accordingly decisions about acquisition, hardware brand selection, software and applications may have been made by a number of different end users. If guidance was not offered by or sought from IT departments, the result in many organisations may be:

— a proliferation of different and possibly incompatible hardware models;

— computers which are inappropriate to the required purpose;

— a considerable and probably unrecognised amount of time wasted on duplicated research and experimentation; and

— unstructured and disorganised information systems development.

7.3.2　Strategy for Small Computer Systems

A team of designated individuals should be made responsible for implementing a corporate information systems strategy which includes small computer systems. This team should provide post installation advice and guidance to end users. The team might consist of both IT specialists and experienced or interested end users.

The purpose of a corporate strategy for small computing systems is to facilitate co-ordinated and controlled development of such facilities for the benefit of the organisation as a whole and to avoid the proliferation of incompatible and duplicated systems. If it is to succeed in achieving its objectives, the strategy will need to be related to a strategy for centrally managed computing and should take account of the views of the IT department and of end user requirements.

The detailed matters to be taken into account in formulating the strategy should include:

- whether any manual systems would benefit from the implementation of small computer systems;

- whether any central IT systems could usefully be transferred to, or replaced by devolved computer systems;

- which terminal or computer configuration(s) best meets users' present and future needs and whether equipment should be shared;

- whether in-house guidance and support can be provided to end users;

- whether user training will be provided centrally;

- whether maintenance for local IT equipment is to be provided centrally;

- whether activity on small computer systems should be monitored;

- what technological advances can be incorporated; and

- how small computing facilities should be controlled.

The strategy will need to take account of the ways in which the use of small computing facilities may affect existing activities by increasing efficiency, pioneering new developments, consuming resources, or disrupting existing activities. Full consideration should be given to changes in the organisation and its working practices to maximise the potential benefits.

7.4 Controls in Small Computer Systems

7.4.1 Types of Control

The principles of control are discussed in other chapters within these *Guidelines* which for the sake of convenience are summarised below:

- Management of IT resources – Chapter 4.

- Acquisition of IT – Chapter 5.

- General Controls – Chapter 6.

- Development and Implementation of Systems and Packages – Chapter 8.

- Audit of Application Systems – Chapter 9.

- Operating Systems and Systems Software – Chapter 10.

- Audit & Control of Database Systems – Chapter 11.

- Audit and Control of Networks – Chapter 12.

Certain of the issues raised in the above chapters relating to the use of small computer systems are discussed below under the following headings:

- acquisition of small computer systems;

- development and maintenance of systems;

- application controls;

- file control;

- environmental control.

7.4.2 Management Controls

Line management in departments using small computer systems has a duty to ensure that the systems are installed, developed, operated and managed to provide an efficient, secure and effective service. Often, these managers will have had little training in IT management. They may therefore fail to appreciate the special skills and considerations required of them. Auditors should review management training to see that it is comprehensive and effective.

7.4.3 Acquisition of Small Computer Systems

Small computer systems are relatively inexpensive, often costing less than the minimum level at which many organisations' capital expenditure controls apply. If many such items of equipment are purchased, significant aggregated costs can arise throughout the organisation without ever being subject to the appropriate budgetary control and review. Organisations which allow departments complete freedom to select their own equipment are likely to find a wide range of installed systems, many of which may be incompatible with each other. Furthermore, some users may through ignorance or inexperience have acquired equipment and software which is unsuitable or inadequate for its intended purposes, or which proves too complicated for the user to master.

If large scale purchasing of IT is taking place, it may reach a scale where EC directives on purchasing will apply even though the acquisition is taking place in an apparently piecemeal manner at departmental level. It is therefore important that the organisation has a co-ordinated approach to small computer system acquisitions and takes full advantage of internal experience and expertise in selecting or advising end users on suitable configurations.

Software selection

The most important factor in the choice of a small computer system is the availability of suitable software which may also be the most expensive element in the system. Hardware selection decisions should therefore be based on the availability of suitable software to drive the required applications on that equipment.

Software selection is dependent on a number of criteria, including:

- the alternatives available for an existing small computer;
- the nature of the application;
- the extent of its use throughout the organisation;
- the required degree of application controls;
- the extent to which data is shared or may be shared between users;
- the need for compatibility between systems;
- the need for software portability between machines;
- the degree of 'fit' to the users' requirements;
- available user support and maintenance;
- the relative market standing of the package and the experience of other users an indication of program reliability;
- the user friendliness of the package; and
- the inbuilt flexibility of the program to cater for users' particular needs.

7.8

Hardware selection

Although the choice of hardware may depend on the availability of software for a particular application system it is normally advisable to standardise on compatible systems and specific configurations. Considerations in selecting hardware will include:

- the reputation and financial viability of the supplier;

- the reliability of the machine;

- the availability of spares or replacements, components and maintenance contracts;

- availability of software support (for major packages);

- the system's ability to adapt to technological developments: enhanced graphics features, memory upgrades, developments in peripherals etc;

- minimum system configurations, compared with user requirements;

- interfaces to printers, communications and other devices and networks; and

- user friendliness of the machine's operating system.

7.4.4   Development and Maintenance of Systems

Most developments by users will be undertaken with the aid of packages. The low cost and relatively easy availability of such software may encourage users who feel frustrated by the long development timescales offered by the central IT department to develop their own solutions. The advantages of end user package developments are:

- a better appreciation of IT by a wider range of users;

- the ability to respond quickly to demands;

- information tailored for local management; and

- reduced demands placed upon a central development section.

The disadvantages, however, are:

- uneconomic use of resources to develop systems such as senior staff to develop the new system;

- risk of duplication of effort by users with common requirements;

- difficulty in making solutions from stand-alone systems available to other users;

- failure to take the requirements of other users fully into account;

- risk of poor quality and potentially inaccurate programming by inexperienced staff;

    –   maintenance of systems may only be practicable by the author of the system;

    –   difficulty of controlling amendments to programs;

    –   problems of maintaining up to date documentation; and

    –   the security risks associated with the use of interpretive languages.

The enthusiasm which users have for small computers often leads to these disadvantages being overlooked, or given insufficient consideration. Audit should encourage management to:

    –   Adopt an IT strategy which includes clear guidelines on development of systems and sub-systems.

    –   Establish and maintain a user support facility within the organisation to provide a focal point for the provision of advice, guidance on projects and short term problem solving.

    –   Provide users of the software approved by the organisation for local development with short courses or self-teach packages to teach them how to make the best use of it.

    –   Devise and issue simple but comprehensive standards to be followed by users when developing systems. Care must be taken in preparing such material so that it does not assume detailed IT knowledge but nevertheless emphasises the principles and benefits of adopting certain standards in the development of systems.

    –   Ensure that all users are aware of the need to familiarise themselves with development procedures and adhere to standards devised for their use.

    –   Be aware of the implications of the Data Protection Act and the need for users to take the Act into account when developing systems.

7.4.5   Application Controls

Where several users are to share systems which have financial implications (whether developed within the organisation or purchased application packages), then the purchaser must ensure that there are adequate application controls. The principles which underpin effective control over any computerised system are detailed in chapter 9, *Audit of Application Controls*. Among the principles developed there are the following:

    –   Input controls should ensure that data is authorised, complete, accurate, timely and not previously processed.

    –   Processing controls should ensure that the correct data is processed, accounted for and written to the appropriate file and that data conforms to predetermined standards or falls within specified parameter values.

7.10

– Output controls should ensure that all expected output is produced, that it is complete and appears reasonable and is distributed on time and in such a way that confidentiality is maintained as far as is necessary. Procedures should ensure that errors and exceptions are investigated and dealt with properly.

– A complete audit trail should be maintained which allows any item to be traced from input through to its final resting place and any final result to be broken into its constituent parts.

A considerable difficulty which faces management responsible for imposing such control mechanisms is the absence of separation of duties in a typical small computer system. The lack of segregation of tasks increases the risk of accidental errors and deliberate data manipulation or fraud. Where applications are developed by a centrally based unit then there are opportunities to minimise local interference in software by compiling programs and then releasing only the object code. However, unsupervised and unauthorised manipulation of data still poses a risk. Many users also fail to appreciate that routines developed using spreadsheet packages are applications or systems in their own right and the principles of input, processing and output controls still apply and are the responsibility of the user.

Auditors should encourage management to take on full responsibility and ensure that evidence of attention to application controls is clearly presented.

7.4.6   File Control

Where data and programs are stored on local disks then there are significant risks of:

– data and programs being lost or accidentally erased;

– failure to keep backup copies of programs;

– damage to or loss of disks;

– theft of data and programs;

– fraudulent use of data and programs;

– unauthorised copying of proprietary software ('piracy').

Many small computers by their very nature lack sophisticated facilities such as automatic and interference free logging of all activities. Original software programs often reside on a collection of such disks under the personal control of the user. Operating systems in small computers generally lack sophisticated access control facilities and even where more sophisticated facilities are available, managers often fail to implement them properly because they do not understand the need. There are also risks of keeping large amounts of data on hard disks because of unauthorised access and accidental erasure.

Auditors should ensure that management devises standards for file control, back up and recovery so that users unfamiliar with the risks of poor file management can better appreciate the advantages of adopting reasonable controls.

7.4.7 Physical Controls

The portability of small computers increases the risk of theft and accidental or deliberate damage. The auditor should encourage the adoption of controls which include:

- care over the location of equipment to ensure restriction of physical access particularly when the office may be unattended;

- fixing equipment to desk tops and preventing the removal of components or enhancements from within the processor;

- the maintenance of an inventory;

- locking processors, keyboards and power supplies;

- care over the custody and control of access to floppy disks and documentation;

- off-site storage of back-up;

- measures to ensure compliance with the requirements of the Data Protection Act and other relevant legislation.

7.4.8 Maintenance and Insurance

While the organisation may have dealt adequately with maintenance and insurance cover over its main computing facility, this protection may not have been properly considered by departmental users who have acquired facilities of their own.

Maintenance cover for specialised packaged software is often available from the supplier but the main-stream PC packages such as spreadsheets are often supported only by telephone help-lines. Where users acquire a range of hardware or communication equipment from different suppliers, a third-party maintenance agreement may be sought.

Insurance against theft, damage or fraud and losses consequential on any of these may be included in the organisation's general insurance policies, but the auditor should encourage management to satisfy itself that there is neither explicit nor tacit exclusion of small computer systems and that the cover is adequate.

7.12

7.5 Communications

7.5.1 Mainframe Links and Networking

Where a small computer system is linked to a central processor in terminal mode there is an additional risk of unauthorised access to the central system's data and programs. Management should address such matters as:

— whether the computer simply emulates a terminal and has full enquiry, input and update facilities as provided by the on-line system;

— whether the computer can download data for analysis and manipulation – through spreadsheet software, for example; and

— whether the computer can also upload data.

The ability to emulate terminals presents no greater risks than does any on-line system. Where the user can download data then provided the terminal access control facilities are adequate (file amendment being restricted, for example) there is no particular additional risk to the centrally held data. However, it may be possible for a user to download data, process it erroneously or make false amendments to it and use the resulting output as if it were the original, authentic data. With the third option there is clearly a risk that data may be downloaded, edited and uploaded without any evidence of amendments being recorded. For this kind of configuration, therefore, management should consider:

— the precise facilities available to the user and the nature of the risks which they present;

— the need for those facilities and whether that particular method of access and processing have been justified and are appropriate;

— the precautions which the user has taken to provide reliable and consistent evidence of any amendments to data; and

— the facilities which exist on the central computer to compare data files before and after processing by the small system user.

Where small systems are networked and provide access to either other small systems, or central processors or other networks the same considerations apply. The extent of the network, numbers of staff involved and degree of control exercised by line management should be evaluated and risks identified. Appropriate controls can then be more readily determined.

7.6 Office Automation

Much publicity has been given to the concept of the automated office, although the term 'office automation' means different things to different people. For some it conjures up a vision of the 'paperless' office or the 'office of the future' with an image of a revolutionary change in office practice. Others use the term to mean the evolutionary application of modern electronic technology to office work and regard developments such as electronic mail systems as being of the same kind as telephones and electric typewriters.

Whatever the view the primary objective of management should be to take advantage of the potential of IT to serve business goals by raising the productivity of office staff, particularly those who are not specialists in IT by:

- reducing the cost of inputs such as labour, equipment and consumables; and

- improving the quality of outputs such as services, decisions or resource management.

With this in mind, the auditor should be concerned with office automation for two main reasons:

- improving productivity involves investment and there is a need to ensure that the organisation is reaping the maximum possible benefit from the minimum effective investment; and

- the automation of office activities may impact on the control, security and auditability of office systems.

Fundamentally office automation is the application of IT to the routine and clerical processes normally engaged in for the administration and execution of business, Such automation may be provided by a central processor, independent local computing facilities such as microcomputers or a local network. From an audit point of view it is an extension of the concept of user driven computing because its use is exercised locally in the working environment of the user and as stated raises concerns about investment and security and control.

The potential impact of office automation and its relationship with existing data processing technology means that a primary concern is the need for a general strategy for IT and one for office automation in particular. While office automation can bring many benefits, investment must be considered in the light of the needs of the organisation and the resources which are available to satisfy those needs.

7.14

7.7   Audit Approach

7.7.1   Introduction

Before commencing an audit of small computer facilities and office automation auditors should recognise that all such facilities need to be controlled as strictly and as closely as large centralised installations. Unless auditors fully appreciate the nature, potential uses and risks of small computer systems, they are unlikely to be able to assist management in deriving full benefit from such facilities.

The auditor has two broad activities to consider; firstly, the exercise and control of user driven computing generally and secondly, office automation. The emphasis of the first activity is likely to be concentrated on control, whereas, the emphasis for the second is likely to be on the investment and value for money.

7.7.2   User Driven Computing

In planning an appropriate audit strategy the auditor has three broad areas to consider:

- aspects relating to the organisation as a whole;
- aspects which apply to individual machines; and
- aspects relating to particular applications.

Organisation

Matters to be considered include:

- the existence of a management policy on the organisation's use of IT;
- appropriate procedures for the acquisition of hardware and software;
- standards which cover the development of systems, security and the safe and efficient operation of all computers; and
- management arrangements to ensure that facilities are being fully exploited for the benefit of the organisation as a whole and are being used effectively and efficiently.

Equipment

Matters to be considered include:

- their location, manner of use and the types of each machines;
- the appropriateness of individual machines to the overall management strategy;

7.15

- their compatibility with other machines; and

- the end users operating specific machines.

Applications

Matters to be considered include:

- the standards and procedures adopted by the organisation for managing the development of in-house systems;

- the importance or sensitivity of the application to the organisation; and

- the controls and procedures inherent or capable of being added to individual proprietary packages.

Preparation

When preparing to carry out an initial audit of small computing facilities the auditor will first need to obtain some basic background information, such as:

- details of management policy and strategy for the use of small computing facilities;

- personal computing standards and procedures;

- comprehensive details of all user driven computing facilities within the organisation.

- the identity of end users; and

- details of significant applications operating on those facilities.

Audit reviews of the efficient and effective use of small computer systems will need to consider:

- the range of hardware in use and its degree of reliability and compatibility;

- the range, reliability and compatibility of software packages in use;

- available applications and the use made of information which they generate;

- the skill requirements of current systems and the consequent need for end user training and support;

- the adequacy of security, maintenance, standby and insurance arrangements;

- the potential for further growth in and benefit from developing end user computing.

Computing facilities

Installation audits of particular end user facilities should include an assessment of the adequacy of the following:

7.16

 – the security and safety of the physical location;

 – the identity, operating skills and control awareness of all known end users;

 – the access and other system software controls in operation; and

 – any maintenance, standby and insurance arrangements specific to that hardware;

These are discussed further in chapter 6, *General Controls*.

Applications

Application audits will normally include some of the above, but will also cover an assessment of the adequacy of system controls, such as:

 – system access controls (such as passwords);

 – transaction history files and management trails;

 – data checking and validation procedures;

 – system control totalling features; and

 – clerical procedures.

These are discussed further in chapter 9, *Audit of Application Systems*.

Conclusions

In testing management arrangements, installations and applications, the auditor uses the principles and techniques applied to larger computer installations and to systems audits. The main differences are of environment, scale and end user accessibility. The auditor should bear in mind that controls which normally exist in the mainframe environment to protect costly and vulnerable installations from vandalism, accidental damage and unauthorised access and usage, can actually discourage full, efficient, effective and creative use of small computing facilities. The auditor's report should therefore be balanced with all these considerations in mind.

7.7.3   Office Automation

Audit's interest in the automated office lies in the following broad areas:

 – identifying the organisation's strategy;

 – the arrangements for implementing that strategy and for the acquisition of facilities:

 – the organisation of staff and functions related to the provision of office automation and IT generally;

 – indicators of the costs and benefits of office automation; and

       −   the control, security and auditability implications of office automation.

Strategy

In reviewing office systems a first task for the auditor is the identification of the organisation's strategy. This is likely to be a statement of the general direction of developments, the broad needs of all present and potential users and a view of the available resources and estimated future investment.

Such a document or series of documents should provide some indication of the relationship between the development of office systems and those of other IT areas. The auditor should expect these developments to be co-ordinated otherwise, there is clearly a considerable risk of divergent aims, investment and development. A failure to identify these risks may result in equipment being installed and staff trained in techniques and skills which satisfy short term problems only. The opportunity for this investment in equipment and staff to form part of a cohesive implementation of IT facilities may never occur and the full benefits of office automation would not then be realised.

Planning a strategy

The first step in the planning process is likely to be the establishment of a study group with clearly defined terms of reference, the identification of accountable individuals, the scope of the study and an appropriate time frame. It is important that there is adequate representation of all individuals or groups involved. These could be expected to include IT staff, management services, personnel and users. Reporting responsibilities should also be identified and should be consistent with other high level planning procedures (eg IT steering committee, corporate IT strategy). The definition of strategy necessitates the seeking of information and measurements to aid the formulation of solutions. The strategy must recognise the nature of the organisation and its corporate needs and would normally be expected to embrace the following areas:

       −   the nature and business of the organisation;

       −   the availability and use of current office support systems;

       −   consideration of the current generation of office systems; and

       −   the proposals for the implementation of office automation.

Other points which should be considered during the planning of the strategy are:

       −   the extent to which current office systems are dependent upon each other and existing central computing systems. This makes the need for adopting a communication standard essential;

       −   the extent to which uniformity of local office automation systems has been achieved, so far and is desirable for the future. This may be a long term aim following some initial experimentation with different suppliers' facilities. Its advantages are clear within an organisation where interchange of staff between functions is common. It will also ease the task of training and any central technical support and reduce the cost of providing both;

— the procedures which will be adopted within the organisation to determine which office automation proposals will be considered for investment; and

— the provision of guidelines to middle managers on the criteria to be adopted in considering the priority of office automation proposals.

Introducing office automation

The introduction of office automation will also place demands upon support services and this may well prove to be a significant cost. It is inevitable that many costs which previously were readily attributable to the central IT department will drift to users. Keyboard work will be undertaken by more senior staff: the professional manager may be spending time in straightforward data entry.

All of this is a cost to the organisation and the benefits are far less tangible than those which would traditionally be associated with the computerisation of a manual payroll system, for example.

This is not to suggest, however, that a feasibility study is not relevant to office automation developments. It is a very necessary procedure since it will oblige management to identify the benefits, albeit in intangible term such as improved effectiveness or staff morale and then to identify both direct and indirect costs.

The auditor will need to recognise that management may themselves face problems in defining a strategy which is defensible in monetary terms. In many cases management will exercise their judgement as to the worth of intangible benefits. The auditor must be aware of the need for sufficient data to be available to justify a purchase, but be able to balance this against the cost and disadvantages of protracted studies in an area with an ever present degree of imprecision. The auditor's own judgement needs to be exercised to assess whether the value of the 'intangibles' has been assessed reasonably.

When identifying products which are to form the basis of the automated office the organisation must try to assess the stability of the product and the viability of its supplier. The expectations of the user and the claims of the supplier should be considered carefully by the auditor when reviewing the appraisal procedures. The claims of the supplier should be matched with proven demonstrations of results and other user experience although some aspects of integrated office automation are still at a 'green fields' stage of development and organisations must be made fully aware of the risk and the likely additional costs which they will bear if implementing an unproven product.

Where office automation is being introduced into an organisation with little or no previous experience there is a particular need for a mechanism to be installed to monitor the implementation of the new products and their use by staff. This review is not likely to be a once and for all exercise. It is more likely to demand regular 'snapshot' reviews to keep management advised of progress and of particular problems.

Development of office systems

In any data processing environment, there is normally a recognised need for auditors to be involved during the course of system development. Usually, this involvement would be geared towards the review of a specific development project and would encompass:

- system proposal;
- approval for development;
- costs and benefits;
- system design;
- system controls;
- clerical procedures;
- system implementation.

During the course of reviewing the above areas, the auditor would take a view on system and data integrity, the audit trail, ease of maintenance, system continuity and level of documentation.

In the context of development of office systems, auditors need to consider the contribution they should make, just as they would for other computerised systems. In practice there are a number of constraints to be considered.

The equipment itself may not be identified as being acquired to support systems which are of direct interest to the auditor and may therefore receive little consideration. There is a danger too that where an application is judged to be non-financial, it is assumed not to be capable of financial processing although in fact facilities may be provided to support such activity. The devices installed may provide an opportunity for users to develop and run other applications and the auditor must attempt to be aware of subsequent development work.

This may impose a considerable burden upon limited audit resources and, two possible approaches may be:

- to prepare a code of practice for user development; and
- to maintain a register of local developments.

Code of practice

Another option is for a code of practice or development guidelines to be used which details good working practices to be adopted by end users who develop their own applications. This should include specific advice on areas of general interest to auditors as well as wider organisational standards and expectations. It should provide a 'long stop' where auditors and the organisation foresee logistical difficulties in controlling all development activities and possible future operational problems.

Operational systems

There are various considerations for the auditor in relation to operational office systems:

- their financial content, or potential for impact on any significant resource management decision process;

- their interface with other computer systems;

- their dependence upon user development;

- the security and control procedures;

- the procedures for monitoring their efficiency and effectiveness.

Separation of duties

Small computer systems by their very nature are less well controlled than large mainframe based systems. Being small they usually provide limited facilities and are operated by the minimum of staff, often one person. However, the financial importance of an application should not be judged by its physical size or on the cost of the hardware as indeed some important applications will be run within office systems. Management may not recognise the need to retain tight control over these applications, particularly when the capital outlay is low. They may therefore suffer from too few staff being employed to offer segregation of duties. Auditors should be aware of this and should, if possible, take steps to minimise the potential risk. For example where an individual has responsibility for acquisition, development and operation of a system, particularly if it has a capability of linking to another machine holding financial data, then there are clear control implications which must be addressed by the auditor.

Confidentiality

Under the Data Protection Act, use of personal information is restricted to the purpose for which it was originally collected and security must be provided to ensure adequate protection. Individuals are usually allowed access to data concerning them and any inaccuracies must be corrected. If this type of data is to be held on or available to an office system it must be rigorously protected by an access control system that allows various levels of security depending on the standing of the user. Additional measures must be taken to prevent loss, corruption or illegal access. Auditors should ensure that the users of such systems are aware of their legal obligations and of the need to register them.

Loss of the audit trail

There is a tendency for office systems to move towards paperless office environments and when this occurs and a financial system is involved, steps must be taken to preserve an audit trail. This could mean that the auditor will have to ask for a trail to be reinstated to provide the necessary visible evidence or alternatively ensure that the data is saved in an appropriate form on magnetic media.

One further problem of a paperless office is the lack of acceptable evidence in the event of legal proceedings being pursued. Court evidence frequently needs to be in visible or hard copy form and supported by proof of the accurate working of the machine at the time of a transaction was being processed. This may prove particularly difficult to achieve with such systems. The matter can be compounded if the original input was by a third person using magnetic media files or a network for communication.

CIPFA

COMPUTER AUDIT GUIDELINES

APPLICATION SYSTEMS

8 DEVELOPMENT AND IMPLEMENTATION OF SYSTEMS AND PACKAGES

9 APPLICATION CONTROLS

CHAPTER 8

DEVELOPMENT AND IMPLEMENTATION OF SYSTEMS AND PACKAGES

8

Continued overleaf

8.1 Introduction

This chapter addresses the subjects of the development and acquisition of application software for the business activities of an organisation. Its purpose is to provide auditors with an understanding of the development process and an appreciation of the role of the auditor in assisting management to ensure that the primary objectives of the organisation are achieved in a secure manner. The introduction deals with objectives, the options available to meet those objectives. and audit considerations. The second part of the chapter addresses the areas of control and the third part discusses the audit approach.

Readers are urged to read this chapter in conjunction with chapter 5, *The Acquisition of Information Technology* as the principles of project planning and evaluation are similar and, in many instances, the installation of a new system calls for the acquisition of additional IT resources.

8.1.1 Objectives

Management should ensure that the development or acquisition of application software meets the business needs of the organisation, provides users with well designed systems that meet their requirements and are produced or acquired efficiently and cost effectively.

The primary objectives of audit are to establish and verify that the management arrangements and procedures employed will ensure that business objectives are met and in a secure manner. To achieve those objectives the auditor will need to look at the controls associated with the various stages of a development or acquisition project and evaluate and test them. The control areas and matters of interest to the auditor are dealt with in the second part of this chapter.

8.1.2 Options

The development or acquisition of application software to meet business needs makes significant demands on the financial and computing resources of an organisation. Management therefore needs to give careful consideration to the ways and means by which the requirements may be met. The options most commonly available are:

- Bespoke systems – these are developed in-house and hitherto were the traditional method of meeting requirements. Such systems can be tailored exactly to the requirements of the users by permanent professional staff familiar with the requirements and workings of the organisation.

- Shrink-wrap software – is usually provided for PC software and provides the user with a well-tried package which has usually been widely sold. Support and maintenance is usually minimal and this is reflected in the low cost of the package.

— Application software packages – these are produced by commercial trading organisations for network, mini and mainframe users in response to market demands and are chosen more and more often to meet new business needs. They provide management with the option of selecting a readily available 'best fit' solution but which may require tailoring in-house to meet the particular requirements of the user and the operating system.

8.2 Management Control

8.2.1 Introduction

Development control starts with senior management. Rules and structures should be created by senior management that establish how a project is evaluated, who should be involved and what form of approval should be given and by whom. Senior management should thus retain overall control of the investment and decide whether or not development or acquisition should proceed and the priority of a particular project by reference to its contribution to the business needs of the organisation.

The structural arrangements for the exercise of management control and granting of approvals will depend on the nature of the organisation but they should reflect the significance and importance of a proposed development or acquisition and in one way or another the interests of the following groups who should be involved in the process:

— Corporate management: senior officers or members acting collectively on behalf of the organisation as a whole. Such a body could form a project management team.

— IT management: those individuals in day-to-day control of the data processing function and individual project managers who exercise control over specific projects.

— Users: those who will own and utilise the proposed system.

— Line management: those responsible for exercising control over specific functions within the organisation which will be affected by the system.

Priorities will be assigned according to the value judgements but management should take the following factors into account:

— organisational policy and statutory considerations;

— the relative importance of the project to the organisation;

— the net financial and non-financial benefits estimated to be available;

— development resources available;

— timing factors; and

— the total development programme.

Senior management should also determine the process for the appointment of a project leader. The importance of selecting an experienced project leader cannot be overestimated. The project leader has the task of co-ordinating the different personal involved (corporate management, IT staff, user departments and line management) and encouraging and developing the team to achieve the goal based on the resources available. Co-ordination, co-operation and common sense are features which will help to progress a system sensibly and effectively. At each stage in the development, team members need to know when to contribute and when to listen and observe – it requires a skilful project leader to manage each stage and its associated problems in a smooth manner.

The assumptions are that all IT proposals are likely to involve the IT department and that management arrangements require the opinion and possibly approval or backing of the IT department and that authorisation to proceed may only be given by a project management team. It may well be however that the user department as the budget holder has some freedom of action and so while the underlying principles should still be observed, all relevant procedures and activity would occur within the user department, The user department would nevertheless be well advised to obtain professional opinion and advice from external sources, preferably from the IT department to ensure:

— compatibility, if necessary, with other systems;

— provision of access by other users, if required and permitted;

— adequate security of data;

— adequate sizing of the system's hardware, software and other requirements;

— sufficient user support when the system goes live; and proper maintenance and back-up in the event of problems occurring.

8.3 Development Stages

8.3.1 Introduction

The development or acquisition of application software can be broken down into discretely identifiable stages for control purposes even though the stages may overlap and not follow in strict sequential order. The stages are:

    –   The definition of the requirement and initiation of the project.

    –   The feasibility study.

    –   The technical specification for the system.

    –   The technical design of the system.

    –   The production of the system.

    –   The implementation of the system.

    –   The post implementation phase.

8.3.2   The Requirement and Project Initiation

Objectives

The objective of the project initiation stage is to produce a report and obtain a decision from the appropriate authorising body on whether or not a proposal to develop or acquire application software may proceed whether with a feasibility study or the project itself. The starting point is therefore the user's case for the software. The proposal for the development or acquisition of application software should define:

    –   the business need and purpose of the system;

    –   how the end product will meet that business need;

    –   system requirements and how the system is expected to operate;

    –   interactions with other systems and the way in which these will be handled;

    –   the mandatory and discretionary elements of the system; and

    –   how the value of the end product in use will be assessed.

Standards and procedures should ensure that requirements for IT developments are submitted formally and go through pre-defined routes including the IT department. The next stage therefore is for the user to submit the requirement to the IT department for evaluation. The IT department should in turn produce a project initiation report which should include the estimated costs of any feasibility study that may be required and the IT departments comments and recommendations for submission to the appropriate authorising body as required.

Management issues

The advantages of establishing adequate project planning and control procedures are:

    –   ensuring effective use of resources by developing and implementing a system in a phased manner;

8.4

- providing targets in terms of cost, time and performance against which to measure project control;

- setting system boundaries and interfaces with other systems by defining clear terms of reference; and

- allowing management and project team reviews at each phase of the system development to allow corrective action to be made.

Project planning

Initial project planning often exposes the lack or unavailability of accurate and comprehensive information. There is a need for a systematic approach of building up the resource requirements to qualify the cost-benefit analysis. A number of project planning and control methodologies are available to assist in the collection and presentation of all the relevant information. Some methodologies use project management software to provide an analysis of activities and tasks to be achieved against the resources required or available. Large system developments need to be broken down into manageable phases so that shortfalls or slippages can be identified allowing project managers to make decisions on how best to progress the system.

Estimation techniques

Estimating is a task which depends on prudent management and the experience and ability of the project team to build in contingencies based on past experience. A number of common techniques can be used:

- Work unit method: which relates previous performance of individuals on similar projects to the current project and extrapolates an estimate.

- Self estimation average: which uses a project evaluation and review technique (PERT) formula.

- Performance guidelines: which apply a pre-determined rate of productivity to the estimated size of program to be coded.

- Synthetic formulae: which require professional judgement to break each activity into a number of component tasks and build up an estimate.

As the project progresses, estimates can be refined and tailored.

Project control

The elements of a good project control system are:

- Provision for easy and simple recording of actual progress on each activity/task.

- Automatic updating of data based on changes identified ie extrapolation data which shows 'bottlenecks' or deadlines being exceeded.

    —   Ability to display both the activity/task data with the 'resource' (staff) implications.

    —   Provision of key management reports and the ability to extract management information in a number of different ways.

Responsibilities

Management arrangements should ensure that no project will be initiated until the requirements have been jointly discussed by IT and user management. Two teams are invariable established for the development of systems. A project management team which will be a high level group providing an ongoing review function assessing the relative merits of users requests and matching them against the overall strategic needs of the organisation and the resources available. A project control team is more likely to be established for each individual development project and will include representatives of all those involved in the planning production and delivery of the system. The project management team will need to ensure that:

    —   user management is aware of the importance of properly identifying and clearly specifying user needs;

    —   all other persons affected by the requirement will be consulted and allowed to make their contributions;

    —   the 'who' 'how' and 'when' of planning issues are agreed;

    —   sufficient time is allocated for consideration of the requirement before incurring the cost of a feasibility study; and

    —   the appropriate approval to proceed has been obtained.

The user department should:

    —   determine the objective and scope of the proposed project;

    —   determine the terms of reference;

    —   analyse existing systems and working arrangements;

    —   determine the objectives and requirements of the proposed new system;

    —   develop a system outline or proposal with an estimate of the order of cost.; and

    —   produce a project initiation report containing the submission and recommendations and submit it to the project management team for a decision eg approval to proceed with a feasibility study, approval to proceed with the project itself or not to proceed any further.

The IT department should:

    —   evaluate the proposal by reference to business and IT strategies and needs;

    —   advise on the best overall technical approach to adopt; and

— estimate the resources required for any feasibility study that may be required.

8.3.3 The Feasibility Study

Objectives

The primary objective of a feasibility study is to produce a report and obtain a decision from the appropriate authorising body on whether or not to proceed with a project.

Standards and procedures should ensure that requests for new applications or amendments are submitted formally and are channelled through a pre-defined route. On production of the feasibility study report a decision needs to be made by the project management team as to whether development or acquisition should proceed or not. This point may mark the commitment of significant staff resources with associated costs. Careful consideration of the proposed project is therefore required. If the project is not justified it should proceed no further. The decision should take into account costs and benefits of the proposed system including non-financial benefits, priority, available resources and the development time scale. The decision should be taken by or on behalf of corporate management.

Management must also decide at this stage which alternative solution they wish to support. If in-house development is the preferred option, it may be that the time scale of such an option is unacceptable to the user. That situation may arise when insufficient resources are available within the IT department to meet its existing development workload. In such a situation the alternatives available are to place a high priority on the proposed system and divert resources away from current or planned work or to consider alternative solutions such as buying a commercial package, buying-in additional development resources or allowing end users to develop the system.

Management issues

This is the crucial planning phase when system boundaries must be clearly defined. Matters to be addressed are:

— the classification of user needs as imperative, desirable or optional;

— agreement on key system indicators such as speed of operation, ease of maintenance, reliability and security;

— the involvement of users at the evaluation stages;

— the establishment of the structure for technical direction; and

— the use of formal approaches and accepted methodologies for project justification and risk assessment.

Activities and tasks

The user department should in liaison with the IT department:

-    —   appoint a project leader who will be have responsibility for developing the justification for the investment;

-    —   determine the scope and objectives of the project;

-    —   examine the existing facilities and working arrangements and verify the requirements;

-    —   identify and evaluate all the options;

-    —   prepare initial development or acquisition plans; and

-    —   produce a feasibility study report which includes a cost/benefit analysis.

8.3.4   The Specification

Objectives

The primary objective is the production of a technical specification which:

-    —   reflects the user's requirement comprehensively and accurately; and

-    —   provides a sound and well defined basis for the design and production or acquisition of a system that will satisfy the user's requirements.

An important feature of any successful development work is therefore the extent to which users have participated in the development work. That should usually take the form of users agreeing to a system specification and thereafter providing clarification on specific problems.

Management issues

A principal concern of management is to ensure that a clear and unambiguous specification document is produced for in-house design and development or acquisition of a commercial package that:

-    —   uses a formal standard approach;

-    —   is easy to understand;

-    —   contains clear diagrams and examples of reports and screens; and

-    —   has flexibility built in to the specification to allow for changes in requirements during development; and

-    —   completeness of data analysis is verified

Management should ensure that the completeness of data is verified. Management should also consider the provision of hands-on demonstrations of examples of the techniques and routines that are specified for the system.

Activities and tasks

The project control team should:

- determine the specification objectives from a review of the system outline and the suitability of the methodologies and tools to be used;

- complete the detailed data analysis using suitable data modelling techniques and relate the data to other existing systems and databases;

- determine and agree the contents of the specification including such features as data and menu hierarchies and structures, key functional aspects such as input output reports and screen layouts, and security and control features such as validation routines and error correction procedures;

- produce an outline acceptance test plan which includes the testing strategy and acceptance criteria; and

- draw up and publish the formal documentation of the functional specification.

8.3.5   The System Design

Objectives

The requirement for a technical design will depend on whether the decision has been to purchase a package or write the system in house. In the case of a decision to develop the system in-house there is a requirement for the functional specification to be translated into a set of specifications for programs and data files. The primary objectives of management are that:

- either, the selected package will provide the best fit with the functional specification and with the least tailoring;

- or, the in house design will match the requirements and functional system specification and provide a satisfactory basis for the subsequent development and production of the system.

The first objective is considered under the 'Evaluation of Software Packages' whilst the second objective is considered below

Management issues

This is a highly technical phase, so senior management strategy should concentrate on quality aspects by:

- Establishing a 'quality assurance program' under which regular checks are carried out and change control procedures established to handle changes in requirements or the specification.

- Ensuring that the system is broken down into manageable modules to aid control.

- Considering the trade off between performance and the costs operation and maintenance of the system.

- Ensuring that there is a co-ordinated test plan.

- Ensuring that there is an adequate training program.

Activities and tasks

The project control team should:

- Produce the system design by defining the processes involved, each input output and process, each access point and the data flows.

- Define the database or other system data files including file and data structures and the recovery processes required.

- Produce the detailed system test plan including data creation, the resources to be utilised and the timetable.

- Produce the formal technical design document for agreement by the user and subsequent use by the program and system development team.

8.3.6   Development and Production

Objectives

The primary objectives are that:

- the suite of programs and data files and other facilities employed function in accord with the functional specification and meet the requirements of the user; and

- the programming and other development work is carried out efficiently and effectively in a secure manner.

In the case of the purchase of a commercial package the same objectives will apply to any tailoring that is required to implement the package and satisfy more nearly the requirements and working practices of the user and computing centre.

Management issues

The principal matters with which management will be concerned is quality control and ensuring that development proceeds in accordance with agreed plans and timetables and cost. Particular matters which management should address are:

- the awareness of the development team of project plans and deadlines;
- the regular review of progress actually achieved and costs incurred;
- revisions to the project plans etc;
- control over changes to requirements;
- the adequacy of documentation cannot be overstated;
- the production of high quality system documentation and user and operational manuals.

Activities and tasks

The project control team should ensure that:

- the program modules are developed by the production and creation of programs and data files required for the correct functioning of the system in accord with prescribed standards and the project plans;
- a system testing procedure is devised and a system test environment created to ensure that all aspects of the application and operational functions are tested at modular and total system levels;
- the formal documentation of the system is produced including operational and user manuals and guides.

8.3.7   The Evaluation of Software Packages

Objectives

The primary purpose of the evaluation of an application software package purchased as an alternative to in-house development is to determine the acceptability of the package and ensure that it will:

- meet the specified requirements of the users; and
- function effectively in the operational environment of the organisation.

The control of the acquisition of an application software package purchased as an alternative to in-house development is fundamentally the same as that for the acquisition of other computer facilities (see chapter 5). As far as the acceptance of the package is concerned many of the controls relating to system development are equally applicable eg the production of a user requirement and initiation of the project, the production of a functional specification, any design and development work required to tailor the package and the implementation of the system.

8.11

The primary objectives of evaluation in addition to the acceptability of functionality are therefore:

- that the package conforms to the standards of the organisation with regard to security, integrity, reliability, and performance;

- that the package is compatible with the organisations' computing facilities; and

- the package can and will be supported and maintained.

Management issues

The particular issues for management to address are:

- the production of an agreed specification for the application software package;

- conformance of the application software package to the organisations' standards;

- the support and maintenance for the package;

- the performance of the package; and

- the arrangements for evaluation, testing and acceptance.

Activities and tasks

The IT department should evaluate the possible products and agree with the preferred or potential suppliers how the particular requirements of the organisation will be met and assess the functionality of the agreed application package as subsequently produced before taking delivery and establish that:

- software meets all mandatory and discretionary requirements;

- it is written to appropriate and acceptable standards;

- it is adequately documented;

- the package ensures the completeness and accuracy of input, processing and output;

- back-up, recovery and security of files, data and programs meets requirements;

- the package is compatible with existing hardware, operating systems and other systems;

- the performance of the package is acceptable in terms of ease of use, flexibility and efficiency of operation;

- that training is training provided; and

- that support and maintenance of the package is guaranteed and to a good standard.

The IT department and user should jointly test the system before acceptance of the application software package.

8.12

8.3.8   Implementation

Objectives

The primary objectives are to set up the environment in which the system will run and ensure that it is adequately checked and tested and functionally acceptable. The project control team should oversee the exercise which should involve users and IT operations staff.

Management issues

Management responsibilities revolve around ensuring a smooth and painless handover of the new system which necessitates making arrangements for:

- functional testing and evaluation of the system;

- performance testing of the system in an operational environment;

- training all staff involved in the management, supervision, operation and use of the system;

- the conversion or creation of the data and data files for the system;

- the production of all necessary system documentation, operational guides and user guides and manuals;

- support and maintenance of the system including change control procedures.

Activities and tasks

The project control team should:

- set up the production environment and oversee the installation of the required software, hardware and other IT facilities;

- agree the acceptance testing procedures and oversee their execution including such matters as the creation of test data;

- make arrangements for the changeover including the creation and conversion of data files, the training of all staff, the provision of guides and manuals and the provision of operational support;

- conduct the formal acceptance procedure and produce a formal completion of project report for senior management as required.

8.3.9   Post Implementation Review

Objectives

The primary purpose of a post-implementation review is to establish the degree of success achieved

8.13

by the project. The review also provides an opportunity to review the quality of the development process estimating, appropriateness of the project team organisations and procedures and techniques employed.

Management issues

Management should make suitable arrangements for an impartial review to assess and determine whether or not:

- the system meets business requirements ie satisfies the functional requirements of the user;
- the project was completed on time and within its budget;
- the system justified the cost in terms of the actual benefits;
- the systems operational performance is adequate;
- there are any technical problems;
- the interfaces to other systems work properly;
- the documentation is adequate; and
- agreed changes have been properly implemented and recorded.

Activities and tasks

Management should:

- determine the scope of the review;
- define the terms of reference;
- define the criteria to be employed; and;
- appoint the review team.

The review team should in accordance with their terms of reference:

- review the operational system;
- conduct performance and operational tests;
- review the development techniques and methodologies employed;
- compare estimated timetables and costs with actuals and obtain explanations for variations;
- verify that all changes to requirements were properly considered and authorised; and
- produce a report for senior management as required detailing findings, conclusions and any recommendations.

8.14

8.3.10 Amendment Procedures

Objectives

Because of the dynamic nature of software and the dynamic environment in which organisations operate it is inevitable that computerised systems will from time to time require amendment. The need for such amendments may arise in many ways, for example because of:

- changes in the working practices of users;

- changes in user requirements or additional requirements;

- changes to satisfy users wishes and expectations;

- changes in the law or statutory regulations; and

- changes in the structure of the organisation.

The need for amendments may also arise because of:

- errors in initial specification and design;

- program errors or deficiencies not detected during development testing;

- program errors inadvertently caused by amendments to the system; and

- corruption of the system during operation.

Evidence suggests that the main causes for the need for amendments are;

- poor system design;

- poor programming methods and standards;

- inadequate or poor documentation of systems;

- poor operating procedures; and

- ageing of programs and systems.

Whatever the cause amendments make a significant contribution to the cost of maintenance and the demand on the resources available for maintenance. They may also constitute a risk to the security of the system. The primary objectives are therefore that:

- the resources devoted to maintenance are well managed;

- the procedures for amending programs are securely controlled; and

- the causes of errors are identified and appropriate action taken to reduce their occurrence.

Management issues

The main issues for management to consider are:

8.15

— measures aimed at reducing the incidence of system errors and the consequent need for amendments; and

— the application of standards and control procedures for amendments comparable to those that are applied for system design and development.

The consequent costs of executing such arrangements should be commensurate with the significance and importance of an amendment. Significance and importance are measured size and cost of the amendment, security requirements and how essential the amendment is to enable the business needs of the organisation to be met. The same considerations should apply in determining whether or not an amendment should be made.

The matters which should be covered by any control procedures are:

— the formal statement of requirement;

— evaluation;

— authorisation;

— programming and testing;

— implementation.

8.4 The Audit Approach

8.4.1 Introduction

Traditionally the audit of system development controls has been a review of the management arrangements and procedures for the production or acquisition of application software. It is usually conducted at a general level of establishing what the arrangements and procedures are observing what has happened or is happening in practice and evaluating the results.

The role of the auditor in this field has however evolved over the years and many auditors particularly internal auditors are expected either to apply the audit directly to a system under development. They are also invited to comment on system proposals, or be directly involved in system development on a routine basis because of the view that if effective application controls are to be built into new systems then audit needs to be directly involved.

Such involvement should not invalidate the auditor's findings — indeed it may enhance them — nor does it compromise the audit of application controls in the live system. Auditors should however never let such involvement impair their impartiality and judgement or compromise their independence by participating in management decisions. Their involvement should be limited to offering professional comment.

8.16

The role and primary objectives of audit may be defined as:

- to be satisfied that adequate control, audit and security considerations are built into the development and the nominated staff are aware of their responsibilities; and

- to give an opinion on the effectiveness on the management arrangements and procedures for the control of system development.

The criteria for determining whether or not the audit objectives are satisfied are set out in the previous parts of this chapter. The detailed objectives and particular matters that require attention are set out in the remaining parts of this chapter. They are set out under each of the control areas relating to each stage in the development process.

8.4.2   The Requirement and Project Initiation

Objectives

Audit's objectives are to be satisfied that:

- the requirement has been fully defined; and

- proper approval has been obtained for initiation of the development project.

The criteria for the auditor's evaluation are:

- the whole system has been considered and clearly defined including the impact on other systems;

- the proposed system is not in conflict with the business strategy or plans;

- all the possible constraints have been identified and adequately evaluated;

- data details are complete; and

- all persons affected have been consulted and ownership of the proposed system has been agreed.

8.4.3   The Feasibility Study

Objectives

Audit's objectives are to be satisfied that:

- the quality of any feasibility study is of a high standard; and

- approval to proceed with development has been properly obtained.

The auditor should:

  – test for compliance with the procedures for obtaining approval;

  – test the feasibility study document for completeness and compliance with requirements; and

  – examine the cost-benefit analysis for clarity, completeness and reasonableness.

8.4.4   The Specification

Objectives

The auditors' objectives are to be satisfied that the functional specification:

  – adequately reflects and defines user requirements;

  – includes requirements for security and controls; and

  – has been agreed and accepted by all parties concerned.

  The auditor should check the specification and other documentation to see that:

  – all objectives have been stated and quantified;

  – the specification conforms to standards; and

  – all agreements are evidenced in writing.

8.4.5   Technical Design

Objectives

The auditor is primarily concerned with being satisfied that the development project proceeds under control and in accord with established procedures to ensure that the technical design reflects accurately and comprehensively the user requirement and associated operational needs. The auditor should examine the technical design documents and verify that:

  – the design specification complies with IT standards;

  – the design specification reflects the user requirements and that all changes have been agreed and documented;

  – all technical controls governing file and data organisation have been defined; and

  – all security controls over input, processing and output have been included.

8.18

8.4.6   Development and Production

Objectives

At this stage the auditor will be primarily concerned with being satisfied that the arrangements for testing and documenting the system are satisfactory and effective. The auditor should:

-   see evidence that programs conform to the design specification including all changes authorised by users;

-   verify the extent of the test plan including interfaces, re-starts, re-runs, and back-ups;

-   see evidence that all the tests have been satisfactorily completed and conducted in accord with established standards; and

-   verify that the program documentation is clear and complete especially error corrections and treatment of authorised changes.

8.4.7   Evaluation of Software Packages

Objectives

The primary objectives of the auditor are to be satisfied that:

-   the package will meet the requirements of the user and also the operational requirements of the IT centre; and

-   the package will incorporate security and control features.

The provision of controls and procedures within a package is not subject to the internal controls of a particular organisation and as such those aspects of system development controls cannot be reviewed by the auditor. However, the requirements of users still need to be satisfied and the package has to be implemented. Thus the auditor is still concerned with some aspects of internal controls relating to purchases and system development controls.

-   The act of purchasing a package requires the auditor to consider acquisition procedures and controls.

-   Packages may be used independently by user departments and the purchase may be associated with the acquisition of independent hardware. The effect of this is that in looking at such ways of meeting development needs the auditor has to take account of the wider issues.

-   Because a package is substantially complete in itself there is need to evaluate it for functionality, performance and the security features of the package including application controls.

— Although a package may be tailored to meet the particular requirements of a user, the operational procedures within the computer and user departments may require adaptation or modification to suit the package.

The overall matters that should be addressed and considered by audit are as follows:

The Specification

Whether the users' requirements are properly defined and whether the package, when compared with the specification, matches and meets those requirements.

Integrity

The organisation may not be able to examine validation routines and other internal controls directly. It should be possible however to test or check the range and relevance by reference to the documentation that should accompany the package and the printed or screen control output of errors, exceptions and control totals. The control totals should be tested for completeness and accuracy and that they provide for reconciliation of any accounting process.

Reliability and Security

The facilities for back-up and procedures for recovery should be checked. In the absence of such facilities alternative measures should have been set up using existing arrangements. The same considerations apply to the security of files and programs, in particular the security of access and the extent to which users or operators may determine the order and sequence of processing.

Compatibility

The operating procedures and functioning of the package should be compared with the procedures and requirements of existing hardware and software to establish whether or not there are discrepancies, anomalies or other adverse conditions.

Performance

The actual performance of the package should be compared against specifications for response times, volumes and time taken in processing. The package should also be assessed for flexibility and ease of use by reference to such facilities as menu-driven and parameter-driven functions and report generators.

Acquisition Procedures

A methodology for the audit of the acquisition of computing facilities is set down in chapter 5. The principal matters to be considered are the status and reputation of the suppliers; the resources of the supplier and the user base of the package.

Support and Maintenance

Support and maintenance is also dealt with in the methodology. The particular matters to be considered are the terms of the licence and the conditions governing amendments to the package, and the availability of the source or object programs to the users in the event of the supplier ceasing to support the package or going out of business.

8.4.8 Implementation

Objectives

The auditor's objective is to be satisfied that implementation is conducted in accord with established procedures to ensure continued control and the achievement of meeting the users' requirements. The auditor should:

- check the extent of user involvement in testing;

- ensure that manual procedures are tested;

- establish that users are aware of the significance of controls, their control responsibilities and the requisite error correction procedures;

- ensure that the recovery and back-up procedures have been adequately tested; and

- ensure that the user guides are clear, unambiguous and easy to understand.

Audit should remember that inadequate training and testing may well cause considerable operational problems and reduce the probability of user requirements being met fully or in a satisfactory manner.

8.4.9 Post Implementation

Objectives

The key audit issues are:

- analysis of the changes made and their documentation;

- the extent of operational difficulties and their remedies;

- user satisfaction;

- IT operations staff satisfaction;

- the adequacy and performance of the key control and security features; and

- the achievement of aims and objectives.

Although the scope of post-implementation reviews can be expected to vary from organisation to organisation the following methodology provides useful criteria for judging the quality and

8.21

effectiveness of post implementation reviews or the basis for the auditor to conduct one:

- Document the growth rates of file sizes and number of transactions processed by the system. Trends can be analysed and projected to assess whether problems are apparent or likely to become apparent through inefficient file structure or lengthy processing time.

- Assess clerical manpower required to support the system. Estimates should have been made during the system design of the impact of the system on clerical manpower requirements. The auditor should identify current requirements and identify reasons for any variances.

- Identify any system turn-around delays. Delays in processing the system may have consequences in other areas of the organisation. Reasons for delays need to be identified (including any which occur in the user's area) and remedial action implemented or processing time scales adjusted.

- Assess the efficiency of security procedures and quality control checks. Arrangements for file and document security should be documented and checks on quality control of files and output reviewed.

- Review error rates for input data capture. High error rates may indicate inefficient preparation by users of input documents, an inappropriate means of data capture or poor design of input media.

- Review the number of reported program errors.

- Examine any requested amendments to the system. Requests for amendments may be initiated by users, operations or development staff. They may indicate dissatisfaction with the system because of inadequate specification or poor design. Procedural rules may require modification.

- Assess whether there are any external factors which affect system performance. Such factors may be apparent from a number of causes,(eg hardware breaks, sickness of key personnel). Remedial action may be required,(eg more system restarts or more extensive user training).

- Examine the use being made of computer output including any unplanned uses or any redundancies. Obviously production of output not being used, either partially or totally, is wasteful. Unplanned uses may detract from system security or confidentiality. Either may indicate deficiencies in system specification.

- Verify that superseded systems have been discontinued. If redundant systems are still being operated reasons should be ascertained and appropriate action implemented.

- The quality of systems documentation should be examined. This examination should be carried out both in the user and IT departments include such documents as clerical procedures, systems specifications, program listings. Key factors in the examination are adequacy, comprehensiveness and currency.

- Carry out a cost-benefit review of the system to determine:

  - whether anticipated benefits have been achieved or not;

  - whether unplanned benefits are apparent;

  - reference to any long-term benefits not yet realised;

  - whether costs of the system were comparable with estimates;

  - a projection of future costs and benefits.

- Ascertain the user's attitude and comments on the system. Interviews should always be conducted with the users although some aspects may be difficult to quantify, being subjective in nature. Indications may be provided as to where weak areas or bottlenecks are occurring.

- Critically examine operational running costs for the system. This may reveal inefficient programs or processes. It may indicate localised excessive costs although in total, costs may be acceptable.

- Prepare a report of the review making appropriate recommendations. The report should be discussed with users and data processing management while in draft. The final report or a summary may be discussed with corporate management.

8.4.10 Amendment Procedures

Objectives

The primary objective of the auditor is to be satisfied that amendments to programs are controlled and do not adversely affect the security and control features of application software. The criteria for judging the adequacy of controls over amendments are the presence or otherwise of the following procedures:

Formal Statement of Amendment

If a requirement to amend a system arises that requirement must be formally stated. This will facilitate the control of the request as a number can be allocated to the request and a record kept of its progress. It also specifies the problem and usually the preferred solution. This is important because of the number of people that may become involved and the danger of the request being misunderstood. The design of any form should be flexible enough to cater for all types of request, but must be used on all occasions.

Evaluation

When a request has been raised it should be submitted to some form of formal evaluation. Usually such evaluations will be undertaken by the IT department. Upon receipt of the request it should be allocated a number, a register entry opened; and the user should be informed of its receipt and the number it has been allocated. Evaluation of the problem should ensure that user mistakes and misunderstandings are identified and corrected and the request is signed off. It also makes it easier to identify duplicated requests, or requests which relate to other requests already submitted. Such requests should be suitably cross referenced and dealt with together.

An assessment of the resources requirements to effect a change should be undertaken for all requests, and some indication of the relative priority of the amendment should be entered on the request form.

At the end of the evaluation stage the user should be informed of the results, and a procedure should exist to allow the user to dispute the evaluation.

Authorisation

Procedures should be formulated to ensure that all requests for amendments are properly authorised before action is taken.

Because of the varying significance and workload of amendments a suitable hierarchy of authorising individuals should be formulated, and the level of authority of each individual should be formally stated.

Programming

The controls to be applied to the system specification and programming of amendments are the same as for new developments, and include division of duties, adequate testing and documentation. However because of the comparatively minor nature of many amendments testing standards may be relaxed in appropriate cases.

It is important that adequate control is exercised over the accessing of live programs which should be stored in libraries to which access would not normally be granted to programmers. This is particularly important where data is being processed and stored in user departments. Consequently special arrangements are required to allow amendments to these program and suitable procedures are outlined below:

- live program copied into test library on receipt of formal request;

- programmer amends and tests program in test library;

- systems analyst tests program in test library;

- formal request to transfer amended programme from test to live library authorised by

8.24

       suitable individual; and

       program taken onto live library.

Adequate controls must also be applied to the use of powerful utilities usually supplied within the system software, which facilitate one-off corrective amendments. Such facilities are usually used to correct the effect of errors, such as deleting or creating one-sided ledger entries. Access to such facilities should be strictly limited, and their use should be closely monitored by senior staff.

Implementation

Because of the number of amendments that arise, and the need to inform users of the implementation of amendments, many organisations operate a system of releases. Under this procedure release dates are identified and all amendments are scheduled for a specified release date. By this method the user can be certain when his amendment will be effected, management can exercise effective control over the priority of amendments, and management is provided with an efficiency yardstick with which to monitor the performance of the IT department.

CHAPTER 9

APPLICATION CONTROLS

                                        Continued overleaf

9.1 Introduction

An application system is a computer system which performs a specific business function such as payroll. Such systems may be developed in house or purchased as an 'off the shelf' package from an external supplier. It is important to ascertain how the application is processed to enable audit and control considerations to be defined. There are a number of ways that this can be undertaken:

Batch – a process where data is presented to the IT section in batches for conversion into machine readable form and subsequent processing. This process is being steadily replaced by other forms of processing as technology advances.

Batch with on line enquiry – enables the user to display the information input through batch processing but the effect of the new transactions will not be displayed until the next batch processing cycle has been completed.

Batch processing with on-line enquiry and update – the user can enter and amend data at a a user workstation and display what appears to be the updated records. That is achieved by allowing the users to update a copy of the master file. Amendments are stored on a transaction file and the true master file is updated overnight with the day's transactions in batch mode. This requires the use of transaction processing (TP) software (see chapter 10). Controls such as validation are operational at input stage, rather than at processing stages.

Real time – a transaction entered at a user workstation which immediately updates the true master file and can therefore immediately affect any other transaction thereafter.

Real time and on line systems have several advantages over batch processing:

- Input errors can be corrected immediately, thus strengthening accuracy controls.

- Machine readable documents can be used, thus reducing manual work and errors and enabling potential manpower savings.

- Data is more up to date, thus providing better management and customer information.

- The application system can limit sensitive transactions to specific users.

While these advantages are considerable, auditors should appreciate that the consequence of such processing methods is the loss of some of the controls previously exercised in the central IT department. The alternative controls required to overcome any additional risks such processing may cause are addressed in the 'Auditing the Technology' section.

9.1.1 Objectives

The primary objective of management is that applications perform properly the business activity for which they were designed eg payments are made only to valid creditors. The purpose of application controls is to ensure the completeness, accuracy, security and effectiveness of processing. They may be provided either by programming within the application system or by manual controls exercised by users or the IT department.

The overall objective of an audit review of an application system is to review the system to ascertain whether it incorporate adequate internal controls and to verify that these controls form part of the live system when implemented and are effective and that any system amendments do not invalidate them.

The auditor's review of a system's controls may be applied to either a system under development system or a live system. The overall audit objective applies in either case, though in the audit of a developing system the auditor is attempting to ascertain whether the controls to be incorporated within the system will provide adequate protection when the system becomes operational, whereas in the case of a live system the auditor seeks also to verify that the controls are actually in place and are effective. The subject of systems under development is considered in chapter 8.

9.1.2   Types of Controls

The actual form and location of controls will be determined by the operational environment of the application. Most systems now being developed will incorporate on-line processing facilities in one form or another where the user communicates at a workstation connected to a network. Processing is likely to be carried out locally and at the processor to which the workstation is connected. An important matter for the auditor therefore is to consider the appropriateness of application controls as to type and point of action in relation to the operational environment.

Principles and objectives of control

The quality and effectiveness of controls will be determined by whether or not they conform to certain principles and practices as follows:

- the establishment of standards, requirements and definitions of 'norms';

- the recording and monitoring of targets and actual performance;

- the definition and requirements for exception reporting; and

- procedures for corrective action.

The importance of controls should be self evident but they must be cost effective in practice. Risk assessment is therefore an essential element in the evaluation of controls and should be observed by auditors if they are gain credibility with management and acceptance of any recommendations they make consequent upon the results of the review.

The various types of controls are as follows:

- those exercised through line management and supervision.

  those which relate to user rights based on the need for separation of duties. They are particularly important in distributed computing which allows multiple access to and use of data and services or facilities held in common.

- those which may be manual or computerised and are functional in nature and usually performed at the point of entry into the system.

- those programmed controls contained within the application software and exercised during processing including data entry.

Controls may also be classified as follows:

- *Preventive* – aimed at reducing or minimising the risk of unwanted or unplanned occurrences eg authorisation procedures, internal checks and the use of passwords.

- *Detective* – aimed at identifying unwanted and unplanned occurrences after the event eg supervisory checks, control totals, overflow checks, validity checks and exception reporting.

- *Corrective* – aimed at ensuring that the appropriate corrective action is taken in the event that either preventive or detective controls expose an unplanned or unwanted occurrence eg the rejection of data, cessation of processing and the use of recovery journals.

High level controls

High level controls are of interest to auditors in the review of application controls and comprise:

- Corporate control objectives which are management's and auditors primary objectives to namely to ensure that the business objectives of the organisation are achieved eg that payments are only to valid creditors and in an efficient and cost effective manner.

- Disciplinary controls to ensure that controls are monitored and exercised eg supervision, separation of duties, random checks for reasonableness and internal audit activity.

- Statutory controls which are aimed at ensuring that all legal requirements are met such as the requirements of the Data Protection Act, EC decisions and directives, investment regulations and the regulations and requirements of the Inland Revenue and Customs Service.

Low level controls

Low level controls are common to all application systems and are aimed at ensuring that data, its processing and output is complete, accurate authorised, secure and provides a management trail. The verification and evaluation of these controls constitute the secondary and detailed objectives

9.3

of the auditor. They are as follows:

- Input Controls – the procedures adopted to control input to the system should, as far as is reasonably possible, ensure that it is genuine, complete, not previously processed, accurate and timely.

- Processing Controls – the processing controls within the computer system should ensure that the correct data and program files are used, that all data is processed, accounted for and written to the appropriate file and that data conforms to pre-determined standards or falls within specified parameter values.

- Output Controls – the output controls should ensure that all expected output is produced, that it is complete, appears reasonable and is distributed on time and in such a way that confidentiality is maintained as necessary. Adequate controls should ensure that errors and exceptions are properly investigated and re-submissions of data made where appropriate.

- Audit Trail – a complete audit trail should be maintained which allows for both an item to be traced from input through to its final resting place and a final result to be broken into its constituent parts.

Points of principle

There are certain points of principle which the auditor should bear in mind whenever reviewing computerised systems:

- The auditor should not expect a system to contain every conceivable control at every stage but should be looking for a reasonable level of control and balance the cost of including a specific control against the benefit to be gained ie the likely cost of error if control is excluded. Lack of effective controls over one aspect of the system may in the event be offset by strengths in another area.

- The fact that the auditor may have been involved in some stage of the system development process should not inhibit reporting on system weaknesses at the operational stage; indeed the manual controls and procedures may not have been apparent during the system design stage and could not therefore have been evaluated.

- The point at which a control technique is applied, how well it is applied and by whom it is applied, can have a marked effect on its strength.

- Control over data should be established at the earliest possible point in the complete cycle of activity and maintained throughout the system.

- Good application controls may be nullified or negated by poor general controls and vice versa.

9.2 Input Controls

9.2.1 Objectives

The procedures adopted to control input to the system should, as far as is reasonably possible, ensure that it is genuine, complete, authorised, not previously processed, accurate and timely.

Apart from the detailed procedural control techniques which are discussed later in this section, it should be remembered that some general controls are necessary to build on the strength offered by the application system's controls. Within the organisation there should be an adequate division of duties and responsibilities, especially with regard to initiation and authorisation recording and actual custody of the assets. Access to the machine and to the data and program files should be restricted to designated employees.

Controls within the data preparation section should ensure that the data is converted to computer input media accurately, that duplication does not occur and that sufficient information is available to act as a basis for effective control of data throughout the processing cycle. On line input should be reviewed to assess application software verification and validation and additionally management controls applied.

As with any control system, a large part of the strength of the system relies upon the division of responsibility for various control points being properly defined. It is the IT department's responsibility to ensure that all data received by it is properly processed. However the overall responsibility must lie with the user who is required to ensure that all data is collected and passed to the IT department and that the processed results properly reflect that data. An effective rule, if adhered to, is that control should be established at the earliest practicable point within the system.

9.2.2 Areas of Control

Authorisation

There is a need to establish procedures for the authorisation of all material input data prior to its acceptance for input. In addition there should be sufficient control to ensure that transactions or data which are unauthorised cannot be processed.

In computer systems designed to operate on a batch processing basis, authorisation is usually by way of a physical initial signature or stamp.

Where input is through an on-line workstation and authorisation is deemed necessary, it can be either explicit, by way of some signature or initial on the input document, or implicit through a password system tied to levels of authority.

Alternatively data input can be stored on a transaction file which is printed before processing and checked and authorised by a supervisor before data processing is allowed to proceed.

Completeness

Where possible the system should be capable of identifying the fact that input data is missing. This may be performing sequence checks, either through a clerical check or through the programs within the system.

Clerical checks, where operated, must of necessity be concerned less with detail than are machine checks. A clerical check for completeness might be to ensure that an input batch is received from all expected sources, that there are no missing batch numbers in a sequential range, or by totalling particular input fields.

Programmed checks for completeness are effectively processing controls and as such are dealt later in this chapter. An example of such controls might be the testing to ensure data is present in all mandatory input fields. In any computer system it is inevitable that on occasions items of input will be rejected. In these circumstances control over the rejected items should be sufficient to ensure that the reason for the rejection is ascertained and that the item is successfully re-input if appropriate.

Rejected items can be held in a computer 'suspense' file, which effectively maintains control over the clearance of these items since reports can be produced showing movements of transactions both in and out together with control totals for reconciliation to feeder systems as well as any outstanding suspense items.

Checks for completeness arise at different stages within the data collection and input cycle. At the lowest level a clerk may be responsible for obtaining the information from a third party and must ensure that all relevant data is collected. A supervisor may then be responsible for the collection and batching of the section's work and must ensure that all data is forwarded to the IT department in a properly controlled form. Further checks at either a detail or overall level will then be effected within the IT department or by system management to ensure that expected data is received, either directly input or converted to computer input media and passed for processing.

Duplicate input

Controls aimed at avoiding duplication of input may be either clerical or machine-based.

Clerical controls in this area might include the cancellation of documents immediately after the input stage if on-line and a register of input batches recording their progress through the department including reconciliation/identification with relevant input batch.

Machine controls designed to guard against duplicate input of data are described within section 6.4.3. An example of this type of machine control might be a test to identify the input of two amendments to the same item of standing data.

9.6

Accuracy

The system controls should as far as possible ensure that input data is accurate.

Non-computer techniques aimed at ensuring accuracy of input data include form design, clerical procedures clearly defining requirements, training and manual checking.

Machine-assisted techniques to promote accuracy include pre-printed and turn-round documents, checks to ensure that the data is in a valid format and perhaps within a specified range and data collections as a by-product of recording the original transaction (eg production of data from a cash receipting system.)

Conversion

Input controls should ensure that once initially recorded on a computer input form, data is accurately converted to computer input media.

Manually prepared control totals can be used: input validation prints might be compared on a one-for-one basis, though the responsibility for proving accuracy of input conversion should rest with a designated individual.

Computer controls to ensure conversion accuracy include batch total reconciliations, key-punch verification and 'answer-back' procedures in an on-line system.

Custody of documents

There should be clearly defined responsibility for custody of source documents to ensure preservation of the audit trail.

Where source documents do not leave the user department they should be filed in such a way that they are quickly accessible should the need arise. They should, where practicable, be retained in an order which allows the computer input documents to be reconciled with the base data.

Computer input documents should be controlled throughout the processing cycle and the user department should ensure that where input is not initiated by their own on-line system documents are developed to control the processing which will be checked when processing is completed.

Timeliness

Schedules of computer operations should be clearly defined and be co-ordinated with schedules for input to ensure that input is available and submitted for defined scheduled processing.

9.2.3   Input Control Techniques

Authorisation of input data

Clerical procedures should be established which define the authorisation requirements for each different input type.

Authorisation can be at transaction level so that each individual transaction is separately authorised: within each transaction type there may be different levels of authorisation depending upon value or some other criterion. In some instances it may be deemed unnecessary to insist upon the authorisation of individual transactions but desirable that the batch is signified in some way as authorised for processing. In this case the batch header would be authorised and the onus would be on the authorising individual to ensure that the transactions within the batch emanated from an appropriate point in the organisation.

To assist in the control of batched data, some form of transmitted document should accompany completed input batches. This would detail the number of batches and should be reconciled with the batches received by the computer control section (or designated individual) who should also be responsible for scrutinising for evidence of authorisation at the proper level.

It may be possible to use the computer to check that authorisation has been properly carried out, eg where transactions should be within a certain range. Entries outside that range would suggest that the procedures for authorisation were deficient in some respect.

Where a system is designed to cater for on-line data collection the data is often taken straight from the original document and not transcribed onto a standard computer input form. Authorisation must therefore take a different form and unless the clerical procedures can be so designed that only those individuals authorised to input a particular type of transaction are capable of doing so, the computer will play a major part in the authorisation process.

It is possible for all transactions input to be stored and printed out at the end of a period. These might then be scrutinised by an individual who would be responsible for authorising their release into the 'update' phase of the system. Alternatively it may be possible, through a computerised control system, to allocate each individual or group of individuals a password. The control program may then be so designed that particular workstations or passwords are restricted to the input of particular transactions. Any attempt to input a transaction outside those allowed could then be logged and reported to senior management.

Where the system entails input of the information in batches, or individual transactions are input by an input clerk, it will often be necessary to adopt an authorisation system entailing an authorising signature on the documents prior to input.

Completeness of input data

The system should be designed in order to enable the user to be reasonably certain that the input during any particular period is complete: for example, by the use of a schedule detailing the different locations from which input is expected. Such a check could of course be computerised.

It is at the input preparation stage that control is established over input data, by way of batch totals, record counts, sequential numbering, or other checks. These controls should then be reconciled at a later stage to ensure that all data has been completely and accurately converted into machine-readable form.

Accuracy of input data

Controls over data designed to ensure accuracy can be broadened to include those which aim to guard against duplication.

A control group is often established to receive all data for processing and to monitor its progress through the IT department. The group will be responsible for ensuring that input data goes once, accurately, through the data conversion process and that where procedures call for 'verification' during the conversion process, this is actually carried out. Alternatively control numbers may be collated if input is on-line.

There are a number of different methods of guarding against duplication of input. Reliance must be placed on manual controls of source and machine-readable data as well as on application software validation routines. The user might input details after a cancellation has been processed at another location through uncontrolled order of processing.

Control totals established during the origination of the input data can often be used to ensure that all data has been accurately converted to computer input form. Where data conversion is through key to disk equipment it is usually possible to pass the data through a validation phase during the conversion process. Control totals can be agreed at this stage and fields can be tested for accuracy of format, value (by comparison with a predetermined range) and compatibility between input items or values.

At the input preparation stage it may be thought necessary to build in some facility, within the converted data, to allow the input programs to establish that the correct input is in fact being processed ie dates, batch sequence numbers, parameter control cards detailing the number of input files and their correct sequence.

Where systems use on-line data capture (in which an operator within the user department keys in transaction data) there is no reason why batch controls should not still be operated in such an environment. Transactions are often input as they arise and therefore are not pre-batched so control should be established as soon as possible. This may be done by dividing the working day into a number of processing periods so that, for the purpose of control later in the updating process, those transactions input in each period are treated as a batch. It is, however, often still desirable to effect some control at the user end of the system. This may be done by keeping a manual record of the number of transactions of each type input through each workstation, which could then be checked against computer-generated figures.

However carefully the original input is screened, either manually or by computer, errors may still be contained in the input records which go forward to the update stage. These may cause error conditions during processing and the transactions will be rejected. Control over these rejections is of paramount importance since the user must investigate the error and re-submit the transaction where appropriate. Control can be manual (all rejections being recorded and the record marked when they are successfully cleared) or computerised. With computerised control of error rejections, the machine holds a record of each rejection and an input transaction clearing the error would reference the holding record on the reject file and cause it to be removed.

Where a system caters for on-line data collection, a transaction may be processed by a validation program at the input stage. This would allow a high degree of accuracy at data input. If the system, when validating an input transaction, also has the master file available to refer to, it should be possible to achieve almost error free data input. Through validation for format range, etc and validity checks against the master file records, all data errors should be eliminated from accepted input.

Investigation and resolution of rejections is an extremely critical area within a computer system. Often the time scale within which the 'errors' are cleared is critical and further processing may be incomplete without the clearing entries.

Data conversion accuracy

Most software offering validation will request conformation that the user wishes to process the data displayed on the input screen. It is usually possible to ascertain whether verification has been carried out, since the process of verification normally marks the final input record.

The principle of part-verification is often used where not all the data is particularly important, or where a later processing control can compensate and report possible inaccuracy (eg a reference number containing a check digit).

Though in a batch system any errors in conversion on controlled fields should come to light at the data validation stage of the system other errors will go through to the update phase. Where accuracy of data conversion is critical it may be necessary during the data preparation or initial validation phase to produce hard copy of the converted input data which will need to be checked on a one-for-one basis against the original manually- written data.

A designated individual should be responsible for checking controls over the data conversion exercise, either ensuring that verification has taken place, that input documents are cancelled after preparation, or that batch totals produced during the conversion exercise reconcile.

The guidance above has assumed that the data conversion exercise is a manual one. The use of turn-round documents produced by a computer run and annotated by hand with 'this period' figures can make the punch operator's job easier and greatly increase accuracy.

Data conversion can also be an automated process through the use of electronic equipment, designed to read alpha or numeric characters, or possible other markings. Where these characters can be pre-printed by a computer program the accuracy of the data-conversion exercise can be greatly increased through the use of special reading equipment.

An optical character recognition (OCR) device reads numeric and alphabetic characters and whilst the reading of computer printed figures (eg the amount and reference on an invoice) will be almost completely accurate, handwriting can also be read with an extremely high degree of accuracy and at a very high speed.

Optical mark reading (OMR) equipment reads marks made with a pencil and values them according to their position on the document. This is also an accurate and fast data conversion method. Other equipment used may include scanners, direct collection of fax data or the transfer by video image directly into the computer. However, due to the nature of such techniques management should ensure that:

–   only authorised users can gain access to the system;

–   authorised users can only carry out those functions for which they have been authorised;

–   any security violations are detected and reported;

–   adequate back-up and recovery procedures are in operation; and

–   adequate procedures exist to monitor the performance of the equipment.

User procedures

Input at the workstation by users will generally mean the loss of verification of input and the methods of preventing, detecting and correcting errors will need to be considered. The ease of workstation operation, user/machine dialogue, training of operators, workstation environment and the minimisation of the entry of fixed data are all factors which audit should examine. It is difficult to generalise on controls since much will depend on the exact nature of the application, its sensitivity and the capabilities of the on-line software.

If the application is genuine 'real time', where files are updated at the time of data entry, there will need to be a greater emphasis on control at the user interface in order to ensure that errors are detected at that point at the time of entry. In an on-line application where master files are not immediately updated it may be that data can be validated, to some extent at the time of entry but further validation takes place at the mainframe before master files are updated. Any errors detected in this process can then be written to an error file for subsequent correction by the user.

Whilst the use of a password provides an authorisation to use certain transactions, authorised documentation should support each individual transaction and provide a trail for the transaction. The design of the documentation is important since it may be used as a punching document at a workstation. Good documentation layout combined with screen formats that are easy to understand should contribute to fewer errors being made from mispunching.

9.11

Validation

Whilst it is important to detect errors in on-line systems as soon as possible, the degree of validation and checking which can be carried out will often have to be balanced against the resources expended in these operations. Extensive validation may lead to unacceptable response times and so it could be that certain validation is carried out overnight in batch mode. Errors detected at the input stage should be corrected immediately wherever possible. In some cases this may not be easy to do and systems may need to be designed with a facility for errors to be written to a separate error file for later correction. Where this facility is provided the method of error correction should be closely investigated by the auditor to ensure that controls on initial input of data are not by-passed at the correction stage. The auditor should check, for example, whether all data is re-validated after error correction; whether it is possible to alter data other than that which is incorrect, or to add or delete data at the error correction stage and whether a log is produced of error correction transactions.

A particular characteristic of validation through on-line software is the opportunity which may be afforded to the workstation operator to check visually the data entered. On-line software may be programmed to re-display the data after performing the various validation routines and allow the operator to correct any remaining errors.

9.3 Processing Controls

9.3.1   Objectives

Processing controls within a computer system should ensure that the correct and complete data and program files are used, that all data is processed in a secure manner, accounted for and written to the appropriate file, is traceable and that data conforms to predetermined standards or falls within specified parameter values.

Controls in operation at record level should ensure that data conforms to predetermined standards, or falls within specified parameter values. File level or batch level controls should ensure that the correct data or program files are used and that all data is processed in a secure manner and accounted for and written to the appropriate file. Controls should also operate which enable the system to cope with such eventualities as computer equipment failure.

Where processing controls identify errors and/or inconsistencies in data, the resulting action will vary from one system to another. Commonly, erroneous data will be rejected and will require some form of re submission into the system. Re-submissions will of course be subjected to the normal data validation controls and may themselves be rejected if errors are still present. Alternatively if the errors and/or inconsistencies found are not serious then the data may be accepted and an exception report produced containing any relevant warning message. Processing controls can be expected to operate at three levels:

- Record Level – Such controls are designed to be exercised over individual computer records be they transaction or master records.

- Total Level – Controls in this category are designed to be exercised over groups of records, the size of the group varying from a batch of input records to that of a complete file.

- System Failure – Such controls are built into a computer system to allow for recovery when there is a computer equipment failure.

9.3.2   Processing Control Techniques

Record level controls

Control over the data processed by the computer is achieved through various checks on the prime input data and on the data generated as a result of processing. These controls are usually built into the first program in each system, generally known as the 'edit' or 'validation' program. Where key-to-disc input facilities are used it is not uncommon to find that some or all of these record level controls are carried out by programs held within the data preparation equipment itself. Controls of this nature, effective at the time of keying the data, may or may not replace similar checks by the main computer system:

Format Checks

Ensures that data being entered is in the specified form, for example numeric or alpha-numeric. Clearly a letter in an amount field would be unacceptable eg the hours worked on a time-sheet included the letter S or 1234S instead of 12345.

Range Checks

Tests specific data fields to check that the contents are within the prescribed upper and/or lower values. These tests can be used on alpha fields as well as numeric eg weekly net pay for an employee should be within the range zero – £200.

Validity Checks

Checks that the data conforms to an acceptable table of values often held in the program eg an expenditure code of X5371 is unacceptable because it could not be found in the program's table of legitimate codes.

Overflow Checks

Ensures that data cannot be corrupted as a result of overloading the receiving file area eg the result of 1234 x 9876 (12186984) cannot be stored in a single byte area.

Completeness Checks

Checks that each field on an input document has data present in it, where a blank entry would result in inaccurate processing. It is possible to use this technique on computer records other than input documents, but this is rarely necessary eg a line of detail on an invoice for payment must include an amount payable.

Check Digits

One character, usually numeric, of a field represents a mathematical function of all the other characters in the field. Whenever this field is referred to by the system it is possible to re-calculate this check digit and compare it with the character actually present, in order to verify the validity of the whole field. This technique is normally applied to the key reference field of the record, such as the employee number eg using a check digit system based upon a modulus 11 and a weighting of 7,3,1 with the last digit being the check digit, the following number is valid 123454.

The check digit is calculated as follows:

$$1 \times 7 = 7$$

$$2 \times 3 = 6$$

$$3 \times 1 = 3$$

$$4 \times 7 = 28$$

$$5 \times 3 = 15$$

Total: 59

59 divided by 11 = 5, Remainder = 4

Compatibility Checks

These are checks that are used to test the reasonableness of data by relating the contents of one field with the contents of one or more other fields in order to detect unusual or unacceptable relationships eg the sex code and National Insurance code must be compatible in that they relate to one sex.

Exception Checks

Sometimes certain combinations of data may occur in a record which, although unlikely, may not constitute an error. Such combinations may be identified as a direct result of the input data or as a result of computer calculations. In such cases the data is accepted for processing, but a warning issued so that further investigations may be made eg if an employee earns a salary above the overtime limit and yet an overtime payment is required, an exception report is generated.

9.14

Matching Transactions with Master File Records

All transactions used to make changes to the standing data on a master file should contain a field which identifies the nature of the change required. This field is usually referred to as the amendment or transaction type and will invariably signify one of three requirements – a completely new record, an amendment to an existing record and the deletion of an existing record.

Controls built into the update program should ensure that a record with that particular reference does not exist in the case of new additions and that amendments and deletions are matched with existing records on file.

It is important that amendments to standing data cannot be input in such a way as to invalidate or by-pass the compatibility and other tests described earlier.

Further tests on the existing record may be necessary before deletions are actioned. In certain cases a deletion may not indicate the erasure of a record but merely the setting of a marker, often because the record details are required for annual returns or statistics. The auditor should pay particular attention to the proper erasure of such records when they are no longer required and also to the control designed to prevent unauthorised 'resurrection' of such records eg a transaction requesting the creation of a new stock code is rejected if the new code number is already on the master file.

Total level controls

Overall control over processing is achieved through the existence and checking of controls relating to groups of records and usually the complete computer file. The most significant controls of this type are explained below:

Control Totals

Control totals are the most commonly found of the total level controls. They involve the computer in the maintenance of a total of one type or another which is used in later comparison against another independently derived total prepared either clerically or within the computer system in order to help ensure that some aspects of processing had been accurately carried out. The various types of these total controls are:

- Amount control totals – totals of all the occurrences of a specified amount field (numeric, sterling, dollars etc) in a group of records eg total gross pay to date on the payroll master file is £4,123,456.78

- Document control totals – totals of the number of individual documents of a given type input or output to/from the control system eg there are 1,234 time-sheets to be processed in this week's wages run.

- Line control totals – Are totals of the number of individual lines of data to be processed by the system, as opposed to the total number of documents eg there are 5,432 lines of coded amounts to be processed by the creditor payments system although there are physically only 1,876 documents.

— Hash control totals – totals derived from the accumulated numerical amounts of non-monetary information eg the total of all the employee numbers on a payroll is 176,238,154

— Record control totals – totals of the number of computer records that are present in a file (or part of) eg there are 155,328 accounts held on the financial ledger master file.

Maintenance of Totals

The value and effectiveness of the use of control totals may be comprised or nullified if they are not of themselves protected and controlled. Protective measures may be taken as follows:

— Control total record – The most common means of storing a computer control total is to have a specified record on a file allocated for the purpose of holding the totals relevant to the whole file. A variation on this technique is, in addition to the final total record, to have specific control records interspersed throughout the file holding sub-totals (for example a total record for each department on a payroll file).

— Control total file – Another, less commonly used technique, is to have a separate computer file in which all the appropriate control totals are stored for a range of different files and records.

— Run-time totals – It is also possible for control totals to be generated at run-time only and not to store them permanently on a computer file. These totals will normally be printed, or displayed on a workstation for either computer or manual comparison with another total eg comparison with the total from the control total record.

Sequence Checks

Ensure that, where necessary, data is presented for processing in a prescribed sequence eg where stores transactions are being processed against a sequential master file, stock item C1584 is processed before C1597.

Duplicate Checks

Test data which has been sorted in the required sequence to identify whether more than one transaction is present for a given master file record eg if more than one time-sheet is presented for processing against a specific employee then a rejection and/or an exception report will occur.

Run to Run Controls

This technique uses control data generated by one computer process to control the activities of a subsequent process. This control concept is particularly important since control can be exercised over the operation of each element of a computer system by generating input controls at each stage.

9.16

A system can be monitored, therefore, to see that all the constituent programs are operating 'correctly', that the correct files are used and that data is traceable through the system. Where standards have been adopted by the computer installation they should include guidelines on the use of run-to-run controls eg the total of gross pay calculated by one payroll program becomes the input control total for the net pay calculation program.

Reconciliation of Files

An analysis of two different computer files containing substantially the same data, identifying and reconciling the differences eg relating the data on a bank reconciliation file to a series of 'cheques drawn' files.

Summary Processing

An extra process used for calculating the expected results of detailed calculation in bulk and comparing the two eg in a loan repayment calculation program, the total loans in each category/ rate of interest can be generated, totalled and compared with the total of all the individual transactions.

File Identification Controls

These are controls which ensure that, as far as is possible for any given process, all the correct computer file generations are used.

These controls fall into two basic categories. Firstly, where the computer process outputs control information on the basis of brought forward and carried forward figures from (say) week to week for manual verification and secondly, where file header information such as run generation number or week number is used by the computer system. The standards being operated by the computer installation should detail the controls to be imposed over all files used at that installation.

Rejection and Re-submissions

Procedures should be established to ensure that there is control over data rejected to ensure that it is reported, corrected and resubmitted. In addition there should be controls present to ensure that any interfaced systems are also subsequently adjusted. This can be done either by posting to a suspense account or by correction before any transaction within the file is processed.

System Failure Controls

The design of a computer system must enable it to cope with all eventualities including the failure of the computer equipment itself. Clearly if the computer were to fail during a particular process it must be possible either to start the whole process again or to restart at the last checkpoint or a successfully processed item. Most operating systems will provide significant assistance in this area especially in restoring computer files to a known state.

On-line/Real Time Processing Controls

Access and input controls are the key controls for providing a secure on-line environment via the operating system, additional security packages, network control software, database management systems or within the application programs themselves.

Whilst access is a key control it is also necessary to record and log transactions providing not only preventive controls but also detective controls. A log of machine activity will provide a means to enable assurance that only user authorised activity has been processed as well as providing for effective recovery from system failures. Journals should be 'Read only' to prevent unauthorised amendment of logged information.

Transaction Processing (TP) System Controls

The TP system is under the control of the operating system and so the auditor must be familiar with the security and control features provided by the operating system. The TP system may provide controls itself eg limiting access to particular data items via specific user identifier or workstation, maintenance of controls counts and totals, providing logs for interrogation later, the use of programmed instructions to ensure data integrity during multiple record updates.

Controlled Stationery

If a failure occurs during the printing of controlled stationery, particularly cheques, the computer system should, when the computer is again functioning, be able to recommence printing as at the last correctly printed document without producing duplicates and without corrupting the audit trail.

9.4 Output Controls

9.4.1   Objectives

Output controls should ensure that:

– where output of any form should be produced, that output is both actually produced and is complete in itself;

– output which is produced is reasonable, both in quantity and actual format and serves a useful purpose;

– output should be produced in accordance with any agreed timetable and should be distributed in such a way as to maintain confidentiality; and

– errors and exceptions reported by the system must be adequately controlled to ensure a thorough investigation of their cause and re submission where appropriate.

9.4.2   Areas Of Control

Completeness

There are a number of control techniques which can assist in the attainment of the objective of ensuring completeness of output.

Controls can be built into the way the clerical functions within the system are ordered. These controls will be in evidence either in the computer control/operations section, or the user department. With regard to on-line application systems the responsibility for acceptance of output lies with the user.

Similarly, controls can be built into the application computer system itself or use can be made of the operating system resident in the machine being used eg numbering of report pages, messages such as 'NIL' or 'End of report'.

Reasonableness

Output should appear to be reasonable and satisfy the user's expectations.

Responsibility for the initial checking of output for reasonableness lies with the IT control/operations section and control techniques consist mainly of manual checks on the output.

Where the user department itself operates a control section, further checks should be carried out. If a control section is not in being, it should be the clear duty of a responsible person to carry out checks for completeness of output prior to general distribution and usage.

Use

The department for whom the output is produced has a responsibility for ensuring that it is used for the purpose for which it was specified, designed and prepared.

The control section should satisfy itself that all output is distributed to the user and should query the necessity for producing any output if it appears that the user no longer has need of it.

Timeliness and confidentiality

Controls within the IT department should ensure that output is produced on time and that its distribution takes due regard of the need for confidentiality.

It should be remembered that continued confidentiality may rely upon the controlled destruction of output once it has outlived its useful life. The Data Protection Act's requirements should be studied in this respect.

Error and exception control

Rejection of data may occur at different points in processing and procedures are necessary to ensure that each rejection is properly investigated, corrected, authorised, re-input and reprocessed.

It is important that responsibility is defined for the control and re-input of rejections. Division of duties between those responsible for original input and those controlling error investigation is also desirable.

Control over rejections can also be through a computer suspense/error file and this can assist in ensuring that rejected items are not overlooked.

9.4.3   Output Control Techniques

When considering the output control techniques which are available to the computer user, it must be borne in mind that not all techniques can be reasonably applied to all types of computer output. This section is followed by a further section entitled 'Forms of Output' which briefly considers the control techniques which might be best applied to particular output types.

Completeness of output

Clerical controls within the IT control/operations section might include a schedule listing all expected output from each computer run. This would identify the printed reports to be produced and the number of copies of each. It would also detail magnetic media output files, setting out whether they were tape, disc or other media files as appropriate.

Files output to magnetic media would be subject to control by the librarian or another designated person who would be charged with the responsibility for ensuring that all expected output files are produced and properly controlled.

Computerised control techniques designed to assist in ensuring completeness of output might include the numbering of pages by the application program and the printing of a message indicating the end of the report.

Where a report is to be produced and no records actually qualify to appear on it then the program might print 'Nil Report' or similar message.

The computer operating system might also give details of output reports and files produced, together with an indication of the number of records actually output.

The user department might also operate its own clerical controls to ensure that all output is received. Ultimate responsibility for the acceptance of output as complete and/or accurate, lies with the user department.

Reasonableness of output

Whilst the IT department staff cannot be expected to identify in detail whether or not output is correct, there are a number of tests they can apply in order to get an indication of its reasonableness:

> — whether the volume of output produced compares well with the 'norm' for the computer run concerned and whether the processing follows its normal pattern and time scale;

> — whether the output looks right especially when pre-printed stationery has been used;

> — whether the volume of the output is consistent with the indications of size given by control reports produced by the application program or possibly the operating system.

The importance of batch controls, where applied, should not be overlooked when considering this area. These will normally be finally reconciled in the user department, though some initial checking might take place in the IT control section.

Within the user department a particular person may be nominated to test output prior to general distribution and to examine the results of a small number of transactions or look for the effects of a particular change that has taken place (eg change of tax tables, or other fixed rates).

Production and retention of output

Production of output which is no longer used is wasteful and unnecessary. The responsibility falls to the user to justify the continued production of output.. This is particularly important to ensure that the Data Protection Act is complied with Both IT and user departments should satisfy themselves that the reasons for non use of the output are clearly defined and is not due to the user department being unaware of the reasons for the specific output being produced owing to staff changes and the passage of time.

It is also important to have a defined document/output retention policy to ensure only required information is retained. This is also another important area in complying with the Data Protection Act.

Timeliness and confidentiality

If the IT department has a control section then it should be responsible for ensuring timeliness of output. They will keep track of input data as it works its way through the control and data preparation stages (see 'Input Controls') and ensure that it is available in the correct form when the time comes to run the application programs.

The operating system in use is often used to perform the detailed scheduling work and particular jobs are given priority according to a ranking system.

Techniques for ensuring confidentiality include clerical procedures as well as certification to ensure that the output reaches the correct persons, physical controls over output such as magnetic tape and restrictions of access to output at workstations.

Computer output should be clearly marked to indicate its eventual destination. Collection and/or dispatch of printouts should be recorded and a record of receipt obtained where sensitivity of data makes this desirable. Control over output should not be relaxed purely because a later run has produced a set of updated reports or output in another form. Destruction of output may be necessary to ensure continued confidentiality and such destruction must be on a controlled basis where the data warrants it. Where output data is produced on a workstation, there may be a need for passwords, strategic siting to avoid unauthorised viewing of data and techniques to erase data from a screen after a particular time period.

The requirements of the Data Protection legislation outlined in chapter 15 should be borne in mind when arranging for the distribution and display of output.

Error and exception control

A distinction should be drawn between the different types of exception reports which might be produced by a computer system. An exception report is often a term used to describe an item which has been completely processed and is reported as a warning because the data is outside certain tolerance (eg an employee has worked more than 25 hours overtime in one week). An error or rejection report is one which describes an item which has not been accepted by the system and which should be checked, corrected if necessary and re-input to a subsequent run of the system.

It is the responsibility of the user department to correct and resubmit errors and to control this process to ensure all items are dealt with. The IT department control section might, however, be called upon to ensure as far as is practicable in the time available, that rejections have not been caused by actions within their department. Areas to be considered in this respect are punching errors, run submission errors (eg wrong file used), or operating errors.

Where error correction is carried out by the IT department, the user should be aware of the action taken and should eventually receive evidence that it has been carried out.

Within the user department separation of duties is an important consideration and, where possible, if data is at all sensitive, the clerk submitting the original data should not be responsible for acting on the exception reports. If this is not possible, the section supervisor should from time to time examine the exception reports and the action taken on them.

Control of rejections can be effected through the use of a computer suspense file. Items rejected are posted to suspense and are cleared by submission of data which matches the suspense entry and ensures the item is correctly handled. Regular reporting of items not cleared from suspense can then be used to assist in ensuring that all items are dealt with.

On-line systems

Messages printed at workstations can be vetted like other printed documents. A visual check will indicate whether the format is that included in the systems specification and a test check for accuracy is often practicable.

For information displayed on workstations greater reliance must be placed on the accuracy of the computer system, although it is often possible to test check for accuracy by noting or obtaining hard copy of the information recorded on the screen and checking it later.

Confidentiality poses a greater problem but controls are possible depending on the sophistication of the workstation equipment. The siting of workstations can assist in retention of confidentiality. Workstations handling sensitive data should normally be sited so that the screen cannot easily be viewed by other than the user and in such a position that the section supervisor can view the persons operating the workstation.

Hard copy output from an on-line application may often be printed at the user's workstation. The way in which output is controlled will obviously be an area for audit examination since the production of hard copy logs of key transactions, error reports, exception reports and reconciliation reports are an important aspect in the control of the application. The independent checking of output by a person not involved in input, may be the only satisfactory way of ensuring that transactions have been entered in accordance with authorised documentation. Whilst this may not be feasible for all types of transaction it may be necessary for certain sensitive transactions. Other forms of report produced for the application may allow the overall reconciliation of totals on key fields to manually produced totals for a given period of time. The determination of user procedures in this area, particularly the existence of internal check between the various activities, is of paramount importance. The user in an on-line application takes on many functions previously associated with a data control section and has, therefore, a vital role in controlling input and output and carrying out the necessary reconciliations.

9.5 Audit Trail

9.5.1   Objectives

A complete audit trail should be maintained which allows for both an item to be traced from input through to its final resting place and a final result to be broken into its constituent parts.

The term 'audit trail' can be considered as synonymous with terms such as management trail, information trail and data or transaction trail. The term audit trail is used consistently within these *Guidelines*.

In a computer system the trail will not always be as apparent as it would be in a manual system as the data is often retained only on magnetic media and in a form that is intelligible only to the computer programs designed to access it. The occasions when the trail may not be wholly visible include the following:

   —   Output may be limited to a summary of items processed, thus making it impossible to trace an individual transaction right through the system from input to final resting place.

- Magnetic storage devices may be updated by over-writing the equivalent record with the result brought about by the newly input data, thus making visible reconciliation of start, change and finish position impossible.

- Reports may be on an exception basis only.

Though such occasions may arise it should be remembered that though individual transactions are not visibly traceable through the system, the existence of adequate processing controls should ensure that an overall reconciliation of records/transactions input and processed can be made.

In addition controls over input should endeavour to ensure that transactions are correctly and completely entered into the computer system.

The auditor may therefore have to be satisfied with a trail which, while not visible in detail, is nevertheless reconcilable throughout the system. It should be emphasised that the user of the system will have a vital interest in ensuring that the system properly processes all input data and should also be very concerned that the trail is complete.

9.5.2   Testing the Audit Trail

As a general principle, the audit trail is traced by investigating the controls within all the systems, including the operating system and substantiating the path by a limited amount of checking through records and files.

As with other systems, the audit trail in a computer system is best examined at the development of the system or procedure. Where the specification does not appear to be providing an effective audit trail, the opportunity can be taken to improve the trail during system design. Later interest may then be centred on whether the system is still as examined or what effect alterations have made.

If audit is involved in the development of an application it may be able to produce its own test data which can be entered at the workstation. In a development situation the auditor should be able to test validation routines, error reporting procedures, error correction procedures, reconciliation techniques, ease of operation, man/machine dialogue and assess the user procedures to be established around the computer system. This type of audit involvement is invaluable and should greatly improve the auditor's knowledge of the application and assist in developing the audit approach to the system when it goes live. Audit use of test data in a live situation must take account of the risk of files being corrupted very easily. It is likely that many users will be accessing the on-line file and the user would be unlikely to welcome audit testing, which resulted in master files being updated with test data. However, it should be possible to carry out limited testing of validation routines at the workstation with user co-operation. Whilst it may be possible to assess some controls indirectly by considering the state of the data files, it may be that other controls can be more easily assessed by examining the system in operation, for example, if control totals are produced for a document, or if information is not retained on a master file but only used as part of a calculation.

Whenever data that would normally be used in a completed audit is recorded only in a transient manner the investigation should be on a current audit basis. The loss of a visible audit trail may be overcome by checking totals through the system and by the use of interrogation facilities, for example.

9.5.3 Use of Computer Assisted Audit Techniques (CAATS)

Retrieval software, which is further discussed in chapter 13, may be used to interrogate application and system software files and produce samples of transactions for detailed examination by audit. The auditor should be able to trace the transaction to an authorised document and ensure that the user procedures have been followed. It should also be possible to interrogate the files for transactions which do not meet the validation criteria of the application, as mentioned previously. The auditor would need to study system documentation to determine the validation routines purporting to be in operation and devise interrogations to test that no transactions fell outside the parameters.

If transactions are dated, serially numbered or identifiable to a particular period, it may be possible to use retrieval software to produce control totals which can be checked against user control totals and system produced control totals.

The use of a resident audit module is a technique available to audit. Transactions of a particular type could activate a module which would write data to a file to be interrogated by audit at a later date. The use of this technique will depend upon the type of application, the adequacy of the audit trail, the period of retention of data and the capability of audit to interrogate files. If an adequate audit trail exists this technique may not need to be considered. However, where transaction data is not retained for any length of time and sensitive transactions of audit interest can be defined, the technique may be worth pursuing.

The technique of program review may be used to examine the coding of particular transaction modules. However, this obviously requires expertise within audit and can be very time-consuming.

On-line interrogation facilities, providing read-only access to transaction files from an audit workstation, is a technique which will provide audit with considerable independence.

9.25

9.6   Audit Approach

9.6.1   Input Controls

The audit review of input controls is designed to ascertain whether the system does, as far as is reasonably possible, ensure that input is genuine, complete, not previously processed, accurate and timely.

The control techniques available to the system user, the systems analyst or the IT control section have already been described. The auditor is faced with the task of deciding whether or not the input controls in use do achieve their objectives defined earlier. It is, of course, most unlikely that the auditor will ever meet a system in which all possible input controls exist and where there is no possibility at all that errors can go through undiscovered.

One approach is to review the controls in operation within the five areas set out in this section viz authorisation, completeness, accuracy, conversion and control of documents, at the same time not overlooking the organisational controls which may also be in operation.

When considering the controls in operation within a system it is important to remember that inadequate separation of duties can make a control system completely ineffective. Normal audit principles therefore apply within this area and effective separation of the origination and checking functions is most necessary.

The auditor should bear in mind that system modifications may have altered the effectiveness of controls, even those controls which do not appear to be closely connected with any amendments.

It should be remembered that input controls are only part of the overall control system within a computerised system and they should therefore also be viewed in relation to the system as a whole.

The audit checklist should assist the auditor in carrying out a review of system input controls and show the areas to be taken into consideration when assessing whether or not a control objective has been attained.

9.6.2   Processing Controls

Any examination of processing controls should commence with an identification of all the controls that are built into the programs that form the system.

A preliminary discussion with the analyst responsible for maintaining the system should reveal the documentation in which this information is contained. It is important to establish whether documentation is complete and up-to-date before any reliance is placed on its contents.

Record-level controls will be included in the program specifications of the validation and update programs. As far as possible these controls should prevent incorrect data from entering the master files.

Total-level controls will be described within all the program specifications in the system and additional information may be gleaned from the systems specification and user manual.

The manner in which these control totals are produced will be of particular importance to the auditor. When the total printed is the result of an accumulation of the individual fields, greater reliance may be placed on its accuracy.

However, certain methods of processing (eg random updating,) may make this method uneconomic and in such cases it is more usual for control records to be maintained which contain the control totals that are printed.

Under these circumstances the auditor should try to establish whether control totals are ever reconciled with individual fields and if they are not, such a reconciliation should always be performed as part of the audit interrogation of the file.

A description of system failure controls should be included in the systems specification and further details may be obtained from specifications of programs which involve security stationery or particularly time-consuming processing.

Having identified the controls, the auditor should check their proper functioning through the use of test packs or interrogation programs. It is desirable that interrogation routines are devised and written by a member of the audit staff.

When program controls produce output that is meant to be checked clerically, the auditor should ensure that the clerical checks are being done promptly and completely, that there is evidence of the checks having been made and that proper internal check prevails during this process.

The auditor should also ensure that the user is aware of the existence and importance of the various controls and that an adequate audit trail exists to enable the user to verify the proper functioning of programs and the completeness of processing.

9.6.3 Output Controls

In conducting a review of output controls the auditor should examine systems specifications and note from them the program checks built into the system. Auditors should also examine the procedure manuals, identifying the clerical checks specified and satisfying themselves that these are adequate and that sufficient division of responsibility is prescribed so that internal check is satisfactory.

With the aid of software the auditor can test the operation of the system, through selection, analysis or totalling techniques. They may also test the reject/error reporting features of the system by use of an appropriately designed test pack or retrieval software.

Auditors should examine records of program modifications introduced since their previous audit to ensure that these in no way interfere with the in-built program checks.

The information gleaned by the auditor should then itself be reviewed to determine whether or not the overall system output controls go as far as is reasonably possible in ensuring that the output control objective is met.

9.28

CIPFA

COMPUTER AUDIT GUIDELINES

AUDITING THE TECHNOLOGY

CHAPTER 10

OPERATING SYSTEMS AND SYSTEM SOFTWARE

10

Continued overleaf

10.1 Introduction

This chapter addresses an important part of the computing environment in which systems are run. The introduction addresses the questions 'what are operating systems and systems software?' It reviews some of the more important functions of systems software from the auditor's point of view and looks at questions raised by systems software regarding staffing IT departments, implementation of systems software and operating system command languages. This part of the chapter stresses the responsibility of management to ensure that systems software is implemented properly, used and maintained by staff who are adequately trained and supervised, and protected against unauthorised or inadvertent access or use.

In the second part of the chapter, the audit approach is addressed. Audit objectives are suggested and some suggested procedures for examining access control, library control, backup and restoration of files, review of journals, tuning and machine performance.

Finally, the chapter briefly addresses the benefits of audit use of system software.

10.1.1 What are Operating Systems?

Computer operations consists of those processes which keep the computer working and aid its efficiency. These processes may include starting individual jobs running, loading tapes and disks into drives, making data files available to programs, scheduling the workload and dealing with certain events which the programs have not anticipated. Such operations were carried out manually on the very earliest computers, but as successive generations of computers have been able to provide greater capacity and sophistication, many of the routine tasks performed by operators have been automated. The software which carries out these functions is known as the operating system.

Operating systems differ widely in the range of their functions and in their sophistication. The simplest ones merely allow users to initiate programs and provide them with simple commands to perform the various tasks involved in addressing peripheral devices. More complex systems, on the other hand, can run programs for many users concurrently, control their data storage, schedule the running of work and report on their own efficiency, as well as many other tasks. The role of the operating system can be summed up in general terms as enabling users and their programs to interact with the computer hardware and memory resources.

Operating systems usually consist of a series of program modules. The simplest operating system is essentially a program which remains resident in the computer at all times and supervises the running of application programs. In most operating systems there are other subsidiary program modules. As well as controlling the running of applications, the resident control module supervises the operation of its own subsidiary programs, invoking them as they are required and bringing them into memory for this purpose. These modules may perform a variety of tasks such as:

- sharing resources between users;

- sharing processing time between programs;

- maximising machine efficiency;

- automatic work scheduling;

- switching programs and data between main and backing store;

- providing process and access security; and

- security back-up of program and data files.

10.1.2 What is System Software?

As well as the operating system, certain other software plays a central operational role in computer installations. For example:

- networking software to link the computer to other computers and shared peripherals;

- data communications software which handles the transmission of data to and from terminals;

- database management software (DBMS) which is used to control processing and storage of data;

- security software which may be purchased to provide additional facilities to those in the basic operating system;

- diagnostic and performance monitoring software;

- file librarian software to control the movement and use of magnetic media;

- programming language compilers;

- utility programs which may be called by users or their programs to perform certain standard functions such as merging, sorting or copying data.

All this extra software exists and may be used independently of any applications in the installation. Indeed, some applications may cede control to them - for access protection purposes, for example. This implies that in addition to the operating system, there is an operating environment in which the applications work. The applications may use the facilities offered by the environment: equally, the way the environment is set up may affect the applications.

10.2

Taken together, such software and the operating system are referred to as system software, because they are provided at system level, rather than at application level. The scope of the operating environment for auditing purposes cannot be defined as being restricted to the operating system, because in many cases the inter-relationships of one part of the environment with another may also be relevant.

Suppliers of operating systems have tended to provide more and more built-in functionality by including facilities which previously had to be added in as utilities. Many of the functions found under the heading of system software in some installations may exist as part of the operating system in others. For example, one operating system may incorporates access control facilities, a query language and a database management system, whereas another may have none of these built in and installations would have to purchase additional software to provide these functions. For audit purposes it is necessary to consider the whole operating environment.

Some of the more common system software functions are listed in the following table.

Common System Software Functions

Module	Examples and alternative names	Typical functions
Main operating system module	Supervisor Executive Control program	Overall control of computer processing
Device driver	Peripheral controller	Controls interaction between peripherals and programs
File librarian		Records physical location of data and ownership details
Access control module	Security module RACF ACF2	Records user details; links files to owners; records users' access permissions and facilities available to users
File manager	File handler Disk operating system (DOS)	Various – eg file copying & renaming, file deletion, directory management Functions may overlap with file librarian and access control modules

Continued overleaf

Memory manager		Keeps memory allocated to one program separate from memory allocated to others
		Optimises use of memory
		Controls 'paging' of memory between core and fast storage devices
Spooler	Print controller	Temporarily stores files pending writing contents to slow peripherals (eg printers) Controls such peripherals
Database management system	DB2 ADABAS	Controls the storage of data and the relationships between data items

In most computers, the operating system has been designed to permit several users and their programs to work simultaneously. Three groups of system software tasks arise from this. Firstly, the operating system shares the use of the central processing unit (CPU) between users and programs in such a way as to maximise its use. It prioritises the work as efficiently as possible based on the nature of the tasks involved and parameters established by the installation. An operating system function known as scheduling deals with this.

Secondly, memory management keeps track of the users' programs and data in memory, resolves conflicts between competing demands on memory and ensures that there is no opportunity for any one process to access data used by other processes. Two other concepts are related to this function. Virtual memory swiftly swaps 'pages' or sections, of program code or data between main memory and fast disk devices to optimise the use of internal memory. Virtual machine systems dynamically control computer facilities in such a way that the user's jobs appear to users to be running on separate computers.

Thirdly, file management and access control functions maintain information to control access. The file manager records the ownership of files, details of which other users may gain access to them and what activities those users may engage in. Access control ensures that only users known to the system can gain access and it may require users to identify themselves to the system through a log-in procedure. The security module may also control the range of commands or processing facilities available to users. Some operating systems play a more important role in access control than others. Where the operating system's own facilities are weak, the installation may have opted to supplement it with an access control package. The way the access control facility is installed and the parameters used are relevant to the quality of access control at the installation.

In order to interact with the computer, a program must interact with the operating system. The following diagram, although much simplified, gives an impression of the relationship between application software, system software and the operating system.

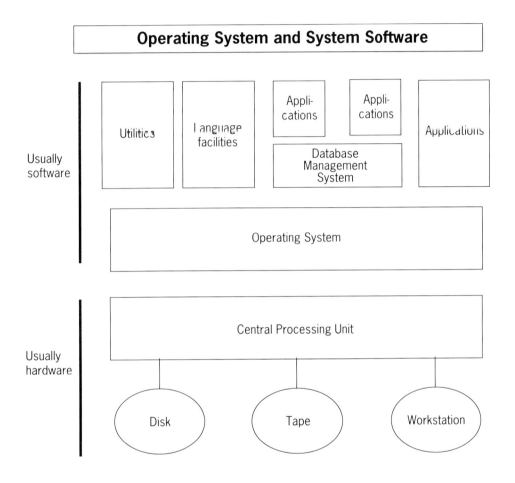

Networking and database management are dealt with in separate chapters in these *Guidelines*. Other functions of system software are further discussed later in this chapter.

10.1.3 Why are Operating Systems and System Software Important?

The operating system and system software provide a variety of facilities which are primarily aimed at facilitating the work of computer programmers, operators and management. Although they often provide the means to enhance control of the computing environment, careless or illicit use of these facilities can breach controls for the whole installation and all the applications run there.

Auditors therefore need to consider:

- how computer installation staff are managed;

- the monitoring and control of changes to system software parameters;

- the controls in place to limit access to system software facilities and operating system commands;

- the control facilities provided by system software and the use made of them for:

- access control: user identities, terminal identities, passwords, encryption, data ownership;

- detective controls: logging access by users, logging access to individual files, access control violation reports;

- system maintenance: error logs, file storage efficiency monitoring, CPU monitoring, backup and restore facilities;

- the means by which deficiencies in system software or careless or unauthorised use of it can jeopardise control and how such weaknesses can be overcome.

10.1.4 Computer Staff

Modern system software has led to the creation of certain specialised roles in computer departments.

Systems programmers

Systems programming staff are responsible for implementing the system software: they tune the system to installation requirements, implement new releases and maintain the system. It is also their concern to make the system software appear to other users to be as simple, helpful and foolproof as possible. It is sometimes also their role to control user access to system software facilities, though other staff, such as computer security officers, may also be involved. To this end they may develop an array of local facilities which will pre-set system parameters to suitable defaults and prevent irregular use of the system. The system programmers possess powerful tools to carry out a variety of supervisory and maintenance tasks which may allow them to manipulate the system software and alter or suppress information.

Systems programmers usually report to senior systems or operations management. However, it is often found that these senior officers have, at best, an outdated or superficial knowledge of the system software currently installed; at worst, they may have no detailed knowledge of its workings.

Often, systems programmers are consulted by application programmers and analysts on methods of programming user requirements and they are often involved in resolving system crashes. As a result they frequently gain some detailed knowledge of applications (many will have been previously employed as application programmers) and have access to data as well as their own powerful facilities and privileges.

The nature of the systems programmers' work therefore gives them both the highest level of technical expertise and the widest possible access in the computer system. The fact that their work is difficult to control and is often largely unsupervised, makes the management of these staff a major audit concern.

Operating staff

Operations staff are responsible for the day to day running of the computer and the efficient and orderly running of its work. Assisted by the operating system and system software, they may:

— start up and close down the system at the beginning and end of the processing day,

— schedule the computer's tasks, including archive processes,

— load and unload tapes, disks and listing paper when required,

— resolve conflicts of resource allocation; and

— initiate recovery procedures in the event of program or hardware malfunction.

There should be formal procedures and instructions governing general operator processes and specific instructions for tasks related to running specific application programs.

Librarian and custodial functions

File librarianship is concerned with the physical control of magnetic media and the logical control of data and programs (making them available to jobs, controlling version numbers, etc.) In modern operating environments control of files while they are on line to the computer is handled by system software. But control of the physical movement of media and organising security copies in addition to those provided automatically remain manual functions.

Another custodial duty is the limitation of access to both programs and data. With less sophisticated operating systems this may have to be achieved by physical means (locked cabinets etc.) With larger operating systems or system software packages, however, software controlled password routines, permissions and security codes are used to augment physical controls. Control of these computer-based custodial duties often reverts to the system programmers. In addition, software-maintained catalogues of files and usage have led to individual volumes (discrete physical units of storage) bearing no external indication of the nature of their contents. Once again, control of this aspect has effectively passed to the systems programmers.

Staffing small computer systems

Smaller computing installations will necessarily employ fewer staff than larger ones: the ultimate reduction being the personal computer (PC) with one user. As a result, the roles described above merge and much of the separation of duties and supervision available in larger installations is not implemented at smaller ones. It is also common for less well qualified staff to carry out these functions: again, the typical PC user is a case in point.

10.1.5 Implementing System Software

Systems software is supplied to the installation by the supplier or software house as a particular release or version. The installation implements that release and can either use the software facilities as provided or tailor the system to meet its own requirements. The tailoring can be achieved in two ways:

- By 'tuning' the system ie altering certain key parameters (eg number of simultaneous jobs, back-up frequency, maximum CPU time per job, access control settings).

- By amending or adding to, the program code of the system software.

Thus, the same software might be used in very different ways, even on similar hardware. Advanced operating systems and system software should not be thought of as having a specific form. The facilities provided by suppliers are better thought of as a 'kit of parts' from which the installation management may select a suitable configuration.

10.1.6 Job Control Languages

Instructions to the operating system to perform its various functions on particular pieces of work (jobs) are issued through a job control language (JCL) which specify who the user is, what is required in terms of resources (eg time, computer files) and what action should be taken in the event of certain occurrences (eg program messages, program failure). Sets of JCL instructions can be fed into the computer through normal input devices or they can be held in store and called by other JCL programs or procedures. In some operating systems JCL is known by other names and different names are also used for job control programs. A complete list of all the expressions used would be impractical, but the following are examples of common variants.

Job Control Languages: system control language (SCL), terminal control language (TCL), proc.

Job Control Programs: procs, macros, batch programs, submit programs, job descriptions.

JCL often provides users with access to powerful and flexible commands which allow the manipulation of data: for example, commands to load and run utility software to edit, erase or copy files. In many systems it is possible to prevent application users from accessing JCL commands directly. This is usually done by creating a link between the user identity (or, less commonly, the terminal identity) and a specific program which will be automatically executed when the user logs on. All further user activity is then controlled by this program, provided both that there is no way of breaking out of it and that all other programs invoked by it return control to the 'logon program' or terminate the user session.

10.1.7 Functions of System Software

Some of the functions of system software are summarised below. This review represents an overview of facilities: it should be remembered that not all systems will have all these facilities, nor will they necessarily make use of features in exactly the manner described. The range of variations allowed to installations through the use of parameters and 'own code' are such that the same software may work differently in two different sites. Installations may also reinforce controls in system software using other control techniques. For example, installations may reinforce access control by requiring written authorisation for certain users to access specified parts of the computer system.

Scheduling jobs

Many operating systems can process several jobs at the same time. To do this, they switch processing very quickly between jobs, giving the impression that each job is running continuously and simultaneously with the others. To avoid processor intensive jobs keeping the CPU busy at the expense of others, parameters in the system software can be set to force this switching to be done after specific time intervals or to limit the total amount of CPU time that any one job is allowed. To avoid all jobs being given equal shares of the CPU time, when in reality some jobs are more important than others, it will be possible to give individual users, jobs or types of job a priority. The system software contains a module called the scheduler, which has four main functions:

- to run jobs in accordance with the priorities given to users and programs;
- to ensure that necessary resources (eg tape and disk drives, memory) are available to jobs as they are run;
- to ensure the most effective use of computer resources by multi-programming, paging etc; and
- to ensure that jobs are not left in the processing queue for an unreasonable length of time.

Running programs

For each job being run, the operating system is involved with:

- running and controlling the application programs;
- acquiring resources and controlling a job's use of them;

10.9

- off-line activity, such as spooling print files arising from a job;

- providing for recovery from errors;

- communicating with operators;

- keeping the program, data and resources separate from those used by other jobs;

- removing certain functions from the on-line job stream to be processed later, perhaps with a lower priority. This is done in order to release CPU resources: these functions usually involve slow tasks like input to and output from slow peripherals, like card readers and printers. This process is sometimes called spooling.

Providing a secure processing environment

Security involves protecting files of data or programs from deliberate or accidental damage or loss and providing the means for recovery should that protection fail. Thus, it includes access control, custodial control and backup and recovery facilities. Files can be protected by the system by means of:

- file ownership structures;

- passwords and access permissions;

- encryption;

- terminal identifiers;

- file identifiers (eg generation numbers, version number or language codes);

- file placement and library facilities; and

- back-up and recovery facilities.

Analysing processing activity

Many operating systems have facilities to report on their own activity and efficiency. This is clearly important to the effective management of a computer installation. Information produced may include:

- overall summary of machine and peripheral usage and performance;

- details of each job run, which may include a summary of the resources used;

- analysis of the budget and usage for each user;

- a detailed log of specific activities such as program amendments; and

- reports from the access control module showing, for example, breaches in security.

It should be noted here that, whilst operating systems and system software may write information to special system files for various purposes, most systems have facilities to limit or modify the information stored and printed out. For example, some systems only log whatever applications programs choose to send for logging. Most systems have facilities for deactivating the logging facility: some have no logging facilities at all, others may automatically overwrite the logging file periodically.

General purpose software utilities

Many systems have additional facilities available. A comprehensive list is impossible in a text of this nature, but examples are:

- report generators and query languages;

- special amendment facilities (for programs and data);

- editors;

- sort, merge and copy software.

10.2 Audit Approach

10.2.1 Overview

Auditors need to be aware of how controls in and around the system software interact with procedural controls in specific applications. They must be aware of the control facilities provided by the system software and more importantly how management makes use of such facilities. Any weakness in the controls provided by the operating system or system software may affect every application for which the computer is used. For this reason, some auditors prefer to conduct separate periodic audits of operating system facilities as part of a general controls review, while others may examine these repeatedly as part of each application system review.

10.2.2 Systems Set Up by Suppliers

Often, smaller computer systems are purchased by users for a single specific purpose as part of a combined procurement of hardware and software. Such systems may be installed and configured by the software house. Users of the system may be unaware of controls provided by the system software: indeed, they may not even know what operating system the computer uses. Auditors, however, must familiarise themselves with the details of the system software to ensure that control facilities and control weaknesses are not overlooked in the operation of the system.

10.2.3 Audit Objectives

The following paragraphs indicate the audit objectives when reviewing control and security facilities provided by system software:

- to assess the extent to which system software is used to control access to the machine and the appropriateness of the access allowed to individual files and groups of files;

- to assess the adequacy of the system software mechanisms for dumping and restoring files;

- to assess the use made of logs and journals by management for job accounting and control;

- to assess the security of the arrangements for installation and tuning of system software;

- to assess the arrangements for monitoring IT resources and the extent to which they maximise job throughput, limit the processing overheads imposed by system software and provide an equitable and efficient service to users;

- to appraise measures which may have been implemented to compensate for weaknesses in the above;

- to recommend appropriate measures to counter weaknesses discovered in the above assessments.

10.2.4 Audit Procedures and Techniques

As stated previously, system software varies from machine to machine in both its sophistication and the range of facilities offered. Some suppliers provide manuals for auditors: for example, IBM produce an audit guide to the RACF access control software and Digital have a security guide for VAX systems. Auditors need to study the technical manuals and any available audit guides on the specific software under review in order to appreciate the range of controls offered and develop an audit approach to them. Where the supplier does not provide specific guidance on security and audit, third party publications such as those in the CIPFA Computer Audit Guidance Note series may need to be consulted.

One technique used successfully by auditors to overcome the difficulty presented by the degree of possible variation in operating systems, was to use the manuals to create a schedule of the control facilities provided by system software. They then reviewed which of these features were designated as mandatory in the organisation, which ones were optional and which ignored. The auditors then reviewed the implementation in greater depth to determine compliance with these criteria. By doing this, they arrived at a view of both the implementation policy and the implementation practices within the range of facilities offered by the supplier.

Control of access to files

User Structure

Files are often held in an hierarchical structure of directories, libraries or accounts under various owners or users. This structure should reflect the authority, structure and responsibilities of the organisation concerned. The level of each user in the hierarchy may decide the level of their control over other users' work, the files to which they have access and the type of access (eg read only, write: see 'Permissions' below).

The auditor should consider the user structure by examining system prints of the user hierarchy and assess whether it reflects the control structure in the organisation. Auditors should be prepared to challenge the level and position in the structure of particular users if a failure of organisational control is implied or because there is excessive unrestricted access to files. The system software may allow users to access files which belong to other users elsewhere in the hierarchy. If this is the case, the auditor should review the appropriateness of all access to so-called 'inferior' users and the type of access allowed.

User Identity (ID)

Many operating systems and specialised access control packages require users to identify themselves with a name or ID code when they initiate jobs. Alone, such codes provide limited control over machine access. However, once in the system, the user identity record is often the key means of controlling facilities and file accesses.

The auditor should be aware, therefore, of the importance of protecting the user ID – usually effected through the use of passwords – and examine instructions and procedures for creating new users. Staff should be instructed to ensure that users will not have unrestricted access.

Special Privileges

Operating systems often have special facilities available to certain users or to pre-defined user IDs which permit by-passing of some security features. For example, one operating system allows a characteristic called ALLACC to be attached to user identities: this permits those users to access any file in the computer as if it were their own. Similar facilities in other operating systems may enable users to access specialised commands, to access sensitive system files, to amend the characteristics of other users and other facilities or combinations of facilities.

Auditors should find out what privileges are available to users, especially those specific to operators, security co-ordinators, technical support staff and field engineers. They should review any list of user descriptions in which such privileges are reported and find out who has access to privileged user IDs, to ensure that they cannot be used to circumvent the security of the system.

Catalogue Software

The file which records the user structure and file system on the computer is sometimes called the 'catalogue'. Some catalogues contain information on file attributes and placements while details on access rights etc. may be part of separate access control software. The 'catalogue' which, for the purposes of this guide includes facilities provided by separate access software, is held in direct access storage media and should be under the control of a senior user of the system. It usually records information about all objects, whether users or files and the relationship between these objects. All files should be recognised as being owned by a specific user. The catalogue should contain information on which other users, if any, may access each file and what tasks they may perform on it (sometimes called traps, privileges or permissions).

When a job requests access to an object before using it, the access control software checks against the catalogue file to ensure that the object exists, that it may be used as requested and that the user is permitted to access the object in that way.

The default for file privacy should be that owners control their own files and no other users have automatic access to them. Some operating systems fail to enforce this basic control and leave files available for general use unless the owner takes steps to protect it. Users and system designers should be encouraged to be careful when setting file access permissions: as a general rule, access should be permitted only on the basis of actual need, though careless designers often set permissions in a number of ways which jeopardise security and control:

- a user is granted access to all files when access is only needed to one;
- a user is granted access to all generations of a file when only the latest generation number is required;
- a user is given all types of access when only read access is required;
- a group of users is given access when only one of them has requested it;
- users are given access 'just in case' when no current need has been identified;
- users continue to have access when there is no longer a need.

The auditor should list the 'catalogue' file (or selected parts of it) by printing or interrogation and should investigate relationships between users and files to check who has access permission to what. The auditor should assess the appropriateness of the relationships and whether permissions granted are monitored and withdrawn when no longer required.

Passwords

Passwords are recorded by the system either in the catalogue or in another system file. The records should normally be encrypted and not readily accessible. Those systems which allow the implementation of password control may do so in a variety of ways.

Examples:

In some systems two-level passwords can be used to control access: the first level may relate to a group of users and the second to individuals. Such a system usually allows users to change their password by means of a terminal command, while a security co-ordinator controls the group passwords. In others systems passwords can be attached to individual files and allow various levels of access .

In order to be effective, password control should take account of the following:

— The presence of a password must be mandatory. Any access path which has no password in an otherwise controlled system is a potential threat to the entire system.

— 'Guessability' in a password system is in part a function of the number of different characters allowed, the minimum password length and the frequency with which change is forced.

— A password system which allows only a single capital letter for a password needs a maximum of only 26 guesses in order for access to be gained to any user account. If the system can distinguish between upper and lower case, the maximum number of guesses is doubled and if other characters such as numerals or punctuation marks are permitted, it increases further. The number of guesses therefore increases with the size of the allowed character set.

— 'Guessability' also increases exponentially with the length of password: while a password consisting of one numeric digit will take up to 10 attempts to guess, a two-digit password can take $100\,(10^2)$ guesses. A minimum password length of 5 or 6 characters is the norm.

— Password longevity affects 'guessability' because longer password lifetimes provide greater opportunity for guessing. In highly sensitive systems, single-use passwords may be employed.

— Guessing of passwords should be inhibited by the system software. Normally, this is done by disabling the terminal or the user id after a certain number of wrong guesses. It will only discourage determined efforts to guess passwords if all cases are investigated. As part of staff training, this feature of password control should be carefully explained to staff, so that they understand their responsibility to remember passwords and enter them accurately.

— If changes to passwords are carried out automatically by the system, management should ensure that users are notified of such changes confidentially.

— Passwords should not be shared by individuals. In the case of breached security, even when accidental, it is important for management to know the individual whose password has been compromised. They may then take appropriate educative, supervisory or disciplinary action.

— The frequency of password change will depend on the sensitivity of the applications and facilities to which the password allows access. For example, users requiring high security (such as the security administrator for an installation) may wish to renew their password daily, while users who have no updating permissions and can access only non-sensitive data may need to change only quarterly. For many commercial systems, password changes are normally forced after 30 days or less.

— On staff terminations and changes of duties, existing user identities or permissions should be amended immediately. Where staff are on notice to leave as a result of their dissatisfaction or of disciplinary action, their access permissions should be revoked immediately.

— Password control can be self-defeating. Some systems generate passwords which the user is required to memorise. However, if the generated words or phrases are of such length or complexity as to be difficult to remember, staff will be likely to write down the password. If such systems are adopted in order to provide additional security for sensitive applications, extra care should be taken to educate staff so that they appreciate the need for difficult passwords and the requirement to keep them secure.

— Users should be instructed to select passwords which meet reasonable standards and they should be encouraged:

— to mix non-alphabetic characters with letters, to add random and not easily guessable features to their passwords eg cof3fee, a*tit!ude;

— if they use common words as passwords, to mis-spell them deliberately eg coffie, attichude;

— not to use a 'system' (eg the names of sports or television personalities, towns, flowers) for password selection: should the system become known, the passwords would be more easily guessed. Other commonly used words to be avoided are words associated with sex, power (eg God, boss, master) and the word password itself;

— not to employ words or numbers associated with themselves or the organisation as passwords: this includes details of names, addresses, relatives, pets, telephone numbers and dates;

— not to re-use passwords: often, the system software can be made to prevent a user re-using a password within a certain number of changes by keeping a list of their most recently used passwords and prohibiting the selection of any word on the list;

— to bear in mind the importance of password length. Although the system may impose a minimum length, users may be encouraged to use words of different lengths from time to time;

— to keep all passwords secure since, once the password is known to other users, they

10.16

too can log in and masquerade as the owner; and

- to change their passwords at appropriate intervals, as well as when there are staff changes and when a security breach is thought to have occurred.

- Many systems have default passwords, particularly when first implemented or when new users are introduced. Occasionally, these defaults are re-established when new versions of the access control software are introduced or following a visit by service engineers. Such default passwords may include blank spaces, names or words such as 'PASSWORD' or 'EVERYONE'. Some systems even have blank passwords (ie no password is required) as a default for key accounts or default passwords which are shorter than the minimum established by the security controller. It should not be assumed that users do not know of these defaults – they form the basis of every hacker's first attempt to break security. Auditors should find out – from the supplier if necessary – what default passwords are in place and ensure that they have been changed by the technical support team on implementation and following each upgrade and engineer visit.

- The display of passwords on terminal screens should be suppressed if possible, although not all systems have such a facility.

Auditors should familiarise themselves with the level of password control offered by system software and ascertain the policy on use, quality and security of passwords, default passwords, restrictions on password guessing or number of log-on attempts, changing passwords, the monitoring of attempts at unauthorised access and action in the event of a password breach. Auditors should actively promote the best possible password control, balancing ease of use with the need to ensure that access is available only to those who really need it. Auditors should bear in mind the degree of risk represented by password breaches: excessive control in low risk systems may actually devalue the significance of security in the eyes of users.

The auditor may be tempted to test the security of the catalogue by surreptitiously attempting access to directories and files under controlled conditions. However, such action is not part of a standard audit approach and to carry out such a test exhaustively may require considerable specialist knowledge. The co-operation of site management would be essential and assistance might also be necessary to overcome possible difficulties which arose during or after the test.

Permissions

In addition to passwords, there is usually a system for granting various levels of access to files or user directories. This can be provided by the operating system, by DBMS or by other system software.

Some modes of access commonly used are:

Read   –   power to read but not write to the file.

Password Control Checklist

Check	Preferred Answer	Actual Answer
Is the presence of a password necessary?	YES	
What is the password length?	5 char. or more	
Is the password expiry forced after an appropriate period of time?	YES, if the software allows it	
Is the re-use of passwords inhibited?	YES, if the software allows it	
Is the terminal or the user id disabled after a given number of wrong guesses?	YES	
Are passwords shared by individuals?	NO	
Are existing user identities or permissions amended immediately on staff terminations and changes of duties?	YES	
Are access permissions revoked immediately for staff on notice to leave as a result of dissatisfaction or disciplinary action?	YES, without exception	
Where automatically generated passwords or phrases are used, are they of such length or complexity as to be difficult to remember?	NO	
Are users given clear and comprehensive instruction in good password selection?	YES	
Are passwords changed at appropriate intervals and also when there are staff changes and when a security breach is thought to have occurred?	YES	
Does the system administrator or security administrator ensure that no supplier's default passwords are left in place and that engineer's passwords are reset after each engineer visit?	YES	
Is the display of passwords on terminal screens suppressed?	YES	
Is the use of specific terminals or lines restricted to appropriate tasks?	YES	

10.18

Write   –   power to read and write to the file.

Execute   –   power to obey but not amend or print it out (ie load and run program).

All modes –   including power to delete the file.

Individual system software packages may have variants on this scheme. Some systems distinguish only between files which are read-only and read-and-modify; while others may have eight to ten different categories of access to files, determining whether the user can add to, amend, delete, read, execute or even detect them.

Access permissions are granted by the owner or controller of the file library or directory and can be given selectively or generally. In some systems, permissions given at a high level in the catalogue can apply to all subsidiary directories and files, thereby transferring control of groups of files downwards in the organisation and to a wider group of individuals through the use of a single instruction. While this is convenient for technical support teams, a lazy or thoughtless use of this facility may give wider access than is really needed.

In order to access a file, therefore, a user must know either the owner's password or be given the relevant permission. In some systems an additional password may be applied to the file itself. However, free access may still be available through the identity of the file's owner if passwords are not used on certain types of processing, such as background jobs.

The auditor should examine for key system software and applications files, the access granted to other users when the files are first created and what other accesses are subsequently granted. This can be done by examining information in the catalogue file and entries in the control statements of particular jobs. Some system software includes enquiry facilities specifically to perform this function.

'Alien' Files

Sometimes, not all files are known by and recorded in the catalogue and are not, therefore, controlled by the library or access control software. In other systems system software does not control access to any files. Varying levels of physical security and clerical control procedures for such files will be required. The level of security depends on the importance of the file concerned.

If system software normally controls files, the auditor should check the contents and security of 'alien' files which are outside this control. This may be achieved by first determining how alien files are identified and what other physical files reside in the library and then questioning the file librarian about their use. Particularly sensitive 'alien' files (eg BACS tapes) may require special protection. It may also be possible to detect the use of alien files in journal and log records.

A particular hazard when alien files are allowed in a system is that they may be used surreptitiously to introduce unauthorised programs or amendments to programs. Auditors should review the procedures relating to the introduction of alien media to ensure that proper authorisation

10.19

and identification of all files takes place.

Development and Production Program Libraries

Programs in machine readable form are generally physically identical to data files and, without proper control, on-line program libraries can be accessed and altered by any technique which is also suitable for data files.

In some older systems the librarian would ensure that the necessary procedures for development, testing, user approval etc had been followed prior to transferring the program between the development and production program library. Increasingly, installations are automating the maintenance of program libraries, file transfer between them being effected by systems or programming staff using system software, rather than by the librarian. The software which performs these functions is known as 'library software': this may not always be part of the operating system and can be supplied by independent software houses. It must be able to distinguish production programs (or directories) from obsolete, development and test programs (or directories). This allows control by management to ensure that only approved production files are processed.

The order in which different program libraries are searched for programs may be amended by users in some systems. The version used in a run can, in such systems, be completely altered by these changes to individual library lists.

In larger installations, both development and production program libraries should be under independent control and supervised by the control section or operations manager. The librarian function should not be under the control of the system programmers, operators or application programmers. In smaller installations, this separation of duties may not be available and auditors will need to satisfy themselves that programs under development may be kept separate from those in live systems.

Program development should be permitted only in development environments. This may involve the use of access control software to keep live files logically separate from development files (in different directories, for example); it may even mean development has to take place on a separate machine. Access by application programmers should be restricted to those test and development files with which they are concerned. Development staff should only be allowed access to production programs and data under closely controlled conditions in circumstances such as job failures with critical deadlines. Any editing changes to production programs should be monitored by the system and authorised by management and the state of amended files before and after alteration should be recorded for later scrutiny by installation management and for audit.

Changes to programs can be made in two ways. First, the source code may be changed and recompiled into new executable programs (called object programs). Second, the old executable programs may be directly 'patched'. Facilities to do this are often supplied as part of the operating system or can be utilised through operating system facilities. Controls should ensure that any alterations to production programs are to the source code. 'Patching' of executable programs (which is extremely difficult and requires a detailed knowledge of the computer's low level programming language) should be permitted only in exceptional circumstances. Amendments to production programs should always be carefully controlled and documented.

Auditors should pay particular attention to the control of program libraries. Unless adequate controls exist, any other audit activity concerning the examination of programs and the operation of systems may be invalidated. Auditors should assess whether development program libraries (directories) and production program libraries are closely controlled and distinguished clearly in the user structure and catalogue. They should examine the procedures whereby new versions of programs, once tested and approved, are transferred from test to production libraries or directories. Auditors should also consider testing the operation of this control (particularly if it is felt to be weak) by examination of amendment authorisations and program versions. This can be aided by examining directory or library listings for dates of last program updates; the auditor may also consider the use of computer assisted audit techniques such as program comparison and program review. The auditor should test to determine whether on-line programming is restricted to development files, assess the access permissions granted to programmers, examine the adequacy of reports which record programming activity and ensure that these records are properly scrutinised by management.

The auditor should also be aware of the power of various software aids and utilities in the system software which may allow files (data, parameter, JCL) to be accessed, amended or copied and ensure that such facilities are reasonably controlled. Well controlled facilities should produce reports of use which should be examined by staff independent of the users of these facilities. Auditors may examine these reports and seek confirmation from the system log and library documentation that such programs are not used at other times.

Provision for File Back-up and Standby

Management should provide adequate facilities to permit recovery from loss or corruption of code or data caused by hardware or software faults. Backed up files should be stored securely and protected from fire, water and other hazards. Copies of back-ups should be stored away from the computer site.

Many operating systems take back-up copies of files automatically at a frequency specified either by the user or the installation manager. Sometimes this applies only to files currently on line. For systems where automatic backup does not occur users may be wholly responsible for the provision of back-up facilities for all files.

In some systems, security copying of files is handled manually or at least by invocation of separate JCL instructions and great care must be exercised to ensure security copies are taken of all main files at an appropriate time. These arrangements should cover the system software (including system files), production programs and application files.

The frequency of both automatic dumping and dumps of individual files depends on the policies of the site and the nature and volume of the work processed. Site policy should be dictated by the cost of a breakdown in the system, balanced against the cost of providing security and the likelihood of breakdown.

Additional back-up copies of files and programs will be required for use at a standby site, both for testing purposes and in the event of prolonged 'shut down' of an organisation's computing facilities. It is important that all files, including system software files, form part of the periodic test of standby computer arrangements and that decisions have been taken as to what data are required at the standby site and what the security risks may be if the standby facility involves the shared use of a machine and system software, rather than sole use of an alternative computer system.

Security over back-up files – particularly operating system dump files – is important to ensure adequate protection to normal data and special protection for sensitive information (eg lists of passwords, access rights).

The auditor should attempt to assess the adequacy of the back-up and recovery arrangements, both for the system as a whole and for specific applications – particularly those which are time critical. The auditor should determine from operations staff, analysts and JCL listings the stage at which copies are taken, where these are actually stored – whether on-line, in a safe or off-site – and the length of retention periods used. Some of this data may be recorded in the system journal. The auditor should also consider the security afforded to operating system dump files and other back-up files.

Standby computing facilities and data preparation, operating and clerical procedures should be examined to ensure that adequate consideration has been given to restarting processing on a standby computer. This should include the transfer and use of own system software and system files as necessary. Such facilities should have the agreement of staff involved, be fully documented and tested at least once a year.

Gathering and recording information on jobs run

Journals and Logs

System software may provide journal files which can be used for a number of management and control purposes. Standard journals are often provided by the supplier of the operating system and may be used by the installation as supplied or else developed and tailored by 'tuning' or programming to suit individual requirements. However, journals often contain large quantities of data and their use may be limited by the following difficulties:

— mass of technical data;

    —   facilities afforded by the system to 'switch off' (or opt not to 'switch on') journal recording; and

    —   limited file space causing the journal file to overflow and be lost.

It may be necessary to tailor aspects of the monitoring facility by 'tuning' the system, by using packages designed to review the logged information or by 'in-house' software development.

Types of Journal

The following are typical of the basic journal information which may be available from larger systems, although the data will not necessarily be written to separate journal files. The more primitive the system software, the less information is usually recorded:

System journal – contains data giving an overall picture of system activity, including general system data, security data including security violations, error monitoring information and performance data.

Accounting journal – contains data required by the installation for its resource accounting and budgeting. It summarises the resource usage of all jobs.

Hardware error log – contains details of hardware errors for diagnostic analysis.

Job journals – created for every job in the system. These contain details of job initialisation, execution and conclusion for batch jobs, remotely entered background jobs and interactive processing initiated via terminals. The detail may include the amount of memory allocated, CPU and peripherals usage, number of peripheral transfers, job start and finish times, volume of print produced and cost of job. Details of operations including error messages and details of use of run-time amendments to programs may also be included. Prints from the job journal are often returned to initiators of jobs for examination.

User journals – contain information concerning system usage and job monitoring for an individual user name in the system. One user journal can be created for each user name.

Budgets and accounts – a budget is typically the maximum amount of the resource that users or jobs are allowed to consume over a given period. Actual work may be charged to an account, which provides a record of the amounts of specified resources consumed by users. All jobs should be charged to an account. Each application and user group in the system should have a separate account with a budget. Accounts and budgets should be monitored and controlled both by user management and installation management. Charging for computer services may help to overcome the problem of unauthorised use of computer facilities if responsible individuals are required to monitor their budget and computer usage.

Journals can sometimes be printed in natural language format. Some journals can be analysed using interrogation programs, but others are held in a format or structure that makes simple interrogation problematic.

Journal Security

Access to journal files and journal print-outs should be restricted. Each journal file should be set up under the control of the senior user in the access control hierarchy with privacy controls to ensure that journal information cannot be amended or deleted.

Journalised data should be regularly and promptly distributed to those people in the organisation who have an interest in it. Senior management require summary reports, line management require sufficient detail to confirm compliance with laid down procedures and operations staff require detailed indication of the correct function of the system. Users need enough information to be satisfied that their work has been fully and accurately processed and correctly charged to their account.

Auditors should appraise whether journalised data is being produced and whether it is being analysed by the staff responsible and ensure that action is being taken where appropriate. They should assess the adequacy of the journal data produced and whether too little or too much is being collected. They should also ensure that management makes use of information available in the journal files, particularly as a method of checking on unauthorised jobs.

The auditor should be able to examine information produced by the various journalising facilities. The use of journal reporting facilities or, where available, interrogation facilities, should be considered to search journals in connection with examination of file and user security, performance monitoring or utilisation (this information can be either cumulative or on a 'snapshot' basis), job accounting and security violations.

Implementing and tuning

As already described, system software can be amended by additional installation programming, through special entry points in the original code or through 'add-on extras'.

The auditor should determine what version of the key system software is currently in use and ascertain whether any changes have been made. This can be done in discussions with senior management, although other evidence of amendment should be considered (e.g. load time procedures, 'alters', purchase and maintenance documentation relating to added features or new programs, departures from standard system software features or information arising from informal discussions). Proper amendment documentation, including objectives, justifications and authority, should be available for audit examination. Although changed system software facilities may be tested in course of other processing, it may not be possible for auditors to fully probe this area.

10.24

Assessing machine performance

An assessment of machine performance can be derived from statistics compiled either automatically by the system or manually by operations staff. Such an assessment of performance data is likely to be generated from the journals discussed above. It may be required by individual users about the work done by and for them, installation or operations management about the system as a whole or corporate management.

Individual User Job Data

Such data may include:

- terminal session details including the length of time terminals are connected and a record of communications between user and system; and

- transaction processing service details, including start and close time, number of transactions, response times, use of files, record of terminal and other failures and attempted security violations.

Installation Manager and Operations Manager

Required data may include:

Service log – may be compiled manually by operations staff and should show:

- System availability for each shift: routine and extraordinary down-time; and central hardware unit problems (ie down-time) plus comments.

- Transaction processing availability (ie overall time in hours and individual service problems).

- Communications hardware (ie overall availability in hours and individual service problems).

- Terminal users' service record, usually compiled weekly by individual users for analysis and action by computer staff, records down-time and up-time each day and narrative analysis of response time.

System statistics – produced with facilities provided by the supplier of the system software or designed and implemented by installation programmers or derived from software and hardware monitors. The statistics might include:

- Details of the level of service, including the number of terminal and batch jobs in the system; number of transaction processing messages being processed; response items; average length of jobs and average amount of resources used.

- Analysis for each type of job: use of main store and CPU time; transfers per second; and amount of resources being used.

10.25

— Details of hardware usage, including utilisation of CPU and main store, utilisation of peripheral channels and devices and number of transfers per second and messages sent and received on communications lines.

Such information can be written away as accumulated figures of usage or as 'snapshots' of the machine state at regular intervals (eg number of programs in memory). This information can be later printed and analysed, using various types of diagrams and graphical representations to indicate an overall profile of machine utilisation and performance.

The auditor should assess whether adequate statistics are compiled and scrutinised regularly by suitable levels of management and users and that investigative or corrective action is taken where necessary. Auditors should also consider their own assessment of performance statistics and thoroughly investigate any potentially weak areas brought to light.

Other issues

System, Job and User Parameters

Various facilities in the system software may be controlled or limited by the installation. Since the limits applied have an impact on the efficiency of the system software, such areas should be considered by audit. Even when the auditor does not feel personally competent to judge the appropriateness of particular system software parameters, it is often possible to form an opinion:

— if such parameters are only seldom reviewed and adjusted it may indicate weak installation management;

— if terminal response times are slow or file access times are increasing for relatively stable files, one possible cause is inappropriate system parameters.

System limits may include maximum allocations of memory or disk space per user, maximum numbers of terminal connections in any session and CPU time slices.

Jobs may be categorised into different types for scheduling purposes. These categories are known by different names (eg profiles) and define the upper, lower and default limits for a job in that category covering typically:

— constraints on physical resources available to that type of job;

— overall priority in a job queue or priority relative to other competing jobs;

— main store quota and CPU time slice;

— peripheral transfers;

— job timing; and

— output requirements.

It may be possible to change the job category and priority of an individual job during a session. Such changes should be carried out under the direction of the system manager and not an operator.

Based on the detailed performance statistics produced, the system manager should be able to ensure that the upper and lower limits for job categories are reasonable and adjust these limits as necessary to improve efficiency.

Some system software allows an installation manager to ensure that one type of work does not crowd out others and that the machine does not become overloaded. This is done by limiting the number of terminal and batch jobs started concurrently and the number of messages to be processed simultaneously.

The auditor should determine what aspects of the system software can be controlled or limited by the individual installation. The auditor should assess whether the system manager has set up appropriate limits and monitors them in order to maximise performance of the system. Computer resources should be allocated in a way that is both equitable and in the best interests of the organisation.

On-line Files

The allocation of on line file space to users should be controlled by management. In some systems, users are able to leave files in on-line magnetic storage for longer than is necessary and inefficient use of storage facilities may result. The auditor should appraise whether a procedure exists to monitor the allocation and contents of on-line file space in order to ensure the effective utilisation of such resources. This can be done by examining the policy for retaining back-up versions of files, irregularly used and very large files and by examining file (directory) lists for individual users (perhaps on a sample basis). Consideration should also be given to the use made of automatic file deletion facilities (eg all files not accessed for 60 days) for the erasure of old generations. It may also be possible to ascertain from management the general efficiency of file storage on line, the frequency of 'jams' and the success of their efforts to 'prune' on-line file storage.

10.3 Audit Use of System Software

10.3.1 Overview

The use of IT is an essential part of modern auditing and, while the use and exploitation of modern system sof ware require auditors to develop additional skills, they offer improvements in both the scope and efficiency of audit coverage.

10.3.2 Benefits

Use of audit software

System software offers auditors a number of benefits in their use of audit software. Audit jobs can be made easier to run by taking advantage of the flexibility of the file handling facilities and by allowing parameters to be inserted at run time. Auditors can use the operating system to set up jobs to give on-line information retrieval.

Access to utilities

Modern system software offer auditors the opportunity for simple and independent access to a range of suppliers' utilities to conduct a number of standard data processing functions (eg sorting, merging, copying, printing, file editing) without the need for detailed involvement in the full program operating procedures and often with only a limited knowledge of JCL.

These facilities are required almost all of the time for anyone involved in data retrieval and manipulation and are used by auditors during software developments and as part of information retrieval (eg sorts). They are particularly useful where there is only limited knowledge of JCL or underlying software. It is also important for the auditor to gain an understanding of the power of such utilities in order to be aware of the control risks and other audit implications (ie record deletion facilities may be found in some sort utilities).

Some utilities provide the auditor with tools for computer assisted auditing. For example, standard file comparison programs may be used to compare an authenticated copy of an application program with the copy in use; standard query languages may be used for computer interrogation.

Machine and user activity

As already stated, modern system software offers considerable facilities to restrict and control machine and user activity. It may also offer inspection facilities for the audit by management (and audit) of who has accessed the machine and for what purpose and whether unauthorised access has been attempted. Journal and log files can be interrogated and analysed to detect password guessing, production file access and illegal processing or attempts to process. The means are also available, although they must be used with both care and planning, to directly test via a terminal the mechanisms for controlling access to the machine and to specific data files and program libraries.

Consideration of machine and user activity and management control over these areas should form part of a control review of computerised systems and subsequent testing. Audit needs to be aware of the possibilities for control and the obstacles to a fully effective security system. If other work indicates deficiencies or weaknesses are suspected, then the auditor should attempt to test these control features. System files containing details of access etc. may be the only means available to test the use of certain restricted facilities (eg special programs or special system software functions).

Performance measurement

System software, through job accounting software and, in some instances, integral software monitors, can log and output in printed form information on machine utilisation and efficiency. Whilst auditors should encourage installation management to use such facilities to the full, they can also be used in independent audit examination of the performance of the configuration and hardware serviceability. Performance monitoring is, in the first instance, a role of management, but it is suggested that auditor involvement, in what is a complex field of activity, should be considered when it is felt the computer is not performing to its capabilities, where there is no spare capacity or where there seems to be an obstacle (a processing 'bottleneck') to better utilisation.

10.29

CHAPTER 11

AUDIT OF DATABASE SYSTEMS

11

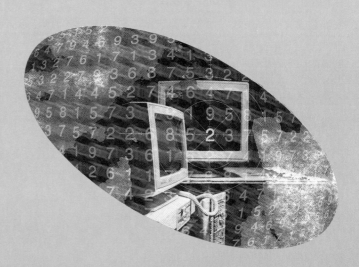

11.1 Introduction

This chapter provides a basic understanding of database systems and of the particular system software associated with them; eg database management systems (DBMS), data dictionaries and query languages. It also describes the objectives of a database audit and the areas of concern to the auditor.

11.1.1 What is a Database ?

A database is a structured collection of data which is intended to enable the organisation to separate the holding of data from the programming necessary to manipulate that data. A term frequently used synonymously with 'database' is 'management information system' which is actually a collection of sub-systems designed to provide management with timely and relevant information upon which decisions can be made. Some of these sub-systems though can be computerised and may use database techniques.

Data held in a database is usually structured according to one of three methods: hierarchical, relational and Codasyl.

Hierarchical systems

These are based on a tree like data structure. Access to individual data is on a top down basis where each layer of records can be related to any number of data record below it in the hierarchy but can only have one record above it.

Relational systems

In a relational database, data is represented as two dimensional arrays that can be formatted and reformatted into relationships. In a truly relational database such relationships would be established at run time by joining two separate records or tables. The record or table consists of rows (records) and columns (data item fields). Row ordering is not of importance, but each row can be uniquely identified by the values of one or more columns and is known as the 'key'. Such a database offers infinite flexibility in the views that could be taken of the data and provides an excellent basis for information management systems and enquiries.

It should be noted that the adoption of a pure relational database could adversely affect performance and the amount of data that may be held. That is because of the greater amount of processing activity involved in accessing the database and careful evaluation of demand and resources is required before choosing a relational database. It is for that reason the majority of relational databases utilise some form of indexing to overcome the performance problems of a true relational database.

Some hardware suppliers have designed their equipment to make maximum use of relational database techniques and only suply relational database products as the means of holding and manipulating data, thus optimising their efficiency.

Codasyl systems

CODASYL is the acronym for the Conference on Data Systems Languages which is an organisation that defines standards for databases to ensure quality and uniformity. A number of proprietary database systems conform to such standards.

Examples of Database Products

Product	Type
IMS, DL/1	Hierarchical
DB2, 4	Relational
ORACLE	Relational
INGRES	Relational
PARADOX	Relational
SEQUEL	Relational
IDMS	Codasyl
IDS, DMIV	Codasyl
TOTAL	Codasyl

11.1.2 Database Strategies

An organisation could place all of its data on one database. That would eliminate all duplication of data items and could appear to offer great savings in the cost of collecting and storing data. However, there is an optimum size for a database which will depend upon the capability of the DBMS, the resources available and the data requirements of the organisation. Few organisations have adopted single databases in practice because their size creates major operational difficulties and an unacceptably high overhead including the cost of reconstituting a corrupted database.

Some organisations have adopted the approach of developing several independent databases which are interlinked by the DBMS with a single data dictionary for locating the required data items. Others have developed separate databases based on major business functions such as personnel, property and financial accounts.

As indicated earlier some organisations equipped with networks of mini and micro computers have opted for a system of distributed databases because it is possible to hold parts of a database at physically remote locations. For example a mini computer dedicated to a debtors system may

11.2

hold in memory a large part of the total income database, with other income data items being held on separate computers.

11.1.3 Why Use a Database ?

In recent years most organisations have faced growing demands for data to be made available not only for corporate applications but also for end-user computing. in addition applications and their data requirements, are becoming increasingly complex and with the use of fourth generation languages are being developed at greater speed. This has led to problems with the availability and accessibility of data.

In response to those problems, managers have looked to integrated information systems for solutions. The main elements of such systems are:

– A data dictionary or directory which specifies what data is and where it is used. It should be a dynamic dictionary which causes all changes to the data held in the dictionary to be automatically reflected in all other relevant places eg other data files and programs which use that data.

– A database or file management system which receives all requests for data from all programs and knows through the dictionary, where the data is, retrieves it and transmits it back to the relevant program. It should give total data independence so that programs are able to ask for data by group or by item. It should also handle requests from all types of programs eg corporate and departmental or end user programs.

– User friendly facilities for manipulation of data and the production of reports including graphics and which:

– allow them to retrieve data through the database or file management system in the same way as corporate applications;

– give the ability to merge this data with their own personal data; and

– give the ability to merge data with text, image and voice.

– An application generation language to increase the productivity of application developers.

In an ideal situation the products in these four areas should be fully integrated. The major problem facing most organisations is the significant investment of time and money in their current range of products, some of which may not be easily integrated. Consequently a smooth migration path to an integrated environment must be defined.

11.1.4 Database Management System Software

To implement database processing successfully it is necessary to describe data at varying levels and providing mappings/relationships between the various layers enabling application software to interface. To achieve this it is necessary to install specialised software which functions along other system software such as the operating system and on-line application software to provide the necessary facilities.

That software is often referred to as database management software and it is used to create and maintain the database, to store and retrieve data in response to application programs and to provide recovery procedures and a degree of security and privacy over data.

The major components of the software are:

–   A data description language which is used to describe firstly the physical description of the whole data base ie its structure and relationships and secondly, the logical representation of the data items available for use by individual application programs often known as the data view.

–   A data manipulation language (DML) which is used by application programs to access the data base. The degree of compatibility between the DML and the language in which the application is written will have a great effect upon the efficiency of the application.

–   A device media control language which is used to describe the physical data organisation of the database and provides a mechanism for reorganising the structure

–   A query language which can be procedural with a formal syntax and vocabulary like COBOL or structured like SQL with high-level data definition and manipulation commands enabling entry into a system at the screen and by batch input, or by embedded commands in batch or on-line mode. The latter type of language enables definition of tables, indexes and views to be structured in order to manipulate data and its output format.

–   Recovery procedures which should include facilities to:

    –   upload and down load;

    –   journalise all types of processing;

    –   automatically or manually recover from failure;

    –   continue process while separate parts of the database are recovered.

–   Integrity routines which will check on the existence of the cross reference linkages between related data items. Usually such facilities will only check for the existence of these links. The organisation may have to develop its own software if it wishes to check that the correct linkages exist. It will also check on the types of records stored and the

11.4

contents of data. The DBMS however cannot check the integrity of the application data. This has to be checked by the application prior to passing the data to the DBMS. Additionally the versions of software and applications can be checked to ensure compatibility.

— Data lockout facilities which will prevent the accessing of data by two applications at the same time.

— Journals which provide logs of transaction processing, performance statistics, failure and recovery details, applications utilising the data base, details of the user, details of operations performed and capacity utilised, details of interventions from computing staff.

— A data dictionary which is a file holding a list of all data items to be found on the organisation's database(s). It includes a definition of the data item and information about its location. A data dictionary can in practice be either free-standing or part of a DBMS and integrated with the database software enabling design, modification and retrieval processes to operate in conjunction with the dictionary. Use of the dictionary improves standards, documentation and the design of a system. It also enables applications to check data using stored validation rules. Thus any changes in the rules need only be entered once in the dictionary rather than changing all applications involved.

11.1.5 Data Management and Administration

Data administration is a policy oriented function concerned with the implementation of the overall strategy for the use of an organisation's data resource whereas database administration is a technically based function with the main responsibilities being the day-to-day management of the data and the efficient working of the DBMS. The two functions are usually combined and the individual appointed to discharge those functions is usually known as the database administrator. The administrator will normally be responsible for setting guidelines for all matters relating to data and arbitrating between all parties concerned. Both functions will have a major impact upon the implementation of a database and the development of any new database applications.

The implementation of a database raises issues of data ownership, rights of access, retrieval, security and accountability. The database administrator should ensure that formal standards and directions are produced for use by the organisation which set out clearly the responsibilities and authority of the various individuals concerned with the collection, processing and utilisation of data and specifying the uses that may be made of data. Control procedures should also be set up for authorising and controlling access to data, ensuring the security of data generally and the integrity of data passed to the DBMS,

Any proposals for the development of new database applications should be reviewed by the data administrator to ensure that the proposed system will be compatible with the data strategy of the organisation prior to the formation and approval of a development team.   During the specification stage the development team will have to ensure that the system complies with the guidelines set out by the data administrator. Subsequently when the application has been specified and agreed and accepted and passed to the IT department the system analyst, who is responsible for designing the application and the database administrator, who is responsible for meeting the data requirement of the system, will need to work in parallel on the project.

In summary, the role and responsibilities of the database administrator are to:

– ensure that the organisation's overall strategy for data is being met;

– ensure that users data requirements are being met;

– control the physical design of the database and its continuing maintenance;

– control the data dictionary and all database related software;

– create and enforce defined procedures and standards for identification and common definitions of items of data and any changes to them, assignment of ownership of data and rights of access and, identify problems and arbitrate on issues arising;

– design and operate integrity controls over the database;

– provide and test backup and recovery procedures including archiving of dormant data;

– review application system changes to confirm compatibility with DBMS requirements; and

– monitor performance of the DBMS with a view to optimal use of resources.

11.1.6 Data Security and Integrity

Security

DBMS facilities may afford additional security for data processed by application programs which interface with the DBMS. It is provided primarily through the function of the data dictionary and the data description language which produces the data view for an application.

In effect the system produces a temporary file containing only those entities or records and data items or fields required by the application. Such data views may only be set up by the administrators if properly authorised. In the absence of such 'data views' then an application program cannot access data. The effectiveness of this security facility will depend upon the control exercised during the setting up and maintenance of data views and the design of the database to prevent back door entry which is the responsibility of the database administrator.

11.6

Data integrity

The inputting of inaccurate or incorrect data into a database, or the inability to trace or access data items within the database, is likely to have a significant effect upon the organisation because of the use made of the data by others.

Whilst the DBMS together with the operating system and networking software should ensure that only approved and authorised applications may update the database, the responsibility for ensuring the validity and accuracy of data passed for entry to the database rests with the owner of the application programs. Application programs should therefore contain adequate verification and validation routines to ensure the integrity of data before it is passed to the DBMS.

Responsibility for ensuring that data is not lost or corrupted once it has been entered onto the database lies with the data administrator using the DBMS for that purpose. A major problem arises when linkages of data items and records become corrupted or broken and subsequently data items are inaccessible because they are not correctly indexed. Such situations may be evidenced in a variety of ways eg:

- the production of inaccurate or incomplete information;

- failure leading to an imbalance of data items with numerical values;

- a 'walk through' of the database undertaken specifically to check the correctness of or completeness of pointers.

Most DBMSs do incorporate integrity checking routines which can be used to identify broken or corrupted linkages. However the running of such checks can make heavy demands upon resources and should be used selectively based on risk assessment. Alternative measures are to make partial and full back up copies to enable corrupted linkages to be restored.

Integrity of processing

The ability to total selected data items throughout the database on a regular daily basis to establish the completeness and accuracy of processing may prove difficult because of the particular design of the database. Alternative techniques may include:

Before and After Imaging

When a transaction is presented to the database, but before it is used to update the database, it may be possible for the application program to take and hold a copy or image of the transaction data and of the relevant record. These images can then be merged by the application program to produce an image of how the record should appear after it has been updated. The actual updating of the record is then completed within the database and the image of the record is then compared with the record held on the database. If they do not match appropriate action can then be instigated (ie abandon the update or continue with the update but flag and report the error).

11.7

Such a check should be operationally efficient, in that it can be completed within an acceptable time scale, as it is applied only to the records which are to be altered. It provides an effective check on the updating of the database and can be applied in either a real time or a batch updating environment.

Control Totals

An application program could maintain control totals for a variety of data fields which could then be compared with the database whenever it is totalled. Any discrepancy could suggest that:

- the database has been corrupted by an illegal action; or

- there is an error in the application program which has resulted in the loss of data or the generation of incorrect data; or

- the DBMS has mishandled data.

The frequency of the totalling of the database and the lack of historic data records may however mean that neither the point in time at which an error occurred nor the records or data items affected may be identifiable. An alternative technique is the use of data segment counts.

Data Segment Count

It may be possible for an application program to maintain a control total of the number of data segments (a data segment is a collection of related data items forming part of a record). It should then be possible to count the number of data segments present on the database which may be done more frequently than the totalling of the database. By comparing the control total maintained by the application program with the actual numbers of data segments on the database, some control can be exercised over the database on a more frequent basis. If a discrepancy exists it should be possible, dependent upon the frequency of the check and the adequacy of historic data files to re create and correct the database.

Such a check will only highlight errors which have resulted in the loss or creation of data segments. It will not detect errors at a more detailed level, ie loss of a data item or the existence of an incorrect figure within a data item.

Control Totalling within Selected Data Segments

The resource requirement for a database totalling routine may be significant because of the large number of records and the large number of data items within each record. While the number of records the routine would have to read cannot be reduced other than by splitting the database into two or more separate databases it may be possible to reduce the number of data items which have to be read.

Dependent upon the number of records on the database it may be possible to total selected data fields at the end of each day or after each update. Traditional control total techniques could then

11.8

be applied.

The scope of the check will be limited to the use of data items which can be efficiently accessed or read. These may or may not include any financial fields, though it will usually be possible to find a field which may be totalled to produce a hash total. Such a check provides a means of exercising a degree of continuous control over the database and would immediately highlight any major errors, thus affording the opportunity to restore and correct the database before any use is made of the data by other applications.

11.2 Audit Approach

11.2.1 Objectives

Introduction

The primary objectives of the management of a database system is to maintain the integrity of the database and to optimise the use of the facilities provided by the system in support of the IT strategies and business needs of the organisation. In turn the primary objectives of the auditor are to evaluate and test the control procedures for ensuring the security of the database and review and assess the adequacy of the management arrangements for the efficient and effective use of the database system.

In pursuit of those objectives the auditor will need to address the following subjects in particular:

- the costs of acquiring and maintaining a database;

- access control features and the integrity and maintenance of the database;

- the development of database applications;

- the control of database applications; and

- the ability to retrieve data from the database.

The underlying principles of the audit of the security of database systems are the same as for the audit of system software dealt with in chapter 10. The particular point concerns the high degree of dependency on the availability of a central pool of information and the accompanying degree of vulnerability of that pool to loss, corruption and improper use and in turn therefore the measures taken and the controls provided to prevent or minimise the risk.

As far as value for money is concerned, not all auditors will feel able to conduct a technical evaluation of a database system but they should be able to make a judgement on the measures taken by management to obtain value for money from the use of database systems including the management arrangements for administration of the database system. To do so auditors need an awareness and understanding of the functional and operational aspects of database systems and their management dealt with in the first two parts of this chapter.

As with any audit the starting point is the gathering of information necessary to understand the subject matter and to determine the audit programme and particular audit objectives. The audit techniques to be employed in the review are no different to those employed in any other technical audit. A particular point to be borne in mind is that the audits of database systems and of applications using the database may impact on each other. The scope and particular objectives of the database audit need to be carefully and closely defined if they are to be achieved.

11.2.2 Acquisition of the Database

The audit of the acquisition of a database and DBMS software should in general terms be treated in the same as the audit of the acquisition of other computing facilities as described in chapter 5. The particular factors affecting database acquisitions to which the auditor should have regard are as follows:

–   The management arrangements for the administration of the database system and creation of a database necessitates the appointment of a database administrator. The auditor should be satisfied that such an appointment has been made and the appropriate responsibilities and executive powers assigned.

–   The consequential cost of the acquisition may be larger than the initial purchase price particularly where the acquisition is associated with the development of an on- line system. Hardware costs may be incurred, for example, because of the additional disk storage for the extra data it will manage.

–   In most organisations there will have to be a major reorganisation of existing data files with the need for a period of dual processing to facilitate a smooth changeover. There will also be an increased administration cost involved with many organisations forming a new data administration section within the IT department and a consequential need to undertake a comprehensive training programme.

–   The organisation's procedures may not be suitable for dealing with such a unique type of purchase (most organisations will only ever purchase one DBMS) particularly the procedures relating to competitive tendering.

–   There may not be sufficient technical advice available within the organisation because of the uniqueness of the purchase and some organisations may feel the need to employ specialist advice when selecting their software.

–   The range of products suitable for use by the organisation may be restricted because of the existing computer configuration although open systems are now an acknowledged standard and therefore this restriction is reducing.

— As with other software products, DBMS suppliers are unlikely to modify their product to suit individual user requirements. It is doubtful that any package will completely fulfil the organisation's technical specification and so the organisation will have to undertake an appraisal of competing DBMS to establish which establish which most closely meets its specification.

— Any purchase must be in accordance with the business and information strategy of the organisation and must be undertaken in accordance with EC Directives and Decisions.

11.2.3 Database Access Control Features and Integrity

The DBMS is only one of several interdependent software packages which combine to produce a safe and secure operating environment. It is suggested that the auditor should not review the DBMS in isolation but as part of a review of all systems software and application controls.

A reasonable degree of technical knowledge and understanding is required before the auditor embarks upon any review of the more specialised facilities of a DBMS such as:

— the adequacy and effectiveness of the lock-out procedures;

— the efficiency and versatility of the query language;

— the adequacy of the data privacy controls provided by the system;

— the frequency with which recovery, reorganisation and integrity checking routines are tested;

— the quality of management information produced relating to the performance of the DBMS and the results of integrity checks; and

— the completeness and accuracy of the data dictionary.

Access to the database structure can be limited by the DBMS to prevent unauthorised changes to the data structure. It is important that only authorised persons have such access and that work done through that access is regularly monitored as a means of control. The primary control objective is to ensure that changes, alterations, reorganisations, deletions and so on, are controlled and traceable thus helping to prevent any adverse impact to applications through uncontrolled changes to the database structure.

Database integrity

Controls should be present to ensure that the DBMS maintains database integrity. The DBMS should have its own integrity checks to identify error conditions such as unwanted duplication of data, references to non existent data, inspection and repair of corruption referential integrity and invalid pointers. The auditor should check that either the DBMS has been set up to carry out automatic checks or that regular checks are initiated by the database administrator. Procedures should also be present to enable an application to be suspended if it fails or corrupts data. Processing controls should be in place to prevent such data errors occurring initially.

Data dictionary

It is important to ensure that the data dictionary is the correct version for the particular database to enable it to properly reflect the structure of the database. Access to the dictionary needs to be controlled and on a need to know only basis. Security copies should be maintained in the event there is a need for recovery.

Maintenance and recovery

The auditor should review the following safeguards to evaluate the adequacy of the provision made for maintenance and recovery of the database:

  — Back-up directory structures: copies should be held of previous file allocation tables and directory entries.

  — Read-after-write verification which if automatically performed after each disk write will provide assurance that the data written is re-readable at the time of verification. An in-situ fix if available will enable the faulty area on the disk to be marked as bad and the data to be relocated to a good area whilst not affecting normal operation.

  — Mirrored drives which enable the activity on one disk drive to be shadowed on another drive.

  — Duplexed drives which provide mirroring and duplication of controllers and power supplies. Upon disk failure a switch is made from the original image to the mirrored image and the data is automatically redirected to another disk area.

  — Duplexed controllers which behave like mirrored drives. If one controller fails the mirrored controller takes over until the failed controller is functioning again.

  — Transaction tracking system which ensures that one change to the database is completed before another is commenced.

  — Automatic roll-back which if a database update fails the database is rolled back to a previous point of consistency.

  — Roll-forward recovery by which in the event of failure the transaction tracking system restores the database to the last successful snapshot state and then applies the archived data to reconstruct the database.

11.12

Journalisation and management trails

Because the costs of management trails and complete journalisation are high their use is often restricted or does not occur in practice. Auditors should ascertain the current practice in the organisation and evaluate the consequent risks of any such restricted or non-practice, The same considerations apply where archiving and security dumps and copies of files are restricted or do not occur in practice.

Efficiency, monitoring and optimisation of the database

The auditor should ascertain what action is carried out by the database administrator to maintain performance of the system such as the regular review of packing density, sizing of buffering space for enquiry facilities and the use of optional indexing facilities. The DBMS reporting facilities should be continuously or frequently to enable prompt re-optimisation of the system if required.

11.2.4 Application Development Procedures

Introduction

The objectives of the auditor in reviewing an organisation's application development procedures are set out in chapter 8. The following additional objectives should be considered if the application utilises an existing database or requires the creation of a new one:

- The adequacy of the existing division of duties between the database administrator and the application development project team and between the database administrator and the systems analysts.

- The adequacy and scope of standards or guidelines issued by the data administration function.

- The compliance of the application development group with those standards.

- The effectiveness of communications between the database administrator, systems analyst and the user.

- The arrangements for the identification of data items requiring additional security which will affect the design of the database.

- The arrangements for testing the implementation of a new or modified database.

Management arrangements

The essence of the auditors' task is to identify what the management arrangements to evaluate them and to test for compliance. The auditor should in particular check that the proposed course of action accords with the strategies and policies of the organisation and the role and functions of the database administrator. Standards and procedures should be checked to ensure that the role of the database administrator is maintained namely the co-ordination and control of all processes to implementation and subsequent performance monitoring. In addition a check should be carried out to verify that written procedures are available and current and that sufficient training has been given to all staff using the system.

Identification of data items

The identification of data items requiring additional security may prove to be a very difficult task as it has to be undertaken at a very early stage in the development of the application. The development group may also be constrained by certain technical limitations particularly if the application will be utilising data from an existing database. While it may be possible to reorganise an existing database to provide the necessary security, the database administrator may have to deal with conflicting requirements from other applications utilising that database.

Implementation and testing of the database

Implementation

The auditors primary objective is to verify that all converted or captured data is complete and correct before the system is operational. Data integrity checks should be made on all data or on a sample of appropriate size. In addition the auditor should verify that there will be adequate logging, data back-up, reporting, management of disk space and facilities for detecting and correcting system errors without disrupting other processing.

Testing

The auditor's primary aim is to verify that the new or modified database is tested and operated with sample data and interfacing in a test environment and only moved into the live system environment when operational integrity, access controls, logging and journalisation and recovery processes are confirmed as correct. Testing should be documented as should any changes made to the database structure. Such records will assist the auditor in identifying default values and controls and to provide evidence of the level and quality of testing undertaken. It is advantageous if users and audit staff are involved at this stage.

11.2.5 Database Application Controls

The objectives of the auditor in reviewing a live system are set out in chapter 9, *Audit of Application Systems*. The following additional objectives should be considered if the application utilises an existing database or requires the creation of a new one:

The following additional objectives arise if the application under review uses database techniques:

— the effectiveness of data security procedures taking into account the inter-relationship with system software;

- the adequacy of data and database integrity checks;

- the adequacy of the procedure for requesting access to data, especially where distributed database systems are supported;

- the applicability and correctness of accesses currently granted to the application;

- the adequacy of data retrieval facilities for use by the user of the system and for audit purposes;

- the adequacy of recovery procedures and the retention of historic data;

- the adequacy of any back-up system for use if the database is unavailable for any reason;

- the adequacy of the control exercised over the updating of the database; and

- the role of the database administrator, data dictionary, the use of database utilities and their effect upon controls and the change control procedures (which will probably need to be more vigorous than in conventional systems).

Data security procedures and the system for requesting access to data should have been defined by the data administration function and set out in standards. The auditor should be familiar with those standards and should conduct tests to verify that the application incorporates the standard procedures and that they are effective.

The auditor should also test and evaluate the frequency with which the integrity of the database is checked and whether it is phased to ensure that if discrepancies are revealed the system can be successfully re-created.

The auditor may also choose to review, test or verify other matters such as:

- Identification of data requiring additional security.

- The design of the database to facilitate such security.

- Error and exception reports produced by the system.

- The documentation generated by a request to access data against established standards for completeness, appropriateness and authorisation.

- User manuals for completeness and adequacy.

- The arrangements for back-up and security copies of data files and their frequency.

The auditor could also obtain from the database administrator details of the established procedures for checking against the development sections' documentation of the application. The compliance test could usefully cover such matters as authorising and checking requests for access, the maintenance of the integrity of the database and the recovery of the database.

The auditor should also review the frequency with which the integrity of the database is checked though such checking should be phased to ensure that if a discrepancy is discovered the system can be successfully re-created.

11.2.6 Data Retrieval

Databases have a more complicated structure than traditional files and contain larger volumes of data; they are also only accessible through the interface with the DBMS. Consequently the interrogation of database files may present the user with difficulties and problems. There are however a variety of software facilities and programs available detailed below which have been designed to overcome such difficulties and problems.

Enquiry languages and report writers

Enquiry languages and report writers are usually part of the DBMS package. Enquiry languages are designed to interface with the DBMS and offer extensive and powerful facilities. They are however very complex and not always user friendly. Consequently such packages often include standard enquiry routines which the user can utilise by inputting selected parameters. Report writers on the other hand provide a quick and efficient means for simple enquiries and accessing random data held on a database file.

Retrieval software

Several of the commercially available interrogation packages have developed special versions capable of interfacing with particular DBMS packages. As with all other applications, interrogations written in these languages pass instructions to the DBMS which are then performed under the control of the DBMS and the results passed back to the application. The method of operation will be transparent to the user, hence there is little difference in the use of the database version of the package. The interrogation of database files by the use of these packages may be inefficient and time-consuming, particularly on a random search of the file unless great care is taken in the design of the enquiries.

High level language

Interrogations written in COBOL or other high level languages are likely to be processed more efficiently than retrieval packages. Such programming languages also provide a more powerful tool for data manipulation.

Database copy utilities

An alternative method of data retrieval is to copy selected data items or parts of the database to a separate traditionally formatted file which may then be interrogated using traditional methods more easily and with greater speed and efficiency than when accessing a database file. Such an

11.16

approach can also increase the security afforded to data as only selected data will be available for interrogation.

The copying of parts of the database may create operational difficulties and increase processing overheads in terms of the additional resources needed for copying and storing the files. There is also a danger in using stored copies of files that the copy file may not at any point in time accurately reflect the data held on the database file. Consequently the frequency of copying may be very high if the currency of the data is crucial to the purpose of the enquiry or interrogation. Current technological developments in database management particularly in the field of the duplication of databases with alternative structures may eventually overcome such problems.

Audit considerations

Whatever facilities an organisation utilises for interrogation and enquiry of databases it should be appreciated that auditors may lose some of their independence if they need to consult and make arrangements with database administrators for the provision of audit data views or the copying of database files.

CHAPTER 12

AUDIT AND CONTROL OF NETWORKS

12

12.1 Introduction

Networks are one of the fastest growing sectors in IT and will continue to develop as the technology improves and as organisations decentralise their services and adopt radical approaches to the provision of IT to meet the demands for new and more sophisticated services.

Networks are a growing phenomenon and many organisations have begun to recognise that while the network carries all their vital information but that it may not be the most appropriate or operated in the most secure manner. Networks have become the main arteries of information and there is a need for managers and auditors alike to understand the technology to be able to ensure that networks are appropriate to needs, properly managed and secure.

12.2 Objectives

The Commission of the European Communities commissioned a report on network security after fears were expressed about the risks that networks pose to organisations. The study looked at a number of major organisations that were thought to have covered such risks and found even there major weaknesses in the network area that echoed those found in the public sector. The shortcomings most commonly found were:

- the administration of network security was a cause for concern;
- the resilience of the network was not always as effective as it should be thus when the network fails, so may the organisation;
- notable weaknesses were found in telecommunication security, contingency planning, and microcomputer security.

It is evident that networks impose additional risks to an organisation and that auditors have a responsibility to ensure that these risks are acknowledged by management and addressed. Chapter 6, *General Controls*, discusses terminal and network security and controls and this chapter focuses upon the wider considerations of networks.

The five objectives of the auditor are to assess the adequacy and effectiveness of:

- the network strategy;
- how the network is planned, constructed and managed;
- the basic security of data;
- the resilience of the network;

— the cost effectiveness of the network.

12.3 Network Strategies

The size scope and complexity of networks create problems in themselves. Organisations may have a multitude of differing networks ranging from a traditional star structure (connecting the mainframe to workstations) or micros linked to independent wide and local area networks each using a different proprietary system.

The primary objective is for an organisation to gain the advantages of 'open information' with a strategy that provides for rationalisation and realistic plans to put the strategy into effect.

There is also a legal constraint to be addressed. Since 1987 the EC under Decision 87/95 has required authorities in the public sector to migrate to open systems interconnection (OSI) which imposes the requirement for all purchases of local and wide area networks to adhere to the principles of OSI.

12.4 Network Management

12.4.1 Objectives

The primary objective of network management is to achieve a reasonable level of control over the operation of the network whilst optimising the use of the facilities against a background of expansion of facilities available and growth in their use. The particular and detailed objectives are to avoid:

— loss of productivity;

— loss of information;

— reduction in revenues;

— sub optimal decisions;

— time and money spent on diagnosis and repair of the network;

— loss of credibility and customer satisfaction.

Apart from the need to be able to manage staff and customers a crucial need of network managers is for reliable information about the network and how it is performing to enable them to avoid or prevent the above risks and consequential costs. Software, or netware as it is known, provides network management tools ranging from low level information from the operating system to sophisticated network management systems (NMS) and in most networks a substantial amount of information is therefore available but it is not always used.

The evidence is that many organisations have little knowledge about their information flows whether these are on paper or computerised. Initially networks may be too small or much larger than required. The first requirement therefore is for information about the basic information flows, which may be available from manual records but the great majority should be available from either the operating system, the NMS or from statistics gathered from network switches. Unfortunately, whilst this information is available in most organisations it is rarely used to its full effect. Thus in many organisations the first indication that there are problems will be the effect on response times.

Network usage

An indication of traffic flows and peak periods should be available from the system on the basis of users and workstations examples of which are illustrated in the following tables.

On-line Usage by Departments for the Month of May 199X

System	Average Number of Transactions	% of Total	Per Hour (8 Hours)
Financial Ledger	13219	23%	1652
Payments System	12745	22%	1593
Payroll	7029	12%	878
Cash Receipting	2809	5%	351
TOTAL	36945		

Usage by Workstation

Workstation Identifier	Dept.	System	Transactions Per Day
VT001	Treasury	Creditors	6538
VT002	Treasury	FIS	13365
VT003	Treasury	Payroll	8756

Such information may provide management with total traffic volumes on a daily weekly or monthly basis, which systems are the prime users of the network and the departments which could most usefully be surveyed to assess the quality of the service provided.

Response times

It should be noted that the normal average daily response times are not in themselves indicative of the effect on the user because they relate only to the time taken for the online processing system to process the users transaction. Additional time will have to be added for transmission over the network and, if telecommunications are involved, the transmission over the circuits.

At some sites hardware and software may be available to obtain the user's view directly; at others it may only be possible to obtain an overview from stored statistics. In the latter case the auditor may have to produce figures manually for particular application system response times.

System availability

Most large organisations will compile system availability statistics to substantiate fulfilment of any service level agreements that the IT section has negotiated. These figures can be misleading since depending upon the time period used, the average availability figures can be inflated, eg by the production of monthly returns which smooth out daily variations. A daily return is preferable, detailing all the major systems and the reasons behind any system falling below say a level of 95% availability. The returns should also show the availability on an hour by hour basis because a fault during the peak period 9-11 or 2-3.30 will have a far greater impact on users than say after 4.30.

Batch updates

The success or failure of the overnight or day-time batch runs will have a significant effect on the usefulness or availability of the online services. Although not technically part of a network review, both the currency of the data and the responsiveness of the system to deal with the user's requirements will be affected if systems are not updated on schedule. Additional batch runs during the day will also slow down average response times and may require the particular service to be disconnected. The impact on the network makes it worthwhile to obtain details of all re-runs, especially those of high usage systems, for examination of cause and effect. The information should be available from the 'system log' along with error codes ie the reason for a re-run and an indication as to whether corrections were made by users or the operators.

A high incidence of re-runs and call-outs by system staff may be indicative of:

— unstable systems;

— a shortage of backing store, ie jobs failing due to lack of space;

— . inadequate operating instructions;

— inadequate scheduling and consequently associated systems not ready for update.

Network management systems (NMS)

It is important that those organisations with large numbers of networked workstations or external departments should have the means to administer and control the network effectively and efficiently.

Network management systems provide such benefits and usually offer the following facilities:

— graphic representation of the network;

— automatic monitoring of each line ie line failures, threshold levels etc;

— collection and analysis of line states;

— the ability to re-configure the lines once a fault has been detected;

— the ability to test the lines eg loop tests and transmission quality tests;

— adequate statistics for current performance and use for long term planning.

Without such data it is difficult for the organisation to determine what action is required to be able to assure itself of a reliable, secure and effective environment for its systems.

The network is of no use to the user if the telecommunication link is faulty. In many organisations the first indication to the IT section that this has happened is a telephone call from the user. In others the NMS will have detected the fault notified the IT section and perhaps re-routed the lines before the user notices a problem.

In either case the network staff should have records of line faults, the time taken to correct them and details of any re-current problems eg inadequate service levels from a particular exchange or nodes on an internal circuit. Experience shows that there can be problems in identifying what is at fault and who should correct it ie the provider of the circuit or the equipment supplier.

12.5 Security of Networks

12.5.1 Objectives

The principles of the audit of the control and security of networks are substantially the same as those for a central mainframe and for many networks much of the security may be provided by mainframe operations. However, with the provision of distributed computing and decentralisation of operations by networking and the variety of network products employed the responsibility for security may be less well defined and the means of providing security dispersed amongst the user departments themselves.

The central IT department may well provide the technology to achieve security or advise on the matter but the initiative for and overall management of network security should come from the users. Initial enquiries should therefore be made to establish whether management has defined its overall security policy and if so how it is administered. If no policy exists then it may indicate that management does not see it as important and therefore it is likely that few staff will take the situation seriously.

Effective security within a network depends not only on the security system itself but also on management's analysis of risk. Networks by definition, circulate all data round the cable thus making it readily available to all potential users, An important first step for management is therefore to decide whether or not the data is required on the network or is better served by a discrete medium. Furthermore, many organisations have a number of networks and whether or not these require to be linked depends upon the requirements of the users. However, even in a multi-network system, availability and access can be restricted to specified users, either by the network software or by the use of the facilities used to connect the networks.

The auditor should ascertain what separation has been established and whether or not it matches the needs for security on the basis of the users' need or rights to know.

Network bridges, routers and gateways

All interworking between networks requires that the various networks can communicate with each other. There are three methods or devices for connecting networks all of which may be used not only to enhance the overall efficiency and effectiveness of networks but also provide security; they are bridges, routers and gateways.

A bridge operates at layer two of the OSI seven layer model (the datalink) and basically acts as a relay between similar types of networks. A router on the other hand operates at layer three (the network) and sets up and routes packages between dissimilar networks. Gateways exist at layer seven (the application) and provides a link between dissimilar architectures such as IBM system network architecture (SNA) and the international standards organisations open system interconnection (OSI).

Security may be obtained by using such devices to filter out or redirect data between and across wide and local area networks (WANs and LANs) or to divide a LAN into two separate parts and distribute data accordingly. Another useful architectural feature is to include bridges at logical points in the network eg between floors or work-groups. Intelligent programmable bridges may thus be used to control specified data flows between the various parts of the LAN.

As far as efficiency is concerned adaptability to the network traffic is also an important factor in large networks. Conditions can vary widely but large volumes of traffic should not be allowed to bring down the network. Some bridges can recognise congestion and correct the situation by temporarily discarding selective packets of data during peak periods. Bridges may also be used to filter out and divert traffic which is passing from one LAN to another and avoid the data having to navigate the whole of the originating LAN.

Protocols

As data is passed between networks or within a network various messages or commands will be attached to the packets of data. Information such as the identities and addresses of the recipient and the sender is required for the system to be able to handle the data flow. Such protocols, as they are known, provide security but if the identity or authority of the sender is not checked at the receiving workstation on the network then one layer of security may be lost. It is therefore important to ensure that each layer of the packet or part of the message is actually checked either by the receiving equipment or by the network software.

Network software and access control

Many networks provide a range of control features similar to those found within mainframe security systems such as:

- log-in procedures which require user identities and passwords to control access to the file server and user directories;

- user hierarchies ranging from full supervisor access to enquiry only;

- user authority profiles to restrict and control user activity within a directory eg open, read, write, and create;

- file authority to control access to files and their uses.

Within such general levels of security some networks provide a number of further restrictions on access either on a global basis or per user basis such as:

- time restrictions often known as slot times;

- access restricted to nominated and identifiable workstations;

- restrictions on the number of concurrent sessions allowed;

- lock-out after a specified number of unsuccessful attempts to enter the system.

12.6 Resilience

12.6.1 Objectives

The dependency of many organisations on the continuous availability of networks calls for a high degree of resilience in the network system. The key questions for management and auditors alike are how long can an organisation continue to function satisfactorily without the network and how long is the mean time to recovery in the event of partial or complete failure? The factors to be taken into account are:

- the ability of the network to detect, determine and correct faults;

- the degree of redundancy present in the system;

- the availability of a transaction log and system journals;

- the skills and experience of the technical support staff and operators;

- how soon and by what means are system failures or errors known eg

  - notification by users,

  - poor response times,

  - from statistical data provide by the system;

  - automatic notification by the network management system.

Network operations and performance should be continuously monitored to ensure that they are able to deal with the message traffic that runs along them and provision should be made to deal with contingencies commensurate with needs and cost. This may involve the provision of duplicate lines where applications are critical to the successful running of the business, redundant circuits and alternative routing.

12.7 Value For Money

12.7.1 Objectives

A value for money review of a computer network may encompass a wide range of objectives starting with an evaluation to determine whether or not an organisation's network strategy is appropriate for its business and organisational needs and finishing with an assessment of whether or not the networks do meet those needs with due regard for the economic uses of resources and the requirement of the EC decision for organisations in the public sector to move towards open systems interconnectivity.

Cost effectiveness

Particular factors which could be considered when evaluating cost effectiveness include:

   -   whether or not the level and complexity of equipment employed matches the purposes and volume of traffic using the network;

   -   whether or not data and voice networks are linked and whether or not they come under one department;

   -   the number of leased lines used and whether the systems could be rationalised by the use of megastream or kilostream lines;

   -   whether or not the use of X25 has been evaluated;

   -   limiting factors such as one switch or piece of equipment which is slowing down the system.

Running costs

A hidden cost in the life cycle of a communications network is that of not having people of the right calibre to manage, maintain and operate the network. If an organisation is operating a network inefficiently or ineffectively it is unlikely to provide a satisfactory service to its users.

Direct cabling

The use of direct cabling is the simplest approach to providing reliable and secure physical connections and is usually preferred but it may prove the most expensive in the long term. If departments or sections using traditional point to point connections move offices then the cables may also have to be moved. For many organisations the provision and management of direct cabling has become a problem with ducts filled with old and often redundant cabling and little information available on the state of such cabling. One solution is to provide totally wired premises. The initial costs are high but considerable savings would be achieved over the life time of the network. It is particularly appropriate for new buildings but may not be a practical proposition in the case of older premises.

12.8 Audit Approach

Development of networks has important implications for auditors not least because of the accompanying decentralisation of control. In general it is no longer possible to rely on an audit of the central mainframe to ensure that access is controlled and authorised. With decentralisation auditors must be assured that each portion of the network is correctly interfaced and is working in a controlled environment. Security may be compromised by the number of network products that an organisation uses, a general lack of standards regarding network security and management and insufficient knowledge of staff using networks.

Auditors also have to assess whether the organisation is achieving value for money from its investment in networks. Data is of no use to users if it is not readily available or if response times are so slow that users waste time waiting for the system. Auditors need to establish that a network is properly planned and implemented and operated in a cost effective manner.

12.8.1 Network Strategies

The starting point for the audit is the gathering of all relevant information about the networking facilities including the factors which will affect the size, scope and complexity of the network or give rise to changed requirements. The first step is therefore to establish basic facts such as:

- the number of workstations and servers utilised and their locations;
- the type and number of transactions, both peak off peak;
- line traffic , ie the level of transaction data plus the network overheads;
- resilience which depends upon the type of traffic and the requirements of the user, eg what is an acceptable delay;
- the physical location of workstations;
- long term plans for system development plus the expected increase in traffic, costs, lines, hardware, software, contractors or in-house and staffing

Such information should be available from reports to senior management and in the case of public bodies to members. A more detailed list of requirements is included in the checklist at the end of these *Guidelines*.

Auditors should also undertake periodic reviews of the operation and workings of the network. Matters which could be the subject of detailed investigation include the integration of voice and data, a quality of service survey of users, or a review of the use of the network to ensure that users with access do actually require such services for their business activities.

Auditors need to be aware that the ad hoc manner in which networks may be developed may lead to an organisation having a number of separate and possibly incompatible networks. In addition in those organisations where departmental computing has been encouraged, multiple telephone lines may be installed, many of which could potentially serve common needs. Auditors should ascertain how much duplication has occurred and what rationalisation can be achieved.

12.8.2 Network Management

The process of evaluation of management arrangements for networking require the auditor to pay particular attention to:

- factors affecting the cost effectiveness and economic performance of the network;

- the elements and nature of running costs;

- the various solutions and options available such as the provision of centralised or decentralised networks the use of direct cabling or public lines.

The audit review should be based on the usage of the network and will need to consider response times, system availability, the effect of batch up-dating, line status and the attributes of any NMS employed.

As far as monitoring network usage, the auditor may determine:

- the main users of the network;

- when the network is most used;

- whether the network charges are realistic;

- which workstations are using what services and also identify incorrect attachments as well as those workstations which are not used.

Once this has been achieved the auditor can then review the service quality using for each selected user department the form of survey provided in the checklist for this chapter. The survey should include a review of the response times that are being experienced although such information should normally available from the operating system or NMS.

12.8.3 Security & Resilience

Having established the security policy, the auditor should seek to establish whether or not the basic elements and objectives of security are present and effective by examining the arrangements and facilities for separation of data flows, network connections, protocols and the access controls provided by the network software.

Auditors need to be aware of the existence of bridges, routers and gateways, know and understand their properties and determine whether or not the uses to which they are put achieve security objectives. The auditor should never assume that network connection devices are working as specified; they should check the pathways in action. Bridges may provide too free an access in practice and allow a user to send a packet of commands to a LAN or part of a LAN and access data or use processing facilities to which they are not entitled.

The auditor should evaluate the security features using risk assessment and comparison against security policies and finally test to see that the features are working in practice.

Auditors should ascertain what measures for resilience of the network have been taken and evaluate them against the security policy objectives of the organisation and the foregoing specified criteria.

12.8.4 Value for Money

Not all auditors will feel able to undertake a detailed technical evaluation of a network but they should be able to make a judgement on the measures taken by management in pursuit of value for money from the computer networks of their organisation. Auditors need to have an awareness and understanding of the functional and operational aspects of networking. Auditors should also review how the network is used and how easy it is to expand or change the network and its uses.

CIPFA

COMPUTER AUDIT GUIDELINES

COMPUTER ASSISTED AUDITING

13 USE OF
COMPUTERS
FOR AUDIT

CHAPTER 13

USE OF COMPUTERS FOR AUDIT

13

Continued overleaf

13.1 Introduction

Advances in IT have transformed the way in which businesses are organised and run. Most organisations rely heavily on technology not only for financial systems but for almost every aspect of service delivery. Technological advances have resulted in batch processing systems being replaced by systems in which transactions are entered directly by the users of the system, and there is a consequent impact on controls. At the same time there have been significant moves away from the centralised IT services towards departmental computing, where individual user departments have their own computing facilities and run their own systems.

These changes have considerable impact for the audit. The auditor cannot afford to ignore the fact that much of the information required for the audit comes from computer files, and in conducting an audit of computerised systems, the auditor will require sufficient information from his tests to allow him to produce objective reports which adequately support the conclusions.

The traditional image of audit staff as 'tickers and turners' is very outdated. Auditors have been making use of computerised facilities for many years, primarily in the area of file interrogation, but the arrival of the microcomputer has provided audit with the opportunity to computerise many more aspects of the audit function.

13.2 Computers for Audit

With the majority of systems now computer-based, auditors can harness the power of the computer to improve the economy, efficiency and effectiveness of the audit. In today's competitive environment, when it is essential for audit to present a professional, up-to-date image to the client, the wide range of facilities available makes it almost indispensable for auditors to embrace the technology.

Today's audit environment is very different from that of even five years ago. Audit departments often have to cope with a shortage of skills, and there is increasing pressure to improve productivity and demonstrate that the audit gives value for money. Many audit managers are adopting a more business-like approach, setting up service level agreements with individual clients and generally operating very much more on commercial lines. For this approach to succeed there must be a reliable source of accurate and up-to-date information so that the audit manager can make sound decisions about, for example, the most efficient allocation of often scarce resources.

The scope for audit to make use of computing is considerable and has the two-fold advantage of improving the quality of audit coverage and providing first-hand experience in using computing facilities.

The uses of computing for audit may, therefore, be considered under two broad headings -

— their application to audit work; and

— the facility to support the administration of the audit function.

13.2.1 Application to Audit Work

File interrogation

Computing offers the same facilities to auditors as to any other computer user and many auditors have recognised the benefits of using data retrieval techniques to extract data from corporate computerised systems. This particular use of computing is discussed more fully below.

Analysis of data using microcomputer software

The microcomputer spreadsheet package provides considerable benefits in analysing data without the need for computing skills. The availability of relatively easy to use programming languages which use database-style data structures allow the auditor to design, process and display data quickly and effectively. Statistical work can be performed quickly and easily, using specialist packages or general purpose spreadsheet or database packages. Auditors may also be able to perform or repeat calculations such as loan repayments and discounted cash flow estimates; interrogate records in client systems, or exploit similar features in their clients' microcomputer based systems.

Facilities are available, too, to 'download' mainframe data onto microcomputers and directly into certain spreadsheet or database formats. The powerful facilities of such software can thus be applied to both locally and centrally held data.

One use of microcomputing in the business sector is the computerised accounting package. These are relatively cheap and there is a wide range of such software, so the auditor might easily use such facilities: for example, in the audit of incomplete accounts relating to trading-type activities.

Risk assessment

In view of the need to make the most effective use of available resources, it is important when planning the audit to assess which areas of activity pose the greatest risk, and allocate resources accordingly. This requirement has been recognised by commercial software developers, and there are a number of packages available to assist in the process of identifying risk areas. Many audit sections, however, have developed their own risk assessment systems which either form part of the audit planning system or are self contained packages.

Systems reviews

The review of systems is an important part of any audit plan. Many organisations are using the computer to help them plan, support and document the systems review process. By adopting this approach auditors are able to benefit in a number of ways:

- key control areas in primary systems can be identified, recorded and printed as required;

- details of audit tests carried out can be recorded in a standard way: a standard format simplifies the quality review process;

- the approach ensures consistency throughout the audit department or organisation.

Some auditors are beginning to use expert systems, or knowledge-based systems as an aide to their work. These assist auditors by simulating expert knowledge and decision-making ability, and making them available to others through the computer while the experts themselves are absent. Many applications for expert systems exist in business, such as in accounting, auditing and information management.

13.2.2 Supporting Audit Administration

Support functions include:

- those relating to the management of audit resources;

- those relating to the presentation of audit material; and

- those relating to research.

Management of audit resources

Auditors have been quick to recognise the benefits of computerising the information needed to ensure effective monitoring of audit plans and projects. Audit plans can be held on a computer and updated immediately to reflect changes. The auditor could enter details such as the time allocated to projects, staff resources and cost so that the progress of each task can be monitored. This information helps the audit manager to allocate scarce resources in the most effective way and provides detailed information for senior management and clients.

The extent to which audit has now embraced this type of system is demonstrated by the increasing number of proprietary packages on the market for managing and controlling audit projects, although many audit sections have developed their own systems using word processing, database and spreadsheet packages. Standard project management tools are also available and can help in audit planning and control.

Presentation of audit material

Word processing technology has brought significant benefits to managers where there is a need to prepare a well-presented report. The auditor needs to deliver a well argued and properly formatted report to get the maximum impact, and word processing and related software offer a variety of facilities to achieve this.

Memos and working papers held on the word processor can be edited and reformatted into the audit report. The opportunity to edit reports quickly means that the auditor can respond to the client's comments sufficiently quickly with a final draft to avoid the potential problems of having to represent arguments where the passage of time has meant that new issues have arisen.

Many word processors have facilities for using standard styles – pre-defined paragraph or document layouts – which can help to standardise the appearance of an audit team's documentation. Templates – existing documents with set paragraphs to which new text may be added – may be used in some word processors to produce standard questionnaires. It is also possible to purchase 'style checkers': programs which scan text and detect grammatical errors and misuse. The more sophisticated ones will also help users write in a standardised style.

In presenting an argument, the ability to display figures graphically rather than as text or columns of numbers helps ensure a better delivery which is often easier to assimilate, and may therefore appear more convincing. Some spreadsheet software provides the option to display and print data graphically, and many word processors can import these, or have some graphic capability of their own.

Other software, known as presentation software, is available to format text and graphics for overhead projector and photographic slide production.

Research functions

The auditor often has to research into a particular subject to provide better background information and comparative data. The increasing availability of data available through public networks from commercial information databases and other organisations' computers, offers the auditor the opportunity to extend greatly the range of information available.

13.3 Expert Systems and Knowledge Based Systems (KBS)

The advent of artificial intelligence can be said to have changed the computer from a high-speed calculating machine to a machine with reasoning or thinking capabilities. Expert systems are computer programs that exhibit the behaviour characteristics of experts. They can be used to imitate expert knowledge and decision-making ability, and make it available to others through the computer while the experts themselves are absent. Many applications for expert systems exist in business, such as in accounting, auditing and information management.

Many audit tasks rely more heavily on an auditor's interpretation of data than on the data itself. Sometimes there is more than one single interpretation, and it is the auditor's job to make judgements and decisions. Audit skills include the ability to process numeric problems, reason, judge and offer decisions, and this is an appropriate set of tasks for expert systems. They can help auditors make consistent decisions based on previous case work and rules derived from expert decisions of the past.

There are primarily two types of expert systems: rule-based systems and example-based systems. A rule-based system applies a series of 'if ... then...' rules that the human expert uses in reaching decisions. An example-based system is one in which the user enters actual cases and the system tries to find matches between them and prior cases that have been entered into the knowledge base of the system. When complete and detailed records of prior cases exist, it may be best to use example-based systems to solve problems, but when prior cases are incomplete or unavailable, and a body of knowledge can be structured in a set of rules, it is best to use rule-based systems. Rule-based systems are probably the most commonly used type of expert system.

13.3.1 Advantages of Expert Systems

Expert systems are said to provide the following benefits:

Expert systems can do what conventional programs cannot do:

- unprogrammable tasks like configuring computers and managing portfolios;
- be able to produce an answer, although it may not be a certain one, from uncertain and incomplete data;
- make knowledge explicit, ie, examine their knowledge base and provide explanations of the proffered decision.

Expert systems can increase productivity:

- help manage complex tasks while traditional
- improve organisation by ensuring consistent performance of the same task at different times and places, and by different people;
- make optimal decisions quickly, since they have all the knowledge readily available in the knowledge database.

Expert systems offer a way of improving the management of expertise:

- they allow organisations to preserve, replicate and distribute scarce expertise;
- they can facilitate training to guide learning and verify the learner's competence with

standard cases.

Expert systems can perform better than a human in the following ways:

- by constantly practising and rehearsing, to maintain proficiency;

- producing more consistent, reproducible result than human experts;

- they are be easily transferred or reproduced. Unlike transferring knowledge from one human expert to another, which is a lengthy and expensive process, transferring expert systems simply involves the process of copying or copying a program or data file;

- human experts are very scarce and thus expensive while expert systems, though costly to develop, are inexpensive to operate. Their high cost of development is offset by the low operating cost and the ease with which new copies of the system can be made.

Expert systems provide consistent expertise based on the knowledge and experience of veteran auditors. Becoming a good auditor requires practice on many cases in order to develop insight and consistency in decision-making. Unfortunately, such well-trained auditors are rare, because of the years of experience required to reach such a level of expertise. Expert systems provide a means of replicating the expert auditor's skills, making it available to more people for use or training.

Unlike some scientific decisions that have a unique solution, auditing decisions are often complex and do not have a single solution. This characteristic makes expert systems well suited for audit work, since expert systems are especially good at dealing with complex problems and making recommendations and choosing the best solution from many alternatives.

13.3.2 Benefits of Using Expert Systems

Assisting internal control

An integrated expert system is capable of assisting in almost any area of internal control study and evaluation. Expert systems assist internal control in the following ways:

- Expert systems can be built to aid in the audit planning and technical audit procedures, eg deciding the audit programs, determining test sample types and sizes, assessing audit errors, determining a planning level, analysing large volumes of accounting transactions, confirming procedures, and performing analytical reviews. Expert systems can help to improve the efficiency, effectiveness, and speed of the above tasks.

- Expert systems can assist in monitoring the effectiveness of controls and diagnosing errors in information systems, eg monitoring transactions in an electronic funds transfer network.

13.6

     — Where there are many variances that need to be examined, auditors can save time by using expert systems to analyse and detect the significant variances for follow-up and correction.

     — Expert systems can aid in evaluating potential clients in the area of credit rating and credit approval.

Serving auditing standards as a knowledge base

An expert system storing details of generally accepted auditing standards, statements of accounting practice, etc could assist an auditor in selecting the correct opinion for an audit.

Auditor training

Expert systems will not only serve as an efficient research tool for practising auditors, but may modify current techniques used in staff training and development. Expert systems could assist auditor training by teaching the rules and reasoning that an expert in auditing actually uses, so that the quality of training that a new employee receives might improve.

A number of expert systems suitable for auditors are available from academic sources and the large accountancy practices. In addition to these, auditors can develop a customised expert system by buying only a 'shell' (inference engine). The 'shell' allows the user to add personal expert knowledge. This flexible system might be advantageous for auditors wishing to use their own expert local knowledge to design a system to fit their needs for planning and carrying out auditing responsibilities.

13.4 Computer Assisted Audit Techniques (CAATs)

A wide range of computer assisted audit techniques is available, to help auditors conduct their work in as cost effective a manner as possible. This section describes a number of these in detail. Possibly the most widely used is data retrieval, and for this reason, this chapter concentrates on retrieval. However, it would be wrong to ignore other techniques: while they are less widespread, and in some cases require expertise that is often beyond the average audit team, it is important to discuss them to put them into context and describe their main points.

13.4.1 Uses of Computer Assisted Audit Techniques

Some techniques are used to test data, while others are used to conduct tests on procedures or controls built into a system. At the same time, techniques may use 'live' programs or audit programs, and 'live' data or test data. The following table describes the main techniques:

Technique	Type of data	Type of program	What is tested	Comments and restriction
Parallel simulation	Live	Audit	Production programs	Needs programming expertise Either program could be at fault if errors found
Embedded audit module	Live	Audit program in live program suite	Programs or data	Needs special program – cost of development and maintenance
Test data ('dead')	Test	Production	Production programs	More appropriate to system development than to audit
Test data ('live')	Test	Audit program in live program suite	Production programs	Needs special program code Needs exception code built into production programs
Program review, or code analysis	Neither	Production	Production programs	High level of programming expertise required Very time consuming
Program comparison	Neither	Production	Production programs	Skill needed to analyse results Test object code or source code?
Data retrieval (interrogation)	Live	Audit	Live data	Needs skill with language used General purpose languages often specific to one hardware platform

13.8

- **Parallel simulation** duplicates the processing cycle of the real transactions to produce comparable results.

- **Embedded audit modules** insert audit routines into the normal processing cycle.

- **Test data** involves processing test transactions through the application's normal processing cycle.

- **Program review or code analysis** is the detailed audit of program source code.

- **Program comparison** compares different versions of a program, usually using specialist software.

Computer assisted audit techniques which test data, in the above analysis, may be used to validate data, to summarise it, or to produce statistical comparisons.

All these techniques should be regarded as tools in the auditor's repertoire: the auditor should determine the objectives of the audit, review the tools available and select the most appropriate and economic technique.

Auditors with little or no experience of a particular computer audit technique, operating environment or package should be wary of asserting their independence at too early a stage: they should not refuse help from IT departments - indeed, a useful rapport can often be established through an auditor's willingness to learn. For example, the proposed use of retrieval software may require the installation to provide operating instructions and file layouts, and an auditor who is not totally familiar with the software available will probably need guidance on coping with complex file structures or resolving parameter validation rejections.

The auditor should seek specialist training and ensure, as far and as soon as possible, that the techniques or programs are operating as intended. In most cases processing requirements will need to be discussed with the information services department. For organisations using a bureau and for auditors with their own processing facilities arrangements may have to be made to remove files to an alternative processing facility. When removing files the auditor should:

- make every effort to ensure the completeness and authenticity of the data and the correct operation of software used to copy files; and

- give due regard to maintaining the confidentiality of the client's data.

13.4.2 Data Retrieval

Overview

Data retrieval is probably the most widely used, most clearly understood and most easily obtainable of all computer assisted audit techniques. It can be used for extracting and manipulating computerised data, for testing that data and for formatting reports for audit and reporting purposes. It can also be used to test the way programmed procedures and controls have operated on processed live data.

This technique gives auditors an important independent access to computerised information which, in many instances, will be the majority of the information stored by the organisation. It also allows auditors to review and 'work on' much larger quantities of information than might otherwise be possible.

The advantages claimed for general purpose retrieval software are:

- potential 100% review of data, thus overcoming limitations of a 'manual' test;

- speed in processing – once the interrogation has been specified and written;

- flexibility – through use of parameters specified by the auditor;

- accuracy of processing, (subject to the correct specification of parameters by the author);

- a greater proportion of audit time spent analysing results rather than in manual extraction and checking of information;

- independent access to data; and

- relatively inexpensive to use.

Against these benefits it may be claimed that:

- there are the costs of the package (or packages) and of the training required;

- inexperienced users of the package and systems being interrogated may produce inaccurate results; and

- it does not on its own necessarily give positive evidence of the working of controls, as it is an examination of processed data and cannot give information about any controls which are not actually used.

Retrieval software is most commonly used to examine or test transactions in a computer system by:

- selecting cases for auditors for further tests or examination;

- re-performing calculations and processes performed initially by the system;

- stratifying or otherwise examining the scope of an audit population; and

- validation of data used in subsequent calculations (eg asset valuation).

However it can also prove a valuable tool in testing controls by:

- examining the results of processing to test for control failures; and

13.10

- examining the security and utilisation logs of the computer; and

- other general controls.

Selecting audit information

The selection of records for further audit investigation need not imply an error, but merely allows the author to extract a full or selected list of records which satisfy specific criteria (eg arrears greater than £x which have been outstanding for more than y months).

A refinement of this extraction technique would be to use pre-printed stationery to prepare letters to debtors or other organisations, to verify the existence of assets or balances. Testing of the output against known data must be adequate before results are used outside the audit environment. If auditors want only to examine or to verify the contents of computer files, they can randomly select records for such investigation.

Data may be selected to support the audit of financial statements. External auditors, for example, may wish to sample transactions for substantive audit tests, prove a population's completeness prior to sampling, select key items, report exceptional transactions, or conduct detailed tests and calculations to verify accounting figures (eg assets, debtors, and all or selected expenditure heads).

The auditor may also wish to test certain risk areas. The ability of many retrieval packages to search files (eg for duplicate records), to compare files for checks on changes to standing data, to hold running balances or averages, or to indicate records showing major deviations from the norm, are further useful features.

Where the data required by auditors is not immediately available on a file, calculation facilities become essential. For example, average pay can be calculated by taking gross pay and dividing by a week number. The ability to do calculations also enables the auditor to verify, independently, figures calculated by the production program, (eg loan interest, depreciation).

Tracing transactions

Audit trails are often lost or obscured in computer systems by the amalgamation or summarisation of data, and the ordering of document storage which may be different from the magnetic file order. Retrieval software can assist in overcoming such problems by:

- re-performing summarisations;

- selection and printing of individual transaction details;

- providing information on transaction sources to help trace paper records; and

- extracting individual transactions from non-application files, such as database log files.

Sorting and stratifying data

Stratifying, classifying and summarising data by value, source, descriptive or other criteria are very useful in helping the auditor to develop profile of the data to be audited.

Validating data

It is also important for the auditor to determine the quality of data held on a computer file. Retrieval software can compare data with known and acceptable criteria. Reports on data outside these limits may be used, for example, in subsequent calculations (eg asset valuation, depreciation). This may be done to determine the extent of known errors or to search for errors.

The ability of retrieval software to apply a number of tests or types of tests to a record at one 'pass' provides the auditor with the opportunity to devise tests for unexpected occurrences of data on a file. Assurances that payroll files would not contain 'dead' records from a previous year could be checked, for example. The retrieval software could duplicate the processes supposedly carried out by production programs, to check their performance.

Security and utilisation

Interrogation of machine or system logging files can provide information both on machine utilisation and on access control applied to the machine and individual files and programs. Although such interrogations are not always simple because of the often complex record structure, they can prove a valuable source of evidence in testing general controls:

—   times and dates of program runs, for checks on authorisation;

—   reports on use of special programs and utilities;

—   records of access to specific data files; and

—   security breaches.

Some specialist software is commercially available for extracting data from particular logging systems. A number of access control software systems also provide their own report programs.

13.4.3   Alternative Methods of Data Retrieval

There are a number of different methods of data retrieval available including programming languages, general purpose retrieval software (interrogation programs), program generators, microcomputer packages and application generators (fourth generation languages).

Programming languages

Programming languages, such as COBOL or BASIC, tend to be more flexible and offer more powerful facilities than general-purpose retrieval software and well-written audit programs may be more efficient in processing. There are limitations, however:

- the use of programming languages would normally require a degree of technical expertise which may not be available within the audit section;

- more detailed design, compilation and testing stages will normally be necessary – particularly if complex processing or calculations are involved;

- programs may not be easy to amend for future use.

General purpose retrieval software

General purpose retrieval packages are specially-written programs used to select, manipulate and report on computer data. Some simple report generator and utility software could also be considered in this category because of their selection and calculation facilities. Retrieval software operates by processing specific instructions, or parameters, supplied by the user.

The advantages of using such software are:

- it is comparatively easy and quick to learn and use, and does not normally demand full programming knowledge;

- many packages are 'load and go' (ie once the parameters have been validated the program will automatically interrogate the required file);

- stored parameters can be easily amended for future processing; and

- it can satisfy ad hoc enquiries not anticipated in original system design.

Its limitations are:

- it may be less efficient in terms of processing time and less flexible than a programming language;

- it may not readily handle all types of files and records, particularly more complex file and record structures;

- packages are often developed for use with a specific manufacturer's hardware which limits their use in multi-supplier environments: auditors operating on a range of hardware platforms would have to develop expertise in several different packages.

While general purpose retrieval programs have increased in sophistication over the years, there may still be some tasks such as sampling, analysing and summarising data that cannot easily be processed with such packages (particularly on the smaller machines), or are wasteful of computer time. Although this should not inhibit the auditor in developing audit software, it is sometimes more effective or efficient to develop certain audit programs in the programming language used by the organisation. It is sometimes possible to link these specially written modules to standard retrieval programs.

13.13

13.4.4 Availability of Retrieval Software Packages

Few mainframe retrieval software packages have been designed specifically for audit since they have in most cases primarily been developed as report generators and file management aids. The facilities auditors might require within retrieval software are available in a wide range of packages from computer manufacturers, software houses and external auditors as well as software developed by individual organisations.

Several external audit organisations have in the past developed their own retrieval software (including program generators). These are primarily for their own use although often licensed to their clients. The high cost of maintenance of such software for several ranges of machines has tended to militate against development in this field and few such packages are now actively developed and supported; external auditors recently being more inclined to adopt packages marketed by software houses.

Where suitable general purpose retrieval software is not available, some installations have opted to devise their own systems and, in some cases, have made them available to their audit section and to other organisations. There can be advantages in audit using such software wherever possible rather than bringing in one of the more established programs. The advantages include more sympathetic acceptance of the use of interrogation techniques and greater support to users in case of difficulty. Against this the auditor should remember that software developed in-house may not provide such full facilities or the degree of independence and assurance expected from an independently provided package. Auditors should also consider whether their independence is likely to be compromised and take steps to minimise the risk.

Microcomputer packages

The PC provides auditors with significant opportunities for adding value to the audit, as described elsewhere in this chapter. This is particularly true of data retrieval, as there are packages available specifically for auditors which incorporate a number of audit functions – such as looking for duplicate transactions – which are often more difficult for non-specialist auditors using traditional mainframe tools. It is very cost effective to download data from mainframe or minicomputers to a PC and carry out local analysis.

The advantages of using PC-based retrieval are:

- The origin of the data is often immaterial to the package used. This is a significant advantage where the auditor has to cope with systems running on different manufacturer's machines. Such a situation is fairly typical as the move towards departmental computing continues. Many auditors now find themselves having to review systems from a variety of machines and it is often difficult, and costly, to develop expertise in a number of different retrieval packages.

- PC software tends to be more user-friendly than its mainframe equivalents. Although these packages offer a high degree of functionality many of the functions can be carried out without a high level of technical expertise. Amongst other things this can result in more effective use of audit resources as it reduces the amount of training necessary.

–   Once the data has been transferred to the auditor's PC the interrogation can be done in the privacy of the audit room.

–   Using the PC reduces the overhead of running jobs on the mainframe. This often results in savings in the cost of processing which is often recharged to users. It also saves time, as audit jobs would have to be scheduled and compete with other demands on processing time.

–   Retrieval software for PCs has been developed specifically for the audit market and usually incorporates standard audit routines such as duplicates testing.

The main disadvantages of PC retrieval are:

–   It can be difficult to transfer the data from the mainframe to the PC.

–   The packages may offer less flexibility than conventional programming languages.

–   Some processes can be particularly time consuming, depending on the complexity of the enquiry, the size of the data file, and the capacity and speed of the PC.

13.4.5 Transfer of Data

Before any PC retrieval package can be used, of course, it is necessary to transfer the data required for the audit from its host computer to the audit PC. Technically, this is often the most challenging aspect of the job and potentially the most time consuming.

Broadly, there are three options available:

–   direct download using a micro-mainframe link;

–   PC to PC transfer;

–   tape transfer.

Direct download

Organisations are recognising the benefits to users of being able to download data from their systems to analyse locally on a PC. PC software packages often offer superior facilities for analysing data and producing the results graphically, for example, for inclusion in reports. Many businesses have now established direct links between mainframes, minicomputers, networks and PCs to facilitate this work.

Direct download is often the most effective method of capturing data. The data is identified on the mainframe and downloaded either directly to a PC, or to a PC through a network connection, using file transfer software. The data arrives on the PC in a format which can be read by a variety of PC software packages such as database, spreadsheet or file retrieval packages.

PC to PC transfer

If the PC used for the download is not in the audit department then it will be necessary to transfer data from one PC to another, either by copying the data to one or more floppy disks, or by directly transferring the data from one PC to another using communications software. The latter method can be very quick, depending on the package used.

Tape transfer

In some situations the most suitable method of data transfer may be by using an external tape drive. The auditor obtains the data on magnetic tape or cartridge and transfers the required data to the PC using an attached tape or cartridge drive. This method is particularly useful in multi-vendor sites.

13.4.6 Planning the Audit

Whichever method is used to capture the data, it is likely in the first instance that some degree of technical support will be required either from specialists within the audit section or from the IT department. There are, additionally, some points of good practice which should be considered before the actual transfer is initiated.

It is important to be sure of the objectives of the exercise. Before the data itself is accessed it is useful to spend some time identifying the audit tests to be carried out and identifying the data required to perform those tests.

The auditor should be satisfied that sufficient information is available about the system before embarking on the audit. Copies of the latest record specifications should be obtained and examined so that specific data items can be identified. Depending upon the amount of storage available on the PC some pre-selection of data may be required before the data is transferred. The presence of redundant data will adversely affect processing speeds, as well as wasting valuable disk capacity in the auditor's computer.

As well as specialised retrieval packages, the auditor may be able to use other types of PC software for interrogation purposes. Database packages usually support useful selection and reporting facilities: spreadsheet software offers opportunities for data manipulation, formatting and updating which can also be of considerable use to the auditor. Integrated PC packages combine these facilities with others such as graphic representations and text handling facilities to allow the auditor to transfer the results of audit work to formal written reports.

13.4.7 Fourth Generation Languages

Fourth generation languages and application generators are newer tools of the computer department designed to increase programmer productivity by:

- automating repetitive work (eg file creation and manipulation);

- reducing reliance on the detailed procedural nature of conventional programming languages;

- allowing greater user participation in the design of systems and programs; and, in some cases,

- automatically providing documentation.

Fourth generation languages cover a range of products from stand-alone programming tools to systems supplied with specific database products using integrated data dictionaries. They provide a method of design based on interactive VDU screens and simple question and answer sessions.

Most fourth generation languages support powerful report generation facilities, often allowing information retrieval with complex selection criteria. Auditors with such tools at their disposal will find them of considerable benefit, particularly since non-programmers can often produce simple reports. The speed and ease of development using fourth generation languages do not reduce the requirement for caution and care over standards, the validity of the programs created, documentation, adequacy of testing at an early stage and preservation of data integrity (particularly with corporate files).

13.4.8 Audit Techniques

Use of test data

Description

Test data is fictitious data processed using operational computer programs to test the system's reaction and compare it with anticipated results. Audit use of test data is generally intended to test computer programs' compliance with controls, or proving the normal processing cycle produces correct results as part of a continuing review of application controls. Test data is the only positive way to prove that programmed controls operate as specified although it must be remembered that continued correct operation of controls can only be evidenced by further tests or by consideration of the prevailing general controls over access to programs and program amendments.

Test data provides the means for auditors directly to test how systems deal with error conditions by deliberately submitting wrong data.

The auditor may want to:

- verify that a program will not accept invalid or incompatible data;

- check that program controls are operating correctly;

- ensure that exception and error reports are produced as expected; and

- verify a calculation process or that other processes are correctly handled.

Sources of Test Data

Test data can be obtained from a variety of sources and the auditor may have a choice depending on the cost-effectiveness and efficiency of different sources. If up-to-date test data is not available or suitable auditors may choose to devise their own, and this will involve:

- determining the method of processing the data;

- reviewing the standing data in the system and adding test data to it if required; and

- preparing fictitious transaction data for processing with the standing data.

Software packages known as 'test data generators' are available, which allow the user to specify by parameters the format and requirements of the test data to be produced.

In many cases the test data used during systems development or enhancement can form the basis for the auditor's test pack. If the system analyst's test data is available, the auditor must ensure that it takes account of all system and program amendments since the original testing was performed, and that it tests for the full range of conditions in which the auditor is interested.

Methods of Processing Test Data

There are two methods of processing test data: 'dead' processing and 'live' processing.

'Dead' processing (test pack or test deck)

A file is specifically created for testing purposes. This is often done by modifying a copy of a current file. Although the use of test packs does not interfere with the normal production cycle, they can be expensive to maintain and require additional computer time to run.

The auditor should try to minimise the risk of interference and ensure that the current programs and standing files are used by paying close attention to the file references, generation numbers and operating system commands. The security and integrity of the system must also be preserved by restricting processing to ensure that system statistics, downloads or final output (eg cheques, purchase requisitions) are not produced. It may be possible to minimise the disadvantages by making full use of operating system and other software facilities. Where these facilities exist, and the auditor is competent to use them, it should be possible to copy 'live' master files, programs and job control language instructions into an isolated test environment. The auditor can then

13.18

process any of the procedures in an accelerated time scale to include special end-of-year runs.

'Live' processing

This technique, also known as the integrated test facility (ITF) or the 'dummy department', involves the setting up of fictitious test records within the live production files and therefore requires:

- no additional files to be created;

- no additional computer time for the testing stage and very little for the test; and

- use of the normal production programs and standing data.

There are however considerable practical difficulties:

- the fictitious data must not interfere with the production files' live data and it will be necessary either to restrict the scope of dummy record processing by program modification or remove the effects of the dummy transactions by ledger journal or other reversing entries.

- the user and IT departments must agree to their files being used for such purposes;

- management resistance may arise because of the real danger of affecting both the system statistics and producing deliberately erroneous output; and

- if live master files are corrupted, the auditor will lose both credibility and confidence.

The use of ITF is only likely to be suitable, justified and cost-effective by the internal auditors of very large complex real-time systems. Even then the expense and danger of this technique should be carefully considered and fully discussed with financial and computer management.

Both these methods of testing enable a continuous audit of systems and increase the auditor's knowledge of the systems under review, but will demand a high commitment of audit personnel. The design of effective test data will be largely governed by the adequacy of system and program documentation because the author of the data will need to identify the validation routines, the error and exception reports produced by each program, and the presence of control totals at each stage of the processing cycle. Auditors should not be so influenced by the documentation that they fail to take a more objective approach in designing the data to highlight areas where errors are not anticipated.

Advantages and Disadvantages

The advantages of using test data are that:

- they provide positive assurance of the correct functioning of particular program controls in the current live program;

13.19

- if test data is maintained the technique can be used on a continuing basis, irrespective of program changes (providing tests are still relevant);

- if restricted to testing particular program controls (especially if master files are not required), they are not expensive to develop;

- once set up, running costs from year to year are low;

- additional tests can be grafted on to basic test data fairly easily; and

- the contents are variable at will.

The disadvantages of using test data are:

- to ensure that the test data is processed as expected a more detailed knowledge is required of the system than might otherwise be required (often including knowledge of programs not required to be tested);

- to test certain program controls may entail either passing the data through previous parts of the system that do not require testing or writing additional programs to by-pass those parts of the processing;

- processing halts may occur due to the artificial type and small quantity of data used or deliberate errors introduced by the auditor to test the reaction of the software;

- initial set up costs can be high if local test data is not available; and, in the case of ITFs, may require significant work at the design stage; and

- the security risks involved and management concerns normally make it difficult to test data in 'live' files (ITF).

Parallel simulation

Description

The previous paragraphs explained the use of test data to test procedural controls. Whereas test data involves the use of the organisation's programs and the auditor's own data, parallel simulation allows the auditor to reproduce results of processing and calculations using live data or transactions and his own program for comparison with the results produced by the audited system. This technique may be used for reperforming procedures and calculations made by program (eg for substantive testing of calculations of discounts). However, it is unlikely to be cost effective to attempt a complete duplication in the auditor's own programs of all the functions of operational programs. Parallel simulation can be used most successfully to prove critical functions, or to prove a particular control total. General purpose retrieval software packages often contain sufficient manipulative and calculation facilities to create the required simulation routines etc.

13.20

Advantages

- The technique provides a simple and positive verification of any function (eg a calculation) of an individual program or series of programs.

- The cost of running a simulation program will often not be any more than running a standard interrogation.

- The programs can easily be written and do not corrupt live files.

Disadvantages

- Programming skills may be required in the audit section to write and maintain the simulation programs if suitable retrieval software is not available; and this, particularly if simulation was of a complex system, could prove expensive.

- A good detailed knowledge of the systems is required in order to reproduce accurately the programs' functions. The more of a system to be simulated the more detailed the knowledge required.

- The design and coding of the calculation routines may be time consuming.

Embedded audit module (EAM)

Description

This technique, also known as resident audit software, is used to check program activity or data at crucial stages of processing or to select data for further testing. EAM is often described as on-line retrieval. It requires that an auditor's own program code is embedded into the application software. When in use it examines transactions immediately they have been processed by the system to see if they conform to the selection criteria. The main uses of this technique are for very large files (where interrogation or sampling would be very expensive and time consuming) or for real-time systems as a method of sampling or selecting transactions.

Modules fall into two main types:

- Modules 'switched on' or activated by the auditors at selected times depending on the system and flow of data.

- Modules activated each time the application program is used. This could be more expensive in terms of overall processing costs.

Results from EAMs can be presented in three main ways:

- Selected transaction records are 'marked' by the audit module when the selection conditions are satisfied. These markers can then be monitored and reported by the auditor with the aid of retrieval software. This technique is also referred to as tagging and audit indicator, although it negates one of the benefits of EAM in systems with large files.

13.21

- Selected transactions are written to audit files for subsequent examination or printing - often called system control audit review files (SCARF) where ordinary selection criteria are employed or sample audit review files (SARF) where sampling techniques are used.

- Selected transactions can also be routed to an audit terminal as part of a continuous audit.

Examples:

- A random sample of 3% of transactions is required to manually check the accuracy of payments. A parameter is set in the resident software to write a 3% random sample of records to the auditor's SARF.

- Whenever an amendment is made to the payroll manager's pay record a copy of the amendment and the standing information is written to the SCARF.

- Whenever a write-off of greater than £50 is input to the debtors system, a marker is placed in the audit control area of the relevant record.

Advantages

- Data can be extracted for audit examination as soon as a transaction appears in the system.

- The basis for extraction can be either a feature of the master file or a feature of the transaction or a combination of both.

- It reduces the need for separate audit runs, particularly important for very large files.

Disadvantages

- Generally an EAM will have to be inserted during the development of the system.

- The software development may be expensive and may have to be undertaken by the organisation's own programming staff – thus causing a loss of audit independence (this also occurs if computer staff have access to the audit 'code' or the activating and deactivating facility). Audit will need to review regularly the controls governing program access and development.

- The running overheads of the software may be unacceptable, particularly if extravagant use is made of the facilities by running complex coding or selection over long periods or by writing a large number of records to the output file.

- To be effective all items reported have to be followed up with the minimum of delay. This may disrupt the audit plan.

Program review

Description

Program code review consists of the methodical examination of program source code listings in order to determine the manner in which the program is executed. The source listing of the program is not the operational version, of course. It is important to appreciate that once compiled, the source version plays no further part in the day-to-day running of the program. The auditor must be aware that it is possible for a programmer to amend the object program directly without altering the source code in any way.

It would not generally be practical for auditors to examine the object program but it is possible for those with programming expertise to examine source listings to gain an insight into the operation of the program or see whether specified procedures and controls have been incorporated. The auditor must be aware of the limitations mentioned above and take steps to ensure the evidence is appropriate by using an accurate and up-to-date listing, and evaluating the integrity of the source version (by reviewing access controls and program change procedures, or by recompiling the source and comparing the results with the object code). Although it is likely that auditors will spend only a very small proportion of their time on program code review there may be occasions when it is considered a useful technique:

— to verify the accuracy of the processing controls described in the program specification (note that an easier and quicker test of these controls may be achieved through the use of test data); or

— to verify adherence to the programming standards of the organisation;

— to check the accuracy of programming routines that perform critical calculations eg the calculation of gross pay from hours worked and hourly rate of pay – though this should have been done by the analyst at the development or enhancement stage; or

— to ensure that proper programming techniques are used – for example in the production of control totals.

Advantages

— The auditor can gain some assurance that the program functions as specified and on the nature of controls implemented;

— if taken with controls over changes and access, some compliance assurance can be gained;

— the auditor can verify compliance with the programming standards of the installation;

— audit exerts a deterrent to fraud through regular and frequent contact with the computer department; and

— the auditor can develop expertise in the programming language used.

Disadvantages

— the exercise is extremely time-consuming in all but the simplest of cases and it can require a great deal of concentrated effort and technical skill to pursue the author's logic;

13.23

– the auditor could become too engrossed in detail to take the broader perspective; and

– there is no guarantee that the source listing examined corresponds with the object program.

Program comparison

Description

Special comparison software can compare two separate versions of any file to identify differences. Auditors can use such packages to compare copies of programs and check that change controls have operated correctly, or that unauthorised changes have not been made to sensitive programs.

Comparisons can be made of either source or object programs. Once differences are established they need to be investigated. The investigation of differences in source programs, as opposed to object code, is easier to perform since the meaning of source coding is more readily ascertained. As the source versions of a program are not directly executable, a comparison of these versions alone (eg without assurance over program access and amendment procedures) provides less reliable evidence of an unchanged program than comparing object versions.

Object code comparisons are, however, more difficult and time-consuming to interpret, as the compared programs will produce output in hexadecimal (or similar) notation relating to the underlying machine code instructions. Experience has also shown that extraneous features, such as compilation date, can show as differences between otherwise identical object programs and these can be awkward to resolve.

Comparison can realistically be best used to show that two versions of a critical program are the same. For this purpose the auditor should also consider, particularly for critical programs, the maintenance of secure control versions of programs in both source and object form for comparison purposes. The control version would need to be updated with authorised amendments to keep it in line with the live system.

Advantages

– provides a means of evaluating program change procedures;

– programs to make comparisons are relatively easy to use and inexpensive to run; and

– the auditor may gain a better understanding of the system under review.

Disadvantages

– the auditor needs a good understanding of the particular programming language in order to evaluate the effect of changes (although if working with an updated control version it may be enough to detect unauthorised changes); and

– the cost of the software, if not already available, can be high and may well preclude its use by all but the largest organisations.

Other software

A number of additional types of software are available and will be of use to the auditor in particular circumstances:

- **Random number generators** will produce a set of non-duplicated random numbers within a specified population range. These can then be used in manual selection of simple random samples or possibly linked to a retrieval package for computerised selection.

- **Statistical analysis packages** provide a variety of statistical routines for such techniques as regression analysis, standard deviation etc.

- **Modelling packages** allow the effect of changes to known data and relationships to be simulated to support both management, accountants and auditors.

- **Flowcharting software** documents the logical paths of a program in diagrammatic form for subsequent evaluation. Can be used to assist in the documentation of a system when documentation is deficient, or as an aid to program review.

- **Manufacturer's utilities and operating system facilities** (eg copy, sort, print utilities, data dictionary, user file descriptions).

Running audit software

Planning

Efficient planning of the use of CAATs is essential for the production of objective, timely and accurate information. It is important to understand the capabilities of the software and the information required to conduct the work, before beginning to perform the exercise.

When planning the use of CAATs, the auditor should consider:

- the exact objectives of the planned use;

- whether the test is feasible considering the availability of the necessary data in the computer files, the length of time the data remains available, and the possible processing overheads;

- whether sufficient up-to-date information on the layout and internal codes used in the file is available. This can be a problem on files processed by packaged software and wherever possible should be considered at the development stage;

- competence and availability of staff to meet the timetable for the audit;

- the ability of the software to produce reports in a form which is meaningful to the auditor;

- the cost-effectiveness and timeliness of alternatives.

The auditor will need to refer to various documents when planning the use of CAATs: the current file layout, the user manual and functional specifications are all vital to the successful design and processing of computer audit work.

Access and Integrity

The auditor should ensure access to data will be granted by the owners or users, particularly if the data or combination of files have not previously been accessed by audit. Data protection requirements may also enter into the access debate. These considerations are of particular relevance to auditors seeking to remove files, and early consideration of such possible problems is advised.

The auditor should conform to the normal security standards of the installation. Where live files are to be processed auditors should ensure that only 'read' access is granted, as reassurance both to the site management and to the auditor, and to avoid problems should files become corrupted. Where copy files are to be used auditors must be assured of the integrity and completeness of the copy by examining the copying process or hash totals of the data.

General purpose retrieval programs are simply a collection of unrelated routine functions such as read, compare, add and print, and are given purpose only by the incorporation of routine parameters. They could be susceptible to illicit manipulation by the:

- amendments of run time parameters;

- substitution of a 'doctored' file for the required file;

- amendment or substitution of output files or reports; and

- introduction of own-code into the program instructions to identify, for instance the by-passing of specific records and the covering-up illegal or fraudulent data. This, however, is not a major risk with general purpose audit software.

Precautions may be taken against such occurrences:

- by determining whether own-coding amendments are permissible or practical with the package and if so:

- reviewing the control procedures governing access to the retrieval software; if such amendments can be made then the auditor may wish to examine the source (if available) or object versions of the package;

- examining the parameter listings output by the package;

- examining the JCL or operating system log documentation to identify the file being accessed and results of processing; and

- testing the results of the run for reasonableness.

13.26

13.4.9 Audit Documentation

Audit documentation on the use of CAATs should include:

- objectives and results of each test and reference to standard audit files for further investigations;

- listing of parameters – the parameters themselves may well be retained in the auditor's use area or directory and their safe custody should be considered for the cost efficiency and integrity of future uses;

- operating instructions and JCL;

- package or operating system logging information on run times, files processed, and volumes of data read and output performed on those figures and any reconciliations;

- a sample of the output produced.

13.27

CIPFA

COMPUTER AUDIT GUIDELINES

COMPUTER AUDIT AND THE LAW

14 EUROPEAN LEGISLATION

15 NATIONAL LEGISLATION

CHAPTER 14

EUROPEAN COMMUNITY LEGISLATION

14

Continued overleaf

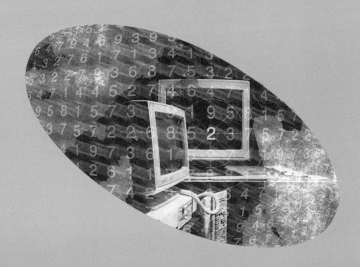

14.1 Introduction

Over the last ten years all member states of the European Community have experienced a continual growth in the influence of the EC and the requirement to comply with EC directives and regulations. None more so than in the lead up to the 'single European market' in 1993 where some 282 white paper requirements had to be in position by the end of 1992. Of these 30 are of direct relevance to the public sector and many more have an indirect effect on the public sector organisations or to their local economy.

Numerous issues therefore need to be considered by all organisations if they are to meet the obligations imposed upon them by the EC and to take advantage of the benefits of membership. Many documents have been published on the general impact of the EC and it is not the intention of this chapter to re-visit these areas. It is however important to understand the effect of the EC on computer audit and to the numerous directives and decisions that have been taken regarding information technology.

This chapter is not intended to be an exhaustive discussion of all directives but is intended to identify the main implications for auditors and to guide them towards more detailed information contained within the directives themselves, government circulars and statutory instruments.

14.2 Background to the EC Directives and Regulations

The United Kingdom became a member of the European Community (EC) in 1973 by signing the 1972 Treaty of Accession. The provisions of which were incorporated into UK law by the passing of the European Communities Act 1972. Section 2(1) of which provided that all directly applicable provisions of the treaties should become part of English law. So, too, would all existing and future Community secondary legislation.

The UK Government signed the Single European Act in 1987, which committed the EC member states to establish by the end of 1992 a frontier free economic area in which goods, services, capital and people could move without hindrance.

14.2.1 EC Legislation

The fields of EC legislative activity which will be of most concern to auditors are:

   —   Tendering and competition for information technology contracts (EC 88/295) and EC

90/531 (Utilities), which was extended in July 1993 to contracts for the supply of services including facilities management (EC92/50).

— The requirement to adhere to an open systems policy and to ensure that purchasers use relevant standards to describe the goods that they require (EC 87/95).

— Legal protection of software (EC 91/250).

— The Compliance Directive (EC 89/665)

— Health and safety at work (EC 90/270).

— The new proposed directive on data protection.

14.2.2   EC Legal Framework

The main EC institutions comprise the Commission (based in Brussels) which draws up drafts of legislation, the Parliament (based in Strasbourg) which submits opinion on proposed legislation, the Council which adopts legislation proposed by the Commission, the Economic and Social Committee (ECOSOC) which is purely advisory; and the European Court of Justice.

In the UK's domestic law, secondary legislation takes the form of statutory instruments. However under EC jurisdiction, secondary legislation is far more extensive and covers everything other than the treaties themselves. The body which has the powers to adopt such measures is the Council of Ministers and for most of the period of British membership of the Community, the Council has worked on the basis that unanimity was required. However, since the Single European Act of 1987 there have been several decisions taken in the Council by majority vote. Since the terms of the treaties are couched in very general language, most detailed Community policy is embodied in such secondary legislation. For example, the complex process of creating a single market by the elimination of non tariff barriers, is essentially being implemented by such secondary legislation.

It should be noted that within UK courts EC law takes precedence over UK law thus where there is any conflict between a national and a European law the European case will prevail (decided in the 'Factortame' case (1990)).

14.3 EC Directives and Regulations

The two principal forms in which new European law is made are directives and regulations. Most major decisions are taken in the form of 'Directives' which require member states to achieve stated results, but leave it to each member state to choose the method of implementation. Other Community legislation however, known as 'Regulations' can be immediately and directly applicable in every member state.

14.3.1 EC Directives

EC Directives are proposals by the EC Commission, accepted by the EC Council, which it is the duty of member states to incorporate into their own domestic legislation, but which are not binding upon individual persons and organisations within a country, until they are duly enacted by the individual national legislatures. Directives are normally accompanied by a requirement from the EC to member states to enact them by a given date, usually within a year.

According to Article 189 of the EEC Treaty, a directive is 'binding, as to the result to be achieved upon each member state to which it is addressed, but shall leave to the national authorities the choice of form and methods'.

Within the UK directives are generally brought into force through Acts of Parliament or ministerial regulations where there is already a UK Act of Parliament that permits such regulations to be made.

14.3.2 EC Regulations

EC Regulations are made by the EC themselves and have legal effect within the Community without further enactment from the national legislatures. There is therefore no opportunity to negotiate with UK ministers about implementation. However, a very large number of EC regulations are only about quotas and levies on specific goods, as distinct from the exercise of law making at large.

Perhaps the most notable regulation of all is Regulation 17 which entitles officials from the European Commission to execute raids in connection with possible breaches of the competition laws of the treaty. The Commission has the power to:

   — enter any company's premises;

   — examine the company's books and business records;

   — take copies of such books and records;

   — demand oral explanations on the spot.

Failure to co-operate with the investigation can result in heavy fines being imposed. The Commission expects persons being investigated to take an active role. They must help the investigators find appropriate records and produce specific documents required.

14.4 Procurement in Europe

14.4.1 Objectives

One of the EC objectives is to eliminate discrimination in the award of contracts on the basis of nationality, supplier or the origin of goods or services. Public procurement in Europe amounts to some 15% of community spending and action in this area is therefore seen to be essential to the completion of a single European market and to increase competitiveness amongst EC producers and suppliers.

The objectives are to be achieved by increasing competition within the single European market by requiring 'contracting authorities' to let contracts over certain financial thresholds after the placing of advertisements and in accordance with prescribed procedures concerning content of specifications, invitation, receipt, opening and evaluation of tenders.

14.4.2 Contracting Organisations

Contracting organisations are defined as bodies governed by 'public law', which includes local authorities, regional and district health authorities and trusts, government departments, education, fire and police authorities. It should be noted that government departments and the health authorities are also required to comply with the general agreement on tariffs and trade (GATT) regulations which impose further obligations on purchasing bodies. It should be noted that the utilities such as gas, electricity and water undertakings are subject to their own specific utility directives which though similar to those of the 'public sector' impose different responsibilities on the organisations.

An obligation is also placed upon member states to comply with directives in the cases of the subsidy of another entity. Additionally, a contracting authority is obliged to ensure compliance with directives where it subsidises directly more than 50% of a works contract awarded by an entity other than itself. Consequently, certain joint ventures between authorities and the private sector will be subject to the EC directives.

14.4.3 Public Procurement

The public procurement directives are based on three main objectives as follows:

- Community wide advertising of contracts so that firms in all member states have an opportunity to submit tenders.

- The banning of national technical specifications liable to discriminate against potential foreign tenderers.

14.4

—   The application of objective criteria in tendering and award procedures

14.4.4 Public Procurement Directives

The following outlines the EC directives that have been issued in respect of public procurement. In particular the rules to ensure that public sector organisations do not favour their own domestic contractors and suppliers. Of these, the first has been in force for a number of years, namely:

—   The Supplies Directive (77/62/EEC as amended by 88/295/EEC) covers the purchase, lease, rental or hire of goods in the public sector where the intention is to let a contract or series of contracts whose value is equal or above the specified limit, which from 1 January 1992 is 200,000 European currency units (ECUs) which equates to £141,431, net of VAT.

—   The Compliance Directive 89/665/EEC allows suppliers and contractors to bring proceedings in a national court of law if they are harmed by a breach of duty owed to them under the works or supplies directives.

—   The Services Directive (EC 92/50) covers a range of professional and technical services where the contract value is above the threshold limit. Unlike the works and supplies directives the intention is to specify different thresholds for different types of services, for example 100,000 ECUs (£70,700) for annual insurance premiums and 200,000 ECUs (£141,431) for design, banking and certain financial services. The Services Directive will have a two tier application, in that requirements similar to those of the Works and Supplies Directives will apply to a range of 'priority services', while less onerous conditions are stipulated for what are termed 'residual services'.

Member states will also be required by 31 October of each year to forward to the Commission a statistical report for the proceeding year concerning the total value of contracts awarded which are below the thresholds (and therefore not covered by the directive).

14.4.5 Thresholds

Thresholds are stipulated for individual contracts above which such contracts may only be let after following certain 'prescribed procedures'. Thresholds are defined in European currency units (ECU).

The currency equivalents are determined for member states every two years, during which time such rates are fixed and not subject to fluctuation. The sterling equivalent of a ECU was approximately 0.66 in 1990/91 and is now 0.707. This figure will apply until the 31 December 1993, when new rates will be determined.

The current thresholds are:

Supplies Directive	:	ECU 200,000 (£141,431)
Services Directive* (except Insurance)	:	ECU 200,000 (£141,431)
Insurance	:	ECU 100,000 (£70,716)

Thresholds relate to the value of individual contracts, not annual values. A contract valued at say £40,000 per annum for example, if let for a term of 4 years, will be deemed to be worth £160,000. If a contract value is not appropriate or cannot be calculated, Authorities are required to assess an equivalent sum by calculating 48 times the monthly value of the appropriate service.

The splitting or undervaluing of contracts in order to avoid the requirements of directives is specifically prohibited.

In respect of supply contracts, if a series of contracts is planned to be let over a period of time in order to fulfil a requirement for the procurement of products of the same type, each contract must be advertised, if the aggregated value of the contracts is over £141,431.

Whereas the Commission is understood to accept that independent procurement by separate parts of a organisation can be treated in isolation for the purpose of applying the aggregation rules, the position is different if individual purchasing officers are required to contract through central purchasing arrangements. It should be noted however that each discrete unit must be independent of the main organisation and have an independent budget.

Where purchases have to be aggregated by department, or by the organisation as a whole, it is essential that officers are able to co-ordinate the organisation's purchases. Otherwise EC thresholds may be exceeded without the authority being aware of it, thereby exposing itself to legal action.

14.5 Prescribed Procedures

Procedures relating to the letting of contracts above the respective thresholds generally include requirements for organisations to :

Follow one of the three tendering procedures :

Open – Where all interested contractors/suppliers may submit tenders following an advertisement in the OJEC.

Restricted – Where following advertisement the required number of firms (minimum of 3) are selected from those submitting initial enquiries and invited to submit tenders. (An 'accelerated version' of the restricted procedures is available where 'urgency' renders the stipulated time limits impractical).

Negotiated – Where contracts may be negotiated with chosen firms. Public bodies may consult between one or more suppliers under the supplies directive and 3 and 20 contractors under the Works Directive.

The 'Services Directive' will introduce a fourth procedure of 'design contests'.

Public organisations in the UK have traditionally preferred the restricted procedure. As well as limiting administration costs, an additional benefit of this procedure is that firms may still be selected from an existing approved list. It should be noted, however, that organisations should not use such lists to discriminate against suppliers. Such action would be a direct contravention of the directives.

It is important to remember that the procedures are not optional. Public bodies must adopt the open procedure, unless a restricted or negotiated procedure can be justified. If an organisation wishes to depart from the open procedures, it must record the reason for doing so. The restricted procedure is usually justifiable by the need to relate procedural costs to the contract value – in effect, where the cost of adopting the open procedure would be wasteful.

The negotiated procedure is permissible, only in certain prescribed circumstances, eg when tender enquiries received under (i) or (ii) above were unacceptable, or because only one supplier is available for technical, artistic reasons or protection of exclusive rights. Other reasons include when additional deliveries by the original supplier are justified or when extreme urgency exists for reasons that were not foreseen.

To publish indicative notices

In respect of supply contracts, large purchasers must give advance information of their procurement plans for each 'product area' which is over ECU 750,000 for the year ahead.

It is noted that there is no obligation to award a contract which has been included in an indicative notice.

Advertise the contract particulars

Organisations must advertise contract particulars in the Official Journal of the European Community (OJEC) and in the Tenders Electronic Daily Database (TED) (for which no charge is made) , to which candidates can gain access through local 'Euro-Info Centres'. Hence, even if tendering is to be by invited tenderers only, every contractor within the Community is to have the opportunity to request an invitation to tender.

The directives include model notices for advertisements and minimum time scales are stipulated for receipt of requests to participate in tendering and the receipt of tenders.

The time limit for receipt of tenders (when following the restricted procedures) may be fixed by mutual agreement between a contracting organisation and tenderers provided that they all have equal time to submit tenders. Reduced minimum time limits are applicable in cases of urgency, although the directives do not define 'urgency'.

If the use of negotiated procedures can be justified, advertisements need not be placed in the OJEC, except when unacceptable or irregular tenders have been received through the open or restricted procedure.

State the award criteria

Organisations must state the criteria that will be used to evaluate tenders, either in the relevant advertisements or tender/contract documentation. Failure to do so will result in the authority being able to only accept the lowest tender received, even if a marginally higher tender that offers say, faster delivery, is available.

Only two criteria however can be stated, either:

— to accept the lowest price only, or

— to accept the 'most economically advantageous tender'.

It is suggested that organisations should always state the second criteria in which case various criteria by which an organisation intends to decide which is 'the most economically advantageous tender' must be prioritised and disclosed eg quality, price, period for completion, running costs, technical merit, after sales service, price etc.

Restrictions in information requested from suppliers

Organisations are required to state in advertisements, the details that they will expect to be submitted by tenders to prove technical competence. Such details may include a list of contracts over the last 5 years, statements on manpower, management, plant and equipment, product samples and officially recognised quality control bodies' certificates. Firms may also be required to supply details of their financial stability such as balance sheets and statements as to last 3 years turnover.

The extent of information required must be relevant to the contract concerned. Legitimate protection of trade secrets must be respected.

Rejection of tenders

Organisations are able to reject tenders from potential suppliers on the following grounds:

— bankruptcy, ceased or suspended trading, operating under court pending settlement with creditors;

— demonstrably guilty of grave professional misconduct;

- unfulfilled obligations regarding the payment of taxes or social contributions;
- serious misrepresentation in supplying information regarding current or past standing, financial or technical capacity .

References to standards

Public bodies are not able to exclude suppliers by reference to particular products although it is in order to refer to a particular product 'or equivalent'. References should be made to UK standards implementing European standards where they exist or common technical specifications, if not it should be stated that the national standard of another member state will also be acceptable. It should be noted that decision 87/95 requires all public sector organisations to purchase IT equipment that adheres to open system interconnection standards. Where an organisation cannot do so it is required to state the reasons for non adherence within its strategy or long term plan. It is also required to state how it intends to implement the requirements of the decision and the time scale. Failure to do so is a direct contravention of the decision and would leave an organisation open to action by the EC or by an aggrieved supplier.

Invitations to tender must contain a technical specification that complies with EC directives. In general terms this means that if standards exist then they are required to use such standards to describe the item or items that are required. Within EC 87/95 the requirement is for all purchases concerning OSI products over 100,000 ECU's to use the relevant standard or where a purchase below 100,000 would effect later purchases of similar products. The directive set out the relative priority of standards in the following way:

1. European Standards
2. International Standards
3. National Standards.

Items subject to EC 88/295 may also require reference to other standards such as noise levels, safety, quality etc.

Pre-award notification

Contracting organisations are required to prepare a full written report for each contract issued under negotiated or restricted tenders. This should contain the reason for the use of the tender method, who was invited to tender, the conclusions and reasons for exclusions. Such reports are to be submitted to the Commission, if requested.

Further, contracting organisations are required to explain within 15 days, at an unsuccessful contractor's request, why they have rejected a bid. In addition they are required to place a 'contract award notice' within 48 days in the OJEC once a decision has been made as to which firm is to be awarded a contract. In this respect if a tender is rejected because it is considered to be too low in price, then the contractor must be given an opportunity to offer explanations.

Records must be kept of all contracts including values, details of tenderers, grounds for using negotiated procedures etc. To facilitate the Commission's monitoring activities, the government of each member state has been required since October 1991 to submit statistical reports on the award of supplies contracts every two years. From October 1993, similar reports are to be submitted in respect of works contracts. Similar reports will be required in respect of service contracts.

Public bodies who expressed concern at the additional work that would be caused by the above, have been assured that the statistics were to be complied from existing documentation, such as contract award notices and should therefore not create any extra burden.

14.6 The Compliance Directive

This directive which came into force on 21 December 1991 is designed to ensure compliance with the Community's rules on public procurement. It requires member states to set up structures to deal with alleged infringements of the Works and Supplies Directives. An appeals procedure, has been effected by the Public Supply Contracts Regulations 1991 (Statutory Instrument 1991 No.2679) and the Public Works Contracts Regulations 1991 (SI 1991 No.2680) in respect of the Supply and Works directives respectively. The regulations allow for the following:

- make compliance with community obligations a duty owed to suppliers and contractors who can bring proceedings if they are harmed by a breach of that duty;

- allow for cases to be taken by the High Court in England and Wales;

- make access to the courts available only to suppliers and contractors from the member states, including the UK;

- require prior notification to the contracting authority of the alleged infringement and the intention to bring proceedings;

- require proceedings to be brought promptly and within three months of the grounds arising, unless leave is granted by the court;

- to provide that, without prejudice to their existing powers, the courts are to have the powers required by the directive;

- to order the suspension of the contract award procedure or the implementation of any decision taken by the contracting authority in the contract award procedure;

- to order the setting aside of any decision or action, or to order the amendment of any document, in breach of the duty owed to suppliers or contractors under the regulations or relevant EC law; and

— to award damages to the supplier or contractor if he has suffered loss or damage as a consequence of a breach.

The directive also provides for the European Commission to notify a member state if it considers that the public contracts directives have been infringed, prior to a contract being concluded. The member state would then be required, either to confirm that the infringement had been corrected, or give a 'reasoned submission' of why no correction had been made, or indicate that the award procedure had been suspended. In the latter case the member state would then subsequently report on how the matter had been resolved.

An aggrieved supplier may complain directly to the advisory committee at the Commission or via a local Euro-Info Centre. Complaints need not take any particular form, a simple letter will suffice. If the complaint is found to be justified, the Commission commences infringement proceedings against the member state responsible for the authority, who in turn apply pressure upon the organisation.

14.7 Health and Safety

The regulations relating to EC 90/270 came to force on the 31 December 1992 for newly installed kit and December 1996 for equipment installed before that date. It is understood that the new directive was introduced to address the growing number of IT related injuries including repetitive strain injury and backache, etc.

Within the UK this has been implemented under the Health and Safety of Work Act 1974. Organisations can be prosecuted under the H&S laws for infringements to the directives and courts have the power to award unlimited damages and to close operations that fail to meet requirements.

Despite its title the directive is not specific to display screen equipment but includes keyboards, chairs, desks, glare and heat from equipment. However, the directive specifically excludes ''portable' systems not in prolonged use at a workstation'. The directive is not however specific as to the length of time 'prolonged use' would entail.

The definition of a 'worker' is defined a worker as 'any worker as defined in article 3(a) of directive 89/391/EEC who habitually uses display screen equipment as a significant part of his normal work'. Employers are therefore obliged to perform an analysis of workstations to evaluate the safety and health conditions of their staff in relation to eyesight, physical problems and problems of mental stress (article 3(1)). They are also required to ensure that the following are undertaken :

- employees receive information on all aspects of safety and health relating to their workstation;

- employees receive training in the use of the workstation before commencing work and if the workstation is substantially modified;

- periodic breaks or changes in activity;

- consultation with workers and/or representatives;

- workers are entitled to an appropriate eyesight test before commencing work and at regular intervals thereafter;

- if necessary further ophthalmological tests and corrective appliances provided for staff.

The directive also lays down minimum requirements relating to the construction and facilities of equipment (the display screen, keyboard, work desk or work surface, work chair), the environment (space requirements, lighting, reflections and glare, noise, heat, radiation and humidity) and the operator/computer interface (software suitable for task, easy to use, systems to provide feedback to users, display of information in a format and pace adapted to operators needs and the use of software ergonomics).

14.8 Areas of Audit Concern

The implications for the public sector are many and varied and therefore there is a consequent need for auditors to fully understand how their particular organisation is to be affected and how they are attempting to conform to the regulations.

If the European Commission considers that a public body has infringed the EC rules, the UK Government will be called upon to justify the authority's actions to the European Court of Justice under article 169 of the EEC Treaty. Auditors should therefore ensure that they are well briefed as to the implications of the EC directives and ensure that their organisations do not leave themselves open to an action either by the EC or by an aggrieved supplier.

14.8.1 Notable Infringements

Auditors should be aware that according to the European Information Service Bulletin No.116 December 1990 some of the most frequent infringements in public procurement are:

- Non publication in the Official Journal of the European Communities

- The misuse of exceptional tendering procedures.

14.12

- The inclusion in tender notices of administrative, financial, economic or technical stipulations, such as an obligation to use standards not compatible with community law.

- The illegal exclusion of bidders or applicants from member states other than that of the contracting authority, for example by fixing discriminatory selection criteria

- Discrimination in the awarding of contracts.

14.8.2 The Auditor's Role

Auditors should review procedures within their own organisation, to ensure that adherence to these directives is achieved with the minimum of disruption and additional cost. In this respect a three point plan of action is suggested as follows:

- Become acquainted with the EC directives themselves. It is also advisable to have the access to or copies of all relevant directives, and government circulars.

- Examine whether their organisation has appointed an 'EC officer', or made an existing officer responsible for assimilating and interpreting EC directives and offering guidance to appropriate heads of department. This is the major key control in ensuring that the activities of the organisation in respect of EC matters are co-ordinated.

- Review the appropriate procedures to determine whether users are aware of their responsibilities and that the procedures ensure that EC directives are actually complied with.

14.13

CHAPTER 15

NATIONAL LEGISLATION

15

Continued overleaf

15.7 Acquisitions   **15.14**
        15.7.1 Overview
        15.7.2 Areas of audit interest

15.1 Introduction

The increased use of IT has meant that existing legislation has, in some cases, had to be used in ways for which it was not originally intended. In addition we have experienced the introduction of specific legislation to deal with new problems and situations created by the use of IT. Add to this the existing legislation that can be applied to the use of IT and it can be seen that this is a complex area to deal with.

This chapter is not intended to (and cannot practically) provide a detailed description of all the current legislation in the UK that relates to the use of IT, rather it is intended to identify the areas generally covered by legislation, with examples and highlight the considerations that need to be taken into account within these broad areas. Legislation covers the following broad areas:

- Control of data

- Computer misuse

- Fraud

- The working environment

- Intellectual ownership

- IT acquisitions.

Legislation is in the main country specific, but within the EC there are also European laws and directives to consider, there are dealt with in detail in chapter 14. Seven important Acts relate to major aspects of the areas identified above viz.

- Data Protection Act 1984

- Companies Act 1985

- Local Government Act 1972

- Computer Misuse Act 1990

- Police And Criminal Evidence Act 1984

- Health & Safety at Work Act 1974

- Copyright, Designs & Patents Act 1988.

Auditors need to be aware of how legislation affects their organisation and one of the main objectives in audit reviews of specific areas of IT use must be to assess whether the degree of control exercised by management is sufficient to ensure that the organisation is complying with the relevant legislation, is protected against prosecution and will be able to provide acceptable evidence if the need to prosecute arises. The controls referred to throughout this section are dealt with in detail in other chapters within this book and are referenced accordingly.

15.2 Control of Data

15.2.1 Overview

Control of data is a basic management responsibility, but often this responsibility is considered to be too important to be left to management discretion and has been made the subject of specific legislation. This legislation identifies two types of data 'personal' and 'business'. Personal data is the subject of the Data Protection Act 1984 and business data is the subject of the Companies Act 1985 and the Local Government Act 1972.

The Data Protection Act 1984 places a requirement on users of personal data to collect, use and maintain the data in a fair and controlled way. This involves registering the use to which the data will be put, identifying its sources and disclosures, ensuring that the information is only as much as is needed, is accurate and up to date and that the security of that data is effective and that it can be demonstrated that such security measures were in force. In order to support these general requirements the Act introduces eight principles which must be adhered to:

—   Personal data shall be obtained and processed, fairly and lawfully.

—   Personal data shall be held only for one or more specified and lawful purposes.

—   Personal data held for any purpose or purposes shall not be used or disclosed in any manner incompatible with that purpose or those purposes.

—   Personal data held for any purpose or purposes shall be adequate, relevant and not excessive in relation to that purpose or those purposes.

—   Personal data shall be accurate and, where necessary, kept up to date.

—   Personal data held for any purpose or purposes shall not be kept for longer than is necessary for that purpose or those purposes.

—   An individual shall be entitled:

    —   at reasonable intervals and without undue delay or expense – to be informed by any data user whether he holds personal data of which that individual is the subject; and to have access to any such data held by a data user; and

    —   where appropriate, to have such data corrected or erased.

—   Appropriate security measures shall be taken against unauthorised access to, or alteration, disclosure or destruction of, personal data and against accidental loss or destruction of personal data.

Subsequent legislation has brought personal health data into the ambit of the Act.

The Companies Act 1985 places a requirement on company directors to ensure that the financial accounting records are accurate, are protected from loss or inadvertent falsification and that means are provided to ensure that any falsification is detected.

The Local Government Act 1972 places responsibility on treasurers or designated financial officers for the administration of council's financial affairs and similar legislation exists to cover health authorities and other public bodies.

15.2.2 Areas of Audit Interest

It is of primary importance to the auditor that the Data Protection Act does not unduly interfere with the accessing of data. Where the auditor is an employee of the organisation and the organisation has registered as a corporate entity then disclosure to the auditor need not be specifically included in the registration. However, if separate departments of the organisation have registered independently, or where the auditor is not an employee or agent of the organisation it may be necessary to include disclosure to auditors in the registration, though certain exceptions are available under S32(4).

As well as being a legal requirement for certain types of data, it is also good practice to control the collection, use and deletion of data in general. While legislation tends to concentrate on personal data and financial accounting data, it is equally important to ensure that there are appropriate controls covering any data that is used by the organisation. The attitude of management to this basic area of control will determine not only the ability of the organisation to comply with legislation specifically aimed at the protection of that data, but will also impact on the ability of management to detect fraud and abuse and produce evidence in the prosecution of those abuses. It is therefore important to ensure that management are aware of the full implications of failing to adopt adequate controls. These controls should cover the following areas:

- Data collection
- Data accuracy
- Data security
- Data disposal.

Data collection

All organisations rely on their data for their day to day operation. It is a fundamental requirement therefore to establish that the data is actually needed and that it is accurate and up to date. To ensure this the auditor must consider the controls applied to the collection of this data.

The first consideration must be to ensure that data collection routines incorporate controls that evaluate the data to ensure that it is accurate, complete and relevant to the purpose in question. To this end the auditor should consider the adequacy of the vetting and validation routines within all systems dealing with personal, financial and other critical or important data. The storage of unnecessary data is not only wasteful of facilities, it will inevitably detract from the efficient use of important data that is essential and useful. It is therefore important to ensure that unnecessary data, including out of date or inaccurate data is monitored and removed if appropriate.

The auditor should consider areas where redundant data might reside and review the procedures which exist for establishing and implementing guidelines relating to the retention of data. It is particularly important to consider the use of free format fields used for general notes etc. as these can effect the efficiency with which systems operate and could expose the organisation to prosecution for the uncontrolled use of personal data.

Data accuracy

Once the auditor has established that only data that is required for an authorised purpose and that has been lawfully obtained is held and used, the question of its accuracy and integrity must be considered.

The adequacy of controls should be reviewed to ensure that processing errors are detected and reported and that there are regular and effective integrity checks carried out. These controls are considered in detail in chapter 9, *Audit of Application Systems*.

When assessing the completeness and accuracy of information relating to corporate data, reference may be made to the data dictionary if one is maintained, or to system documentation and record layouts. The checking of the accuracy of information relating to personal data may be undertaken by interviewing the individuals concerned. Such a review may highlight discrepancies, but the auditor must then determine whether errors arose in the method of collecting the information, an error on the part of the individuals, or a change arising subsequent to the initial collection of information. In every case the particular registration entry requires amendment, but further action will depend upon the source of the discrepancy. If doubt is cast on the adequacy of the initial collection of information, questions may be raised about the correctness of all register entries. Similarly if a change has occurred which could affect a register entry but which has not been reported to the data protection officer the correctness of other entries are placed in doubt. In these situations further checking of other register entries is recommended.

Data security

It is important to ensure that data is subject to appropriate security at all times. This is important not only to prevent data from unauthorised disclosure or amendment, but also to prove that personal data is being properly controlled.

15.4

The auditor should consider the adequacy of individual security facilities, including physical, logical and clerical controls (see chapter 6, *General Controls*) and ensure that there is a corporate security policy. Such a policy is an important document, its function is to lay down the procedures that management consider appropriate to all aspects of the organisations activities, but in addition it may be required as proof that management took appropriate precautions to prevent unauthorised access to or amendment of data in any dispute over the adequacy, or indeed the existence, of adequate security measures.

Data disposal

It is important to ensure that the confidentiality of data be it personal or business is maintained at all times. This responsibility does not end when the data is no longer needed and consideration needs to be given to the way in which data is disposed of.

The auditor should ensure that there are procedures for the disposal of data and that it is carried out in a way appropriate to the nature of the data. Confidential business or personal data should be carefully disposed of, either by physically destroying the data (eg shredding printouts) or by arranging secure waste disposal services. There are companies who will collect waste paper and recycle it while certifying that it will be handled in an appropriately confidential manner. While these services are some times expensive it is often more satisfactory to arrange for the secure storage of data awaiting collection and disposal than it would be to have staff destroying the data themselves and having the resultant waste collected. The auditor should ensure that all the options are considered and that the most appropriate method is adopted.

Data subject access

The subject access provisions of the Data Protection Act possesses three specific problems for organisations, the timely administration of requests and fees, the extraction of relevant data and the presentation of that data in a form which may be understood by the data subject. The auditor should ensure that there are appropriate procedures to deal with these requirements. To date data subject access requests have been limited and it might not therefore be necessary to implement complex procedures, but management should consider the requirement and ensure that any request can be dealt with satisfactorily.

15.3 Computer Misuse

15.3.1 Overview

Computer misuse covers a number of areas including unauthorised access, unauthorised use of facilities and the unauthorised destruction, amendment or corruption of data or software. There are two areas to consider, firstly the prevention and detection of computer misuse, which should be provided by the basic controls detailed throughout this book and secondly the provision of evidence that misuse took place. This second requirement is much more difficult to provide for and in some cases the actual proof that misuse has occurred may cast doubt on the evidence that control mechanisms were working as expected.

The Computer Misuse Act 1990 introduced three new offences to deal with the increase in crimes not adequately covered by existing legislation. The first offence covers simple hacking, that is unauthorised access via a computer to computer facilities. The second covers unauthorised access with criminal intent, that is hacking with the intention of perpetrating a more serious crime. The third offence covers unauthorised amendment or damage to data and covers amongst other things the introduction of viruses and time bombs. The intention is to provide a legal remedy to enable organisations to protect their data and equipment from unauthorised outside interference.

15.3.2   Areas of Audit Interest

The controls necessary to detect and prevent computer misuse are a combination of the controls identified throughout this book and are dealt with in detail in the appropriate chapters, but they can be identified here in general terms.

Physical access

The basic control to prevent physical theft of or access to computer equipment is to physically restrict access to the equipment. This can range from large purpose built computer suites to protect mainframe computers to a small sturdy lockable cupboard to protect a portable PC and will need to be reviewed in light of the individual equipment and the specific needs of the users and data owners (see chapter 6, *General Controls*).

Logical access

Once physical access has been gained to the equipment the next line of controls are the logical access controls which require a login routine including a password to be provided before access can be gained. These procedures will vary in complexity depending on the nature of the data or software being protected and level of access that can be gained through the equipment (see chapter 6, *General Controls*).

Clerical controls

If access has been gained and unauthorised amendments have been made the clerical procedures around the computerised system should pick up these changes. These controls should involve run to run balancing, checking of transaction totals and reconciliation with other systems. The scope and effectiveness of these controls will vary considerably and the auditor needs to be aware of independent totals that can be used to cross check totals.

15.6

Management trails

Whenever unauthorised access or amendments are suspected, there are various management trail facilities that can be used to trace the actions of the intruder. These range from specific management trails provided within applications, to the journals provided by the operating system software. It is important therefore to ensure that there are procedures to ensure that all necessary management trail facilities are switched on at all times and that they are used and reviewed properly (see chapter 10, *Operating Systems and System Software*).

Evidence of computer misuse

With the wealth of controls and recording devices available it might appear that even if an intruder did gain access to data, the recording facilities would be able to determine what was done, where it was done and when it was done and by whom. If all the controls are in place and they are all operating properly, this might well be the case, but if access was gained by an outsider the vital piece of information, who the intruder was, may not be available or may be misleading especially if that intruder gained access to a valid user ID and password.

This raises the problem of what to do to secure really sensitive or vital information. It is not currently possible to control every possible avenue of attack, but by applying all the currently available controls it will make the intruder's life more difficult and it will therefore take longer for the intruder to gain access. If unsuccessful access attempts are monitored, the system can be set to raise an alarm at an operator console after a predetermined number of attempts so that the intruder can be challenged while still attempting to gain access.

Once misuse has been established and the suspect identified the problem of providing evidence remains. Evidence produced by a computer is not of itself admissible, it requires that a responsible person is available who can be cross-examined on the accuracy and integrity of the data. This is a serious and unenviable undertaking.

The complexity of today's computer systems is such that there are individual experts dealing with individual elements of the network and each element of the network could have a bearing on the operation and effectiveness of controls run on or applied to another element. When considered in these terms it might seem impossible to say that at a specific moment in time all the controls were working correctly as intended and all the equipment was functioning correctly and as expected.

It is in this context that the need for comprehensive control procedures must be seen, it is not only important for providing evidence for court cases, but equally if not more importantly for providing management with evidence that their systems are functioning properly and as intended on a day to day basis.

To have any chance of producing effective evidence from a computer system it is necessary to establish that all the appropriate controls available are in use and where they are not available risk

15.7

analysis should be used to provide management with information on the consequences of those omissions.

15.4 Fraud

15.4.1 Overview

Computer fraud attracts interest as a potential high risk white collar crime. Some argue, though, that the term itself is misleading, as the number of instances of 'pure' computer fraud (ie the manipulation of software) is relatively small and a more accurate term is computer-assisted fraud or even computer-aided deception.

Purists may argue, therefore, that the term 'computer fraud' refers to frauds which could only have been perpetrated using a computer and which therefore involved the manipulation of programs and data files. A wider interpretation seems more appropriate; one which reflects the impact of computerisation on the organisation and its controls and procedures and the subsequent creation of fresh or additional risks. Thus a payroll cheque which has been put aside in a drawer because it was unclaimed but is then misappropriated, can hardly be described as a computer fraud merely because the cheque was originally prepared by a computer. A wages time sheet, however, which is only checked and certified and passed to the computer control section for data preparation, but which is altered immediately before being punched, should perhaps be classified as a computer fraud because advantage is taken of poor controls within the computer section's data handling procedures.

The interpretation also needs to reflect that whatever the sophistication of computing technology, computer programs can seldom match the human capability for testing or assessing the credibility of data and results of processing. This function, though, is often taken over by programs or displaced by computerisation and thus fresh opportunity for fraud is created and detection is made more difficult.

Computer fraud should embrace any act where there is misappropriation or misrepresentation, together with an ability to obtain cash or goods and where a computer was involved. This was defined by the Audit Commission's Computer Fraud Survey as 'any fraudulent behaviour connected with computerisation by which someone intends to gain dishonest advantage'. A computer fraud could thus include unauthorised alteration of computer input, destruction or suppression or misappropriation of output, theft or alteration of master-files, theft or alteration or misuse of programs, or theft or misuse of computer time or resources.

Existing legislation relating to fraudulent acts covers most frauds carried out using computers and there is not therefore specific legislation for computer fraud, however the prosecution of frauds involving computers often rely on computer generated evidence and this is subject to legislation in criminal proceedings. This section looks therefore at two subjects, finding and providing evidence of computer abuse and a more general look at computer fraud and its implications.

15.4.2 Areas of Audit Interest

Evidence of computer abuse

The Police And Criminal Evidence Act 1984 is not about a single type of offence, rather it is about what is admissible as evidence. In this context we are concerned with its implications with regard to IT. Computer files cannot be cross-examined by counsel in a court of law and therefore additional requirements must be met before it can be accepted by a court. The requirements are basically that a responsible person is available who can be cross-examined on the correctness and integrity of the data in question. This would usually require some demonstration that the procedures undertaken ensured the correctness of the data and had been correctly operating at the time in question. This is normally done by providing a section 69 certificate signed by the appropriate person stating that the computer was working normally.

In civil law the breadth of evidence admissible is wider and so unless specifically excluded by statute, computer evidence would be admissible without a section 69 certificate.

Whereas the dramatic growth in computers is well documented, the growth of computer abuse is more difficult to quantify and, while much has been written on the subject, there are relatively few examples of computer abuse within the UK.

There is no doubt though that the increasing dependence upon computer processing by more and more organisations does mean that there is also a significant dependence upon adequate controls and security procedures. The need for such procedures is to protect an organisation from deliberate actions, though accidental disruptions to facilities may well prove to present an even greater risk and consequential cost.

The risk of computer fraud should, therefore, be viewed against the background of all other forms of disruption, whether accidental or deliberate and which disturb the organisation's computer processing cycle. Analyses of such disturbances are likely to show that human operator error may well account for the major hazard, with the effects of errors in system design and hardware malfunction also being significant contributory factors.

The risk of deliberate abuse must therefore be seen in perspective.

The trend towards user-driven computing presents an increased risk of computer abuse. Whether users use independent microcomputers or are linked by intelligent terminals to remote mainframes, a primary responsibility for minimising risks of abuse lies with user management.

They will need to install adequate safeguards to compensate for the lack of central data preparation and central data control and the potential loss of separation of duties (see chapter 7, *User Driven Computing* for further details).

User-driven computing is dependent upon various types of software provided potentially by a number of suppliers. The user will be insulated from his data by several layers of software which typically may include an operating system, database management system software, transaction processing software, interactive computing software and application software. Each of these may be provided by the computer supplier, a software house, or by the organisation itself.

While overall responsibility for secure systems lies with the organisation, there is also an onus upon suppliers of externally provided software. Their products should provide the user with an assurance that the accuracy and integrity of his data will not be impaired by inadequacies within the product.

Users will become more dependent upon such software particularly as the automated office becomes commonplace and increased use is made of electronic fund transfers between organisations and financial institutions. Users will need to be assured that the provider of the particular hardware, software and computer services can demonstrate that their products can guarantee the integrity and security of the data will be preserved. (For more detailed discussion of issues relating to user-driven computing see chapter 7).

UK computer fraud surveys

The first survey of computer fraud in the UK was undertaken in 1981 by the Audit Inspectorate and then repeated in 1984, 1987 and 1990 by its successor body, the Audit Commission. The objectives of the surveys were:

- to identify those aspects of computing which posed the greatest risks;

- to assess the potential incidence of such risks within the local government sector; and

- to provide an authoritative survey of UK computer fraud for the benefit of management and auditors within both the public and private sectors.

The pattern of the types of frauds reported in the 1990 survey proved to be similar to that reported in the earlier surveys. Frauds which involved the fraudulent manipulation of data during its input into the computer processing cycle predominated and represented approximately 75% of the total cases. This outcome serves to emphasise that the absence of basic controls provides opportunities which some feel unable to resist. Improvements in fundamental controls and safeguards could significantly reduce the risk of such cases recurring.

The 1990 survey disclosed that over half the frauds were discovered by internal control procedures and this should serve to emphasise that audit should endeavour to prevent fraud by encouraging management to install sound internal control. 'The main responsibility to prevent

15.10

and detect fraud lies with management and there is no measure available of the number of frauds prevented thanks to the imposition of effective controls' (1981 Survey).

15.5 The Working Environment

15.5.1 Overview

This area of legislation is fairly industry specific and lays down quite rigid standards in some areas, it is therefore important that the legislation relating to your area of work is examined in detail to pick up all the relevant information. In this book it is only possible to consider the very general areas that are covered in all the legislation and which relate to or can be applied to the computer environment. The items relating to environmental controls are dealt with in more detail in chapter 6, *General Controls*.

The Health & Safety at Work Act 1974 places a duty on employers to provide a safe work-place for their employees and to ensure that safe working practices are adopted. These responsibilities cover the provision of safe plant and machinery, proper training in the safe operation of machines and that proper precautions are taken to prevent fire and explosion and to protect against danger from electrical equipment and radiation. It should be noted that more complex and much stricter regulations apply to factories, mines and railway premises and are covered by other legislation.

The main area that all legislation to do with the working environment is concerned with is personal safety and as far as the auditor is concerned common sense will alert you to any problem areas and detail can be checked with the designated health and safety expert within your organisation.

15.5.2 Areas of Audit Interest

There are strict requirements relating to the risk of fire and the facilities for evacuation in the event of a fire. The auditor should ensure that there are adequate procedures in existence and that they are tested and kept up to date. In this area effective training is the single most important area of concern as effective training will highlight all the possible areas of concern and will ensure that staff are aware of safety procedures and report breaches before they become a threat.

Fire is not the only threat in a computer environment, in the past Halon gas was used as a fire extinguisher and is in certain forms lethal. While the use of Halon is being phased out it is still in use in some areas and needs to be considered carefully when a review of the environmental controls is being undertaken.

The other important area for consideration is training in the safe use of equipment and

15.11

machinery. This could cover PC maintenance and the safe use of electrical equipment to the correct use of shredding equipment for the destruction of confidential computer waste and needs to considered in the context of who is performing the task and if they have been properly instructed and where appropriate trained in the use of equipment. It is the employer's responsibility to ensure that all machinery is safe to use and that staff are properly trained in its use. It is important therefore to ensure that there are effective procedures to ensure that dangerous equipment or tasks are handled by appropriately trained staff at all times.

In addition the EC are drawing up directives which will set out ergonomic standards for office equipment such as PC's and monitors, so consideration needs to be given to the way in which purchases are made and how the organisation will be able to incorporate there future requirements into their purchasing procedures.

15.6 Intellectual Ownership

15.6.1 Overview

The Copyright, Designs & Patents Act 1988 provides the same rights as literary, dramatic and musical authors to authors of computer programs. This allows the author to charge a fee for the publication or performance of that work and covers piracy of software as well as unauthorised use.

Intellectual ownership or copyright provides authors with rights over their work, enabling them to decide who can use their work and in what way. Computer programs are treated as works of literature (creative writing) and therefore computer programs have the same level of protection as books and those rights extend for the life of the author and for fifty years after the author's death.

This legal protection has two main concerns for the auditor. Firstly whether software purchased under licence is being used in accordance with the agreement and secondly whether programs written for the organisation belong to the organisation or the author.

15.6.2 Areas of Audit Interest

Software is not (in day to day terms) sold outright to the purchaser, only the right to use it as laid down in the user licence. With most small applications this will be for a single user and it is expected that only one person at a time will have access to and use the software concerned. Indeed, certain software suppliers have simplified the wording of their licences to liken their software to a book, which can be purchased at work but also used at home or by another person in the same way as a single copy of a book could be.

The auditor's role in this first case is to determine how many copies of the various software packages exist and ensure that it corresponds to the total purchased. Often this will not be an easy task, as original disks may have been lost, or software may have come with two sets of disks (5.25" and 3.5"). The auditor may find that if purchases are made through a single supplier or a few suppliers, they might be able to provide details of purchases over a period of time; in addition orders for software can be found and a list drawn up from them. In an ideal world and in the occasional well run department, a list of all hardware and software will be available and if that is the case it will be a simple, if long, case of checking the list to the physical machines.

Software copying has been such a problem that many of the manufacturers have banded together to form the Federation Against Software Theft (FAST) who investigate reports of software piracy including illegal manufacture and sale of copied software and investigate organisations who have been reported as using illegally internally copied software. These investigations and subsequent prosecutions have been very successful and have covered public as well as private sector organisation. FAST state that they would rather co-operate with organisations to "clean up" their software use rather than prosecute and have produced free software to enable organisations to systematically audit their PCs to determine the software installed on them and have started a corporate membership scheme which provides advise and assistance in rectifying known problems.

It is important to ensure that there are adequate procedures to prevent illegal use of software and to ensure that people are aware of the problem, because under the copyright legislation the individual is liable as well as the body corporate.

The second area of concern is that of the ownership of programs or systems written for your organisation by outside parties. Under normal circumstances anything written by an employee in the course of their work is automatically the property of the employer. The problem comes when a third party such as a consultant or software house or even a contractor working in the IT department writes computer programs for the organisation.

Generally it is accepted that contractors and consultants will be working as agents for the organisation and will be producing programs specifically for the organisation, but unless the contract specifies who retains the copyright on the programs there could be legitimate claims made against the organisation.

The auditor should therefore ensure that all contracts between the organisation and any one working on the organisation's behalf to produce computer systems or to write computer programs includes a section which states categorically who retains ownership of the copyright.

15.7 Acquisitions

15.7.1 Overview

Public sector organisations are subject to EC directives concerning the acquisition of computer equipment. This covers two main areas which are dealt with in detail in chapter 5 acquisition of IT namely the price level above which acquisition orders have to be advertise in EC journals and the type of equipment and systems that should be purchased.

15.7.2 Areas of Audit Interest

The auditor should ensure that all IT acquisitions are subject to review to ensure that they are conforming to the EC advertising and tendering requirements and that as part of their overall strategy they are moving towards open systems and have a strategy for migration. There is considerable advice and information available form the Department of Trade and Industry covering all aspects of open systems.

EC legislation now provides the European Commission with the ability to impose mandatory requirements on all public sector bodies this currently includes the requirement to move towards the implementation of open systems and the requirement to make greater use of competitive tendering for the acquisition of IT.

CIPFA

COMPUTER AUDIT GUIDELINES

APPENDIX (General Controls)

BIBLIOGRAPHY

ABOUT THE AUTHORS

INDEX

APPENDIX

GENERAL CONTROLS

Continued overleaf

General Controls

Organisational Control

Responsibility for computing

- Obtain details of the organisation of computer department staff including their respective responsibilities

- Identify from discussion with senior staff whether overall responsibility is vested in one individual or a management team

- Determine whether computer services are provided for or by other organisations and the effect of any such arrangements upon the staffing structure

- Identify by reference to staff organisation details and from discussion, who exercises day-to-day management for the computer department and also for the disciplines within the department

- Identify the chain of command within the disciplines within the computer department

- Assess whether the arrangements for managing the organisation of staff demonstrate a well-organised department.

Separation of duties

- Determine whether staff involved in the development discipline have quite separate duties and responsibilities from those working within the operations discipline – and vice versa

- Determine whether management actively encourages a separate of duties throughout the computer department

- Where separation of duties is inadequate, determine what precautions are taken by user departments to verify the data they submit to and receive from the computer department

- Visit remote locations to determine whether separation of duties is actively pursued by users who design, develop, operate and manage their own computer facilities

- Assess whether separation of duties is effective and generally promotes a high standard of internal control.

Job descriptions

- Obtain a copy of job descriptions and determine whether they are up to date, comprehensive and reflect the current staffing structure

    — Determine whether staff are provided with a written copy of their job description

    — Assess whether job descriptions do contribute to effective separation of duties.

Standards

    — Obtain a copy of the computer department's standards and verify that they are comprehensive and up to date

    — Determine from discussion and inspection whether staff are aware of the presence of standards and that there are effective procedures for monitoring adherence to them

    — Determine by inspection whether standards have been prepared for users of computing facilities and that they are comprehensive and up to date

    — Assess whether standards do help in promoting efficiency and effectiveness.

File and Software Control

Magnetic file storage

    — Identify the types of magnetic files used throughout the organisation including those used by remote users of mini and microcomputers

    — Identify the location of tape and disk units and the storage facilities

    — Visit the locations and assess the adequacy of the arrangements for access to files and for protection against hazards

    — Enquire of the arrangements for issuing and receiving files out of normal office hours - particularly night shift operators requiring access to back-up copies in the event of an emergency

    — Assess whether the arrangements for storing magnetic files provide adequate safeguards against the risks of accidental and deliberate damage.

Housekeeping

    — Determine whether there are defined and written procedures for the general housekeeping of files, eg:

    retention periods of files include current, back-up and archived copies, management of disk space

    media failures

    — View the records maintained and obtain evidence of current and accurate housekeeping

    — Assess whether the housekeeping arrangements provide adequate safeguards against the

Appendix 2

risk of accidental and deliberate damage.

File librarianship

— Identify who has responsibility for file librarianship and whether these duties extend to remote users

— Obtain a copy of the job description/operational procedures for file librarianship

— View the general environment for file librarianship and assess its overall effectiveness

— Determine whether file library records are wholly manual, wholly computerised or a mixture of both

— Inspect the records to assess their completeness, the general updating arrangements and their currency

— Where there are remote locations not included in any central file librarian arrangements repeat the above tasks for each such location

— Assess whether the file librarian function provides adequate safeguards against risk of accidental and deliberate damage.

Access to files

— Determine the arrangements for controlling access to files through discussion with the systems programmer, file librarian, chief programmer or computer manager

— Determine whether the controls over the physical files extend also to data and programs held on those files (particular attention should be directed at JCL and spooled data held under the control of the operating system and where the physical placement of those logical files will be unknown to users)

— Determine whether facilities are provided by the operating system or access control software, or by specific file librarian software

— Through discussion and reference to software suppliers' documentation and sight of reports produced by access control software, ascertain the completeness and currency of the records and the reliance which can be placed upon the facilities to restrict access

— Identify those files which may be regarded as susceptible to high risk of deliberate damage through theft or fraud and the adequacy of access restrictions

— Ascertain the procedures for overriding security facilities in an emergency and for recording such activities; the availability of passwords which provide a wide range of access facilities should be reviewed

— Identify the procedures for controlling the availability of documentation which discloses

Appendix **3**

the access provisions of files. View the documentation and assess the sensitivity of its contents

— Where files are held in remote locations and not under the control of the general access control and provisions, ascertain the adequacy of access arrangements; visit the locations and view the documentation and assess the adequacy of file access restrictions.

Back-up and archive routines

— Identify the arrangements for retrieving back-up and archived data and determine whether the arrangements have ever been implemented

— Determine whether systems with long processing times or running permanently on-line, include facilities to reconstruct files without at frequent intervals incurring significant delays; identify the systems with such facilities and the frequency of use of reconstruction features

— Identify the routine back-up arrangements and view the record of such activities

— Visit remote locations and determine whether back-up and archive routines are used and assess the adequacy

— Assess whether the back-up and archive routines provide adequate safeguards against the risk of deliberate and accidental damage.

Operational Control

Operations management

— Discuss with the operations management the overall organisation of data conversion, operating and data control functions

— Obtain a copy of staff organisation structure, standards documentation, processing schedules and procedural instructions governing the operations function

— Determine whether the operations procedures apply to all applications or whether certain complex applications demand different arrangements.

Data conversion

— Identify through discussion with the operations management the methods of inputting data into computer-readable format

— View the organisation of data conversion facilities in the central data section and in remote locations

— Determine the completeness of the procedures for verification and validation of data

—   Ascertain whether validation programs are available at the data conversion phase key-to-disk or terminal based systems and whether these complement such routines within the application's programs

—   Determine who has responsibility for developing, amending, operating and over-riding data validation routines on key-to-disk or terminal based systems

—   Determine the respective responsibilities of user departments, data preparation and data control staff for authorising, batching, submitting, receiving, punching and checking data

—   Identify the procedures for identifying and correcting data input errors

—   Assess whether data conversion procedures promote the completeness, reliability and timeliness of processing and minimise unauthorised input of data.

Data control

—   Determine the responsibilities of the data control function throughout the organisation including the central and remote locations

—   View the documentation for scheduling processing and for providing instructions on the requirements for each job to be processed under central operations control

—   Observe the general procedures for controlling the passage of data from users through the various computing functions and then back again to users

—   Determine the arrangements for providing a data control function outside normal hours (particular regard should be had to facilities for recording emergency activities and to management's inspection of such documentation)

—   Assess whether the data control function ensures the completeness, reliability and timeliness of processing and minimises unauthorised processing.

Operating

—   Determine the facilities provides by the operating system for scheduling processing

—   View the documentation for scheduling processing and for providing instructions on the requirements for each job to be processed under central operations control

—   Identify jobs which are initiated remotely without the assistance of central operations (consider the effectiveness of control exercised by local management over such activities)

—   View the documentation maintained by operations staff and recorded by the operating system which provides evidence of all processing and of the files accessed

—   View the documentation and review the procedures for logging machine breakdowns and interruptions in computing service

– Assess whether the operating procedures and supporting documentation ensure the completeness, reliability and timeliness of processing and minimise unauthorised processing.

Terminal Control

Communications management

– Identify the individual responsible for managing the communications facilities

– Determine the extent of communication facilities and the types of terminal equipment including the use of microcomputers linked to other computers

– Identify the location of all current (and planned) terminal equipment and the individuals responsible for each terminal or group of terminals (particular regard should be had to portable equipment)

– Identify those terminals used for:

inputting data, initiating processing and updating files,

program development,

user enquiries

– Assume that every terminal is an access point to the most critical system in the organisation until satisfied otherwise.

Physical access

– Visit terminal locations and view the general location, ease of access and control documentation available

– Consider whether terminal activity is authorised

– Observe the use of physical identification devices, key locks and other means of restricting access and consider their appropriateness and effectiveness and the procedures for issuing and controlling their use

– Determine the means of connecting terminals to the computer system whether public or leased lines are used and whether auto connection facilities are used

– Consider the effectiveness of controls over the issue and use of portable terminals

– Assess whether physical access controls ensure that the risk of unauthorised inaccurate and inefficient processing is minimised.

Software restrictions on access

- Identify, through discussion, the facilities offered by the operating system and telecommunications software to manager terminal activity

- Determine for each application offering full file processing the facilities for:

  identifying the terminal equipment,

  identifying the use,

  identifying the file,

  restricting connection time

- Determine the procedures for devising issuing and changing passwords, particularly when staff changes occur

- Identify the documentation available from the operating system and related system software to record terminal activity

- Assess whether software restrictions on access minimise the risk of unauthorised, inaccurate and inefficient processing is minimised.

Environmental control

- View the location of the central computer facilities and assess the risks of potential accidental and deliberate hazards

- Assess the adequacy of safeguards for each of these hazards, viz.

  contingency planning,

  standby arrangements,

  insurance cover,

  maintenance cover,

  staff netting procedures

- Determine whether advice has been sought from specialist agencies (eg fire service, insurance companies, computer supplies)

- Visit locations and assess the risks and safeguards

- Assess whether the environmental controls provide protection for staff, computer equipment, data and documentation against deliberate and accidental hazards.

Systems Development Controls

Management control

- Determine who exercises control over the development of systems and the constitution of any such management team

- Select recent projects and ascertain the extent of management control by reference to appropriate documentation

- Determine whether the computer manager or other individual has delegated authority to approve developments which are otherwise determined by a management team

- Determine the extent of user involvement in centrally-developed systems

- Determine whether management exercises control over maintenance as well as new developments; ascertain whether the computer manager has delegated authority to undertake maintenance work without reference to a management team.

Standards

- Determine whether written standards exist; that there are arrangements to ensure that they are up-to-date and that they are adhered to

- Obtain a copy and assess whether the standards are complete and adequate and whether, if appropriate, they take account of developments by users

- Select recent projects and ascertain whether they conform to the standards.

Project planning and control

- Select recent projects and determine whether there are defined stages in the development of projects

- Determine whether stages are costed in finance and staff resource terms so that delays in satisfactory completion of stages can be assessed

- Determine the procedures for managing project control and observe the documentation used to record and measure progress and to identify deviation.

Post-implementation reviews (PIR)

- Where PIR's are conducted, examine the PIR programme and determine the number of systems to be covered and the priorities assigned

- Review the PIR reports and assess their comprehensiveness, objectivity and impact of their conclusions

- Determine management's reaction to the PIR conclusions and recommendations.

Appendix **8**

Where PIR's are not conducted, assess the need for audit to review certain projects to demonstrate to management the value of such an exercise.

Development and Implementation of Systems and Packages

Generally

- Establish procedures to ensure that audit is aware of intended developments
- Determine the organisation's strategy for developing systems (developed in-house by computer department acquisition of packages, developed by users).

Externally acquired packages

- Compile a review checklist based upon the needs of the user and taking account of the following issues:

  processing requirements,

  system software,

  file and record management,

  suppliers utilities,

  program development aids,

  documentation,

  auditability,

  training,

  reliability of supplier

- Consider the procedures governing the acquisition of software
- Assess whether due regard has been had to the acquisition of packages and that the advantages and disadvantages of individual software have been fully evaluated.

Developments by computer department

- Establish the scale and volume of forthcoming developments to assess the extent of audit involvement necessary and available taking account of the views of auditors responsible for particular systems
- Determine the nature of involvement in individual developments and bring this to the attention of the development team(s)
- Plan the nature of involvement within the different stages of the development cycle

Appendix **9**

– Assess for each system under development whether the audit involvement made a positive contribution to the satisfactory completion of the project.

Developments by users

– Determine the volume and nature of developments by users; the software tools used; the equipment on which the programs will run; and the location of the users

– Determine whether development standards have been prepared for and issued to users and obtain a copy

– Determine whether for each of major applications developed by users, sufficient regard has been had to the adequacy of:

systems design and implementation,

controls,

compatibility,

recovery and back-up,

documentation.

Application Controls

Generally

– Determine the nature of processing used for the application under review (eg batch, online, database)

– Determine the availability of the specification; the user and system documentation; all amendment and test data results

– Identify the individuals within the user and computer departments who are most familiar with the application to be reviewed

– If the application uses online facilities, determine whether the terminal controls relating to that application have been evaluated recently, and whether any online system software which supports the application has been tested.

Input controls

– Identify the procedures for authorising the inputting of data and view those procedures and the use of any physical authorisation techniques

– Identify and view the procedures for minimising the duplication of input

– Identify and view the procedures for ensuring the accuracy of data presented for input

Appendix **10**

- Identify and view the procedures for ensuring that data is converted accurately
- Identify and view the arrangements for preserving the audit trail through the custody of data
- Verify the completeness of the audit trail through the input cycle
- Evaluate whether the procedures adopted to control input to the system ensure that it is genuine, complete, not previously processed, accurate and timely.

Processing controls

- Determine whether processing controls have been designed to provide control:

  at the record level

  at the total level, and

  when system failures occur

- Identify the validation routines and establish the nature of record level controls
- Identify the procedures for compiling total level controls throughout the processing cycle
- Identify the procedures for minimising breaches in control in the event of a system failure
- Verify the completeness of the audit trail through the processing cycle
- Evaluate whether processing controls ensure that the correct data and program files are used, that all data is processed in a secure manner, accounted for and written to the appropriate file, and that data conforms to predetermined standards or falls within specified parameter values.

Output controls

- Identify and view the procedures for ensuring completeness of output
- Identify and view the procedures for ensuring reasonableness of output
- Identify and view the use made of output by users
- Identify and view the arrangements for ensuring the timeliness and confidentiality of output
- Identify and view the procedures for dealing with error and exception reports
- Verify the completeness of the audit trail through the output cycle
- Evaluate whether output controls ensure that all expected output is produced; that it is complete and appears reasonable; that it serves a useful purpose; is distributed on time; and in such a way that confidentiality is maintained.

Microcomputers

Acquisition

- Obtain details of the organisation's strategy relating to microcomputers

- Consider the checklist for acquisition of computer facilities relating to micros.

Systems development

- Determine whether a central user support facility to provide help and advice to users has been provided

- Determine whether there are adequate user training programmes in the use of micro hardware and software

- Identify whether any user-friendly standards have been issued for users when developing systems

- Determine whether users have been made aware of the requirements of the Data Protection Act when developing systems.

Application controls

- Determine whether in user-developed systems, there are adequate controls exercised over input, processing and output

- Determine whether management ensures that evidence of attention to application controls is clearly presented.

File control

- Determine whether standards have been devised for file recovery, back-up and recovery and whether they are adhered to.

Environmental control

- Determine whether there are adequate controls to minimise the risk of theft, accidental or deliberate damage to hardware and software.

Maintenance and insurance

- Obtain details of the maintenance and insurance cover relating to microcomputers and identify whether they have been regularly reviewed.

Office Automation (OA)

Strategy

- Obtain a copy of the organisation's office automation (OA) strategy document(s)

— Identify who has responsibility for defining, renewing and implementing the OA strategy and consider the extent to which senior corporate management were involved

— Assess the adequacy of the strategy document in terms of the expected key components

— Select recent OA development projects and assess the extent of co-ordination of these developments and their relationship with the defined strategy.

Implementing OA

— Identify what procedures exist to determine which OA proposals will be implemented and determine whether an adequate reporting mechanism exists to ensure that the decision makers are fully appraised of progress and general OA activities

— Determine what criteria have been adopted in considering OA proposals and whether these have been communicated to middle managers

— Select recent OA projects and determine whether there are defined stages in the development or projects

— Review the manner in which the feasibility of the projects were considered and their predicted costs and benefits determined, paying particular regard to less tangible costs and benefits

— Determine whether adequate regard was given to:

system and data integrity,

the audit trail,

ease of maintenance,

system continuity,

level of documentation required

— Determine procedures adopted for acquiring hardware and software paying particular regard to:

clear specification of the organisation's requirements which should include minimum performance measures,

appraisal procedures which should include relevant demonstrations of the facilities offered,

references from other users of the facilities offered where appropriate,

contractual arrangements which should explicitly refer to representations made by suppliers on matters such as performance, development or delivery timescales

Appendix **13**

- Determine the nature of senior management involvement in the planning, development and implementation of an individual project and consider whether the human and organisational issues were given adequate and timely consideration

- Determine whether a post implementation review or a series of reviews have been conducted and consider management's response to the reported findings.

User developments

- Determine whether a register is maintained centrally of local development work by end-users and determine what procedures exist to reduce the risk of duplicated effort

- Determine whether a code of good working practices has been adopted and whether end users and their managers are aware of it and abide by it.

Audit review of existing OA systems

- Review the mechanism by which internal audit become aware of corporate and local developments and assess whether it enables timely audit input where appropriate

- Evaluate the relative potential risk of each OA system by determining:

  the financial 'content', or potential for impact on resource management processes,

  the existing or potential links with mainframe and other computing systems,

  the dependence upon end-user development,

  the extent to which personal and confidential data is stored or processed,

  the extent and nature of potential access from local and remote workstations and the environment in which they are used,

  the number of potential users and the nature of their use

- Prepare, for each workstation, a security checklist in order to identify its potential capability and to assess the degree of risk of unauthorised access to critical or sensitive applications

- Review the adequacy of physical and software security measures, administrative procedures and level of internal check that exists to control the use of the facilities, the operation of the applications and to ensure continuity of operation

- Identify procedures by which management monitor and control the effectiveness and efficiency of the systems and facilities in use.

Acquisition of Computer Facilities

Computer strategy

- Obtain a copy of the acquisition strategy to determine whether it is well-defined, applies to the whole organisation, and includes departmental as well as corporate computing

- Identify who has responsibility for defining and implementing computer facilities acquisition strategy

- Determine the terms of reference for those involved in the decision-making and implementation process

- Determine whether there is an adequate reporting mechanism which ensures that those responsible for decision making are fully appraised of progress and general activities.

Establishing the need

- Determine how a need to acquire facilities is usually identified and whether the mechanism

- Determine whether adequate consideration has been given to satisfying the need by organisational or procedural changes.

Feasibility study

- Determine whether there are formal procedures for preparing a feasibility study

- Determine who has responsibility for the preparation of such studies

- Determine whether the study report includes:

   a statement of objectives,

   a statement of existing arrangements,

   identification of alternative solutions,

   a proposed course of action,

   regard for audit and security issues,

   financial implications, and

   a schedule of implementation

- Ic'entify whether decision are taken on the actions to pursue as a consequence of the feasibility study.

Specifying the requirement

- Determine who has responsibility for specifying the requirements and whether there are delegated powers for small projects and for projects initiated and developed by user departments

– Determine whether a project management team has been appointed to exercise overall management control over the project; and if so, identify the members of that team and assess how representative it is of those likely to be affected by the project

– Determine whether a project control team has been appointed to implement the management team's policy and to control the day-to-day activities of the project

– Obtain a copy of the specification and assess whether it has sufficient regard to:

the existing and future applications,

the hardware needs,

the software needs,

the modes of operation, and

the conditions of supply

– Identify the tendering procedures and how responsibility over the selection of appraisal of tenders

– Determine the arrangements for evaluating tenders

– Confirm whether the evaluation process includes:

a technical appraisal,

a financial appraisal,

a comparison of tenders submitted, and

a contract appraisal

– Determine who has responsibility for selecting the successful supplier.

Installation of facilities

– Identify who has responsibility for organising the installation of the new facilities

– Confirm that regard is had to:

identifying the areas affected,

planning the installation programme,

conversion work,

maintenance and insurance arrangements, and

staffing implications

— Determine the arrangements for disposing of any existing facilities and for adjusting the maintenance and insurance covers.

Post-implementation review

— Determine whether post-implementation reviews are conducted and whether sufficient attention is given to:

effects on hardware,

effects on software,

effects on costs, and

user satisfaction

— Determine whether a report is produced and obtain a copy to view its comprehensiveness.

Acquisition of micros

— Determine the acquisition policy for micros and related software

— Determine whether there are adequate procedures to ensure that all equipment is compatible and conforms with the computing strategy

— Where users acquire their own facilities determine whether there has been computer department involvement

— Determine whether the user has provided a specification of requirements, that the tendering and selection procedures are adequate, and that adequate maintenance and insurance cover is arranged

— Assess whether the arrangements for acquiring micros ensure that the purchases are in accordance with an agreed strategy.

Networks

General

— Determine whether a network strategy exists, who produces and agrees it

— How was the network planned

— What did it cost to buy, what does it cost to maintain

— How many networks are there, are they independent or linked

— Are they compatible or do they require protocol conversion to tranfer data from one network to another.

Details of the network

- What is the extent and complexity of the present network
- Is there a complete map of all equipment/cables
- What are the predicted increases in the following:

  BT Lines,

  Mercury,

  terminals (internal and external),

  use of kilostream/ megastream

- How is the network constructed
- What are the main components of :

  the internal circuits,

  local area networks,

  wide area networks.

Network control

- How is the network controlled

  manually,

  network analysers,

  protocol analysers,

  network management system,

  via the operating system,

  via the PABX

- What level of control does this give
- What security provisions have been implemented
- How are these achieved
- Is it monitored
- Is it manual or automatic
- Does it secure both LANS and WANS

Appendix **18**

    –   Does it secure the central network (from mainframe/mini)

    –   Is there a network strategy , who determines ,agrees and monitors it.

Resilience

    –   What preventative measures are taken to prevent downtime

    –   What duplication is there in the network:

    lines,

    alternative routing,

    equipment

    –   Can the network be re-routed centrally, in flight etc.

    –   Does the organisation have a complete set of wiring maps

    internally,

    external circuits.

Performance

    –   What monitoring systems are in operation

    centrally,

    by users.

    –   What information does this provide, it sufficient

    –   Does the organisation use the secondary channel for monitoring

    –   Does the organistion use diagnostic modems

    –   Are performance 'norms' established and monitored

    –   What diagnostic information is available

    at what level,

    at what cost,

    how regularly is it produced,

    what is it used for,

    who uses it

    –   What network management statistics are produced:

    line states,

response times,

transmission rates,

line failures,

mean time to repair,

mean time between faults,

availability of network,

availability of systems,

use of the network (where, how much, when).

Value for money

- Do you know the cost of the network

- Would you say that it was value for money

- Is the structure appropriate for the type of traffic

- What quality of assistance do you receive from:

service desk,

analyst/programmers,

operations,

technical support,

management

- What bandwidth is being used , is it enough

- How helpful are BT/Mercury

- Is the organisation able to dial into their fault determination circuits

- What contact and at what level is there with the supplier

- How quickly do they repair lines , are records kept

- How much leeway is there to re-configure the network , how long would it take

- What are the line speeds

- Is information obtained on the following:

data flows per terminal,

data flows per application,

Appendix **20**

- Does the organisation cost downtime

- What workload projections are made , are they tested

- What problems have been identified

  which areas,

  how long did they take to resolve,

  how were they identified.

BIBLIOGRAPHY

Bibliography

There is a wide variety of publications on the subject of computer management, computer auditing and computer security. The list below cannot be regarded as definitive but it is intended to point the reader to other publications which may be helpful.

Title	Publisher
Managing Computer Audit (1991)	CIPFA
BACS Guidance Note Third Edition (1992)	CIPFA
Computer Survival Guides (1991 & 1992)	CIPFA
Computer Audit Training Package (1991)	CIPFA
Computer Audit Control & Security Guidelines	Institute of Internal Auditors (UK)
Government Information Systems Audit Manual (1993)	HMSO
Systems Auditability & Control	Institute of Internal Auditors Research Foundation (USA)
Surveys of Computer Fraud & Abuse	Audit Commission

ABOUT THE
AUTHORS

About the Authors

Grateful thanks are due to the following CIPFA IT Audit Group members who devoted their time, effort and wide-ranging experience to the compilation of the 4th Edition of *Computer Audit Guidelines*.

MARTIN ADFIELD

Beginning his career as an economist with the Department of Industry, Martin held a variety of public sector accounting/auditing posts before joining the Audit Commission in 1983. He is now Senior Computer Audit Manager with the Audit Commission and Chairman of CIPFA's IT Audit Group. Martin is currently researching into the IT needs of the National Health Service.

PAUL GARNER

Originally a teacher, Paul moved to the NHS where he became a founder member of the NHS Computer Audit Unit in 1980 and later Computer Audit Training Manager. He now works with the Audit Commission where he has both training and research and development responsibilities. Paul was a member of the panel which developed the qualification in computer auditing.

PETER JOB

Peter has specialised in computer auditing in local government for many years. Previously he held IT and audit responsibilities with an electricity board. He is actively involved in computer audit training in the south west and has been a member of CIPFA's IT Audit Group since 1989.

ROWENA JOHNSON

Rowena has worked with London borough, county and district authorities, progressing her career through accountancy and internal audit to the position of Head of Audit Services for Hart District Council. She is currently responsible for internal audit services, data protection and computer security. On the strength of her extensive experience of computer auditing, Rowena was invited to join the CIPFA IT Audit Group in 1990.

DAVID LANG

David was trained in computer auditing at the National Audit Office where his duties included writing and running interrogation software. After a spell at Touche Ross, where he managed computer audit activities for a number of large private and public sector clients, he moved to

Mercury Communications Ltd, part of Cable & Wireless plc. David has had a long association with CIPFA, involving himself in training as well as publications.

TIM NICHOLS

Tim has held a number of local government posts in Surrey, including the London Boroughs of Sutton and Richmond upon Thames. He has specialised in computer audit for seven years and is now Computer Auditor with Woking Borough Council. Tim has been an active member of the CIPFA IT Audit Group since 1989.

KEN ODGERS

Ken Odgers has been Senior Auditor with the Corporation of London since 1988. He had previously worked in the internal audit divisions of the London Boroughs of Brent and Camden and within the finance department of the London Borough of Enfield. Ken is Chairman of the CIPFA Contract Audit Group and has a special interest in EC and national computer audit legislation, particularly concerning the acquisition of IT.

VERNON POOLE

After acquiring computer skills in local government, Vernon moved into consultancy and is now Head of IT and Audit with Aid to Industry (ATI), part of Touche Ross, where he specialises in internal audit training for major companies and public sector organisations. As well as serving on CIPFA's IT Audit Group, Vernon is an executive member of the Electronic Data Processing Auditing Association – the USA/Canada institute for computer auditing .

DIANE SKINNER

Diane is Computer Audit Manager with the Audit Commission in Bristol and has responsibility for the provision of computer audit support services and the development of the use of computing, particularly microcomputers, within the District Audit Service. A regular lecturer on Audit Commission computer audit courses, Diane is currently Chairman of the UK IDEA User Group and Secretary of the BULL Audit Group.

INDEX

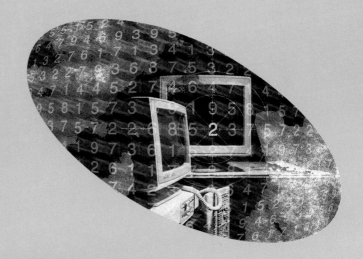

INDEX

A